# Science Fiction from China

# SCIENCE FICTION FROM CHINA

## Edited by Dingbo Wu
## and Patrick D. Murphy

### Foreword by Frederik Pohl

PRAEGER

New York
Westport, Connecticut
London

**Library of Congress Cataloging-in-Publication Data**

Science fiction from China / edited by Dingbo Wu and
Patrick D. Murphy ; foreword by Frederik Pohl.
    p.    cm.
    Includes index.
    Bibliography: p.
    ISBN 0–275–93343–1 (lib. bdg. : alk. paper)
    1. Science fiction, Chinese—Translations into English.
2. Science fiction, English—Translations from Chinese.  3. Chinese
fiction—20th century—Translations into English.  4. English
fiction—Translations from Chinese.  I. Wu, Dingbo.  II. Murphy,
Patrick D., 1951–
PL2658.E8S36  1989
895.1′30876′08—dc19       89–1986

Library of Congress Catalog Card Number: 89–1986
ISBN: 0–275–93343–1

First published in 1989

Praeger Publishers, One Madison Avenue, New York, NY 10010
A division of Greenwood Press, Inc.

Printed in the United States of America

The paper used in this book complies with the
Permanent Paper Standard issued by the National
Information Standards Organization (Z39.48–1984).

10 9 8 7 6 5 4 3 2 1

# Contents

# Foreword: Science Fiction and China

## FREDERIK POHL

It is about time a sampling of Chinese science fiction was presented to an American audience. I welcome this one.

Americans tend to think of science fiction as a peculiarly American invention (though they may give a little prehistoric credit to the Englishman, H. G. Wells, and the Frenchman, Jules Verne). Yet there is a rich literature of science fiction that originates in other languages—indeed, that originates in almost every language, or at least in the language of every country large enough to support much of a publishing industry in the first place. (I once had some correspondence with a man who described himself as "the second-best science-fiction writer in Iran." That clearly implied that there were at least two—though I must say that nothing has been heard from either of them lately.)

In fact, many countries—for example, Japan, Germany, Poland, Italy, France, the Soviet Union, and a number of others—have scores or even hundreds of native science-fiction writers actively practicing their careers. Unfortunately, with no more exceptions than you can count on the fingers of your hand (Stanislas Lem in Poland, the Strugatski brothers in the U.S.S.R., and hardly any others), they are rarely translated into English at all, and when they do appear they seldom reach a wide audience.

What is least pleasing of all is that when a work from almost any "minor" language is translated (the word "minor" being taken in the sense employed by most of the publishing industry, that is, to mean almost any language that doesn't happen to be French, German, or English), it is all too often translated only once directly from its original. Subsequent translations may be made not from the original tongue, but from the first translation; so that a lot of, for instance, Eastern European science fiction reaches American readers only after it has first been turned into French or German and then retranslated into English after that. There is an Italian expression, *Traditore, traduttore,* which means "To translate is to betray"— and those unfortunate works are thus doubly betrayed.

There may be hope for the future. The organization World SF (the international association of persons professionally connected in any way with science fiction) has inaugurated a series of awards that are specifically intended not for science-fiction works themselves, but for the quality of their translations. The awards are called the "Karels" (after the Czechoslovakian science-fiction writer, Karel Capek). I think this is the first international project aimed at recognizing the work of the best translators of science fiction. With any luck at all, they should encourage publishers to seek out the good translators and try to avoid the bad ones . . . or, at least, to try to tell the difference.

If original works from most of the world have had little recognition in America, the situation in regard to China has been even worse. To be sure, the life of a writer of any kind in China has never been easy. The country has never had a copyright law, so until the Communist revolution it was next to impossible for anyone to make a career out of writing. Nor did the pursuit of such a career get much easier even after 1949. The Great Leap Forward threw the country's economy into turmoil; the Cultural Revolution made intellectual activity of any kind dangerous. In that vast convulsion, most of China's best writers were "struggled" or exiled to remote areas, or jailed, or worse. A whole generation of students lost their school years. A whole generation of writers lost their right to be published.

Even since these sorrowful episodes have become history, the writer's choice of subject materials has been far from free. There have been periods of thaw. For example, the short story "The Scar" opened the way for countless works about the excesses of the Cultural Revolution; that was clearly a momentous step toward freedom of literary expression in China. But then cultural controls were imposed again—relaxed briefly for a time later on—then reimposed.

Even the periods of thaw did not encourage very much science-fiction writing. It was tolerated sometimes as a form of children's literature, seldom accorded much respect. The small amount of science fiction that saw publication at all was often subjected to hostile political criticism, and almost never given recognition as "serious" writing.

Yet the forces that impel some people to the writing of science fiction are nearly universal; they are, put simply, the need to understand the complex interactions between science and technology, on the one hand, and the lives of human beings, on the other, and to try to imagine the future these interactions will produce. When I visited China I was not surprised to meet writers and students from many parts of the land who shared my own lifelong interest in science fiction, and to discover that a recognizable body of Chinese science fiction did in fact already exist.

After all, China is *China*. It is immense—nearly a quarter of the human race lives within the borders of the People's Republic—with a history of culture that began while the Americas and most of Western Europe were trackless forest. As much as Europe or America, or any other part of the world, China needs all the help it can get in making this century's revolutionary transitions into a technologically sophisticated era—and science fiction is uniquely able to provide that sort of help in literary form.

Ever since I first visited the country I have been waiting for someone to bring a part of this literature into English so that I could read it for my own information and enjoyment. Now it is here, in this volume. I thank each one of the individual Chinese science-fiction writers whose works are included here—and all those others who could not be included—for their devoted efforts to bring to the Chinese people those special insights and understandings that science fiction, of all literatures, is best able to provide. And, particularly, I thank Patrick D. Murphy and Wu Dingbo for their labors in preparing this volume so that the English-speaking part of the world can share the results of their efforts.

# Looking Backward:
# An Introduction to
# Chinese Science Fiction

## WU DINGBO

Fiction originates from mythology and legend; science fiction as a prose genre is no exception. Ancient myths stand as the ancestors of science fiction while epic, romance, utopian speculation, and imaginary voyages—whether fantasy or satire—are all its near relatives. China has a long tradition of the fantastic that prepares the way for and leads up to modern Chinese science fiction, which in turn builds on, respects, and challenges that tradition. If one accepts this lineage and ancestry, rather than naively imagining that a new genre springs up *ex nihilo,* then the pedigree of China's science fiction can be traced back to the earliest Chinese literature, such as the *Shan hai jing* (The Book of Mountains and Seas, 500 B.C.), "Tian wen" ("Heaven Questions") in *Chu ci (The Songs of the South)* by Qu Yuan (347–278 B.C.), "Hou Yi sheri" (Hou Yi Shoots the Suns) and "Chang E benyue" (Chang E Goes to the Moon) in *Huai nan zi* by Liu An (197–122 B.C.), and others. As mountains and seas are fertile grounds for myths and legends, *The Book of Mountains and Seas* is full of tales about mythological encounters, unusual experiences, and extraordinary adventures. "Heaven Questions" is a collection of cosmological queries asking heaven 172 questions about the creation of the world, the nature of light and darkness, the locations of heaven's nine divisions, and the motions of the sun and the moon. "Hou Yi Shoots the Suns" tells of a time when ten suns appear in the sky scorching the crops so that the people can hardly survive. To save the people from starvation, a hero named Hou Yi comes forward and shoots down nine of the suns, leaving only one in the sky, the same one we see now. "Chang E Goes to the Moon" tells of Hou Yi's wife, who flies to the moon after she drinks an elixir of immortality that she has stolen from her husband. This tale is very probably the world's earliest fantasy about space travel.

Robotics is one of the conventional themes of science fiction. The earliest robot story, as a matter of fact, appeared in China in the fourth century. In Zhang Zhan's "Tangwen" in *Lie zi* (The Book of Lie Zi, circa 307–313), there is a story about Yanshi's robot. Yanshi is a clever craftsman who produces a robot capable of singing and dancing. While entertaining the Zhou emperor, however, the robot constantly stares at the queen. This so enrages the emperor that he issues an order to kill Yanshi. Before his execution, Yanshi requests permission to open the robot's chest. When the emperor sees with his own eyes that all of the organs inside the entertainer's body are made of artificial materials, he is greatly relieved. With his jealous anger turning to appreciative joy, he praises Yanshi for his craftsmanship.

Robot stories can also be found in other historical records. From the seventh century, in Zhang Zhou's *Chaoye qianzai* (The Complete Records of the Court and the Commoners), there are two robot stories. One is about a robot monk who stands in the street begging money from pedestrians. Whenever his alms bowl is filled he utters vocal thanks to the donators. The other is about a robot girl who is able to entertain a drinker to his heart's content. Shen Kuo (1031–1095) also told a story about a robot rat-killer in his *Mengxi bitan* (Sketches and Notes by Dream Creek). Filled with artistic exaggeration, these stories reflect China's level of technology and mechanization in ancient times. Whether depicting robots or natural beings, whether having their characters soaring high into the skies or diving deep into the seas, these tales present beautiful visions that have been cherished by the Chinese people for thousands of years.[1]

Some classical novels also display the fantastic tradition of Chinese literature precursive of modern science fiction. *Xi you ji ( Journey to the West)* written late in the sixteenth century by Wu Chengen; *Feng shen yanyi* (The Canonization of the Gods) written at the end of the seventeenth century by an unknown author; *Liaochai zhiyi* (*Strange Stories from a Chinese Studio,* 1679) by Pu Songling; and *Jinghuayuan* (Flowers in the Mirror, 1828) by Li Ruzhen are all fine examples. The Chinese tradition of wondrous stories includes tales of extraordinary events, fairy-tale romances, supernatural interventions in secular human affairs, heroic explorers on holy missions, unusual experiences during journeys, and close encounters with aliens of various kinds. Such stories all depict people's pursuits of fantastic possibilities in alternative worlds. The subject matter of these stories has been constantly borrowed and extended by modern science fiction writers.

The above mentioned myths, legends, fantastic voyages, and utopias, however, can only be regarded as prototypic predecessors of science fiction because this genre is a distinctly modern form of literature, the child of the scientific era. The industrial revolution in England ushered in the rapid development of science and technology, which in turn brought about tremendous changes in Western life. Human knowledge of the world and the universe greatly increased, and human exploration of fantastic possibilities was intriguingly stimulated. Science fiction emerged as the times required, and it emerged first of all in the West.

In that same historic period of industrialization, China was forced to yield to the powerful military machines of the Western countries in a series of disastrous wars. The nation was fast disintegrating. People, especially young intellectuals, became worried about China's future. They hated foreign aggression, but when they compared China's backwardness with Western power and wealth, they could not but admire its accomplishments in science and technology. They came to see the importance of science and technology for a nation's civilization and development, became aware of the inexorable laws of nature, and realized the need to cope with them both.

In order to stimulate people's interest in science and technology, some enlightened intellectuals discovered sicence fiction and began introducing this new literature to the Chinese reading public, mainly in four magazines. Lian Qicao's *Xin xiaoshuo* (New Fiction) was inaugurated in Yokohama, Japan, in 1902, later moved to Shanghai, and ended in 1903, producing twenty-four issues altogether. Li Baiyuan's *Xiuxiang xiaoshuo* (Portrait Fiction) was inaugurated in Shanghai in 1903 and ended in 1906, with a run of seventy-two issues. Wu Woyao's *Yueyue xiaoshuo* (Monthly Fiction) began in Shanghai in 1906 and ended two years later after twenty-four issues, while Huan Ren's *Xiaoshuo lin* (Fiction Forest) was also produced in Shanghai in 1907–1908 but ran for only twelve issues. They carried almost all of the early translations of foreign science fiction stories produced during these years. Among the major translators of the time were Lian Qicao, Bao Tianxiao, Rue Yi, Xiu Yu, Wu Woyao, Pi Fasheng, and Lu Xun. Lu Xun (1881–1936), China's greatest modern writer, highly praised science fiction in the preface to his 1903 translation of Jules Verne's novel, *From the Earth to the Moon:*

More often than not ordinary people feel bored at the tedious statements of science. Readers will doze over such works before they can finish reading. It is simply inevitable because these readers are pressed to go over them. Only by resorting to fictional presentation and dressing them up in literary clothing can works of science avoid their tediousness while retaining rational analyses and profound theories. . . . So far as the Chinese fiction is concerned, if we talk about the love story, historical story, social story, and the fantasy, they are too numerous to enumerate. Nonetheless, only science fiction is as rare as unicorn horns, which shows in a way the intellectual poverty of our time. In order to fill in the gap in the translation circles and encourage the Chinese people to make concerted efforts, it is imperative to start with science fiction.[2]

Thus, translations of Western science fiction began to reach Chinese audiences one after another beginning at the turn of the century. Chinese readers first came into contact with science fiction not through original creations but through Chinese translations of Western stories. The dissemination of Western science fiction in China played a very important role in the emergence and development of its Chinese counterpart. Among the earliest of translations is that of Jules Verne's *Around the World in Eighty Days*. It was interpreted orally by Yi Ru and put down in writing by Xiu Yu, and published by Shiwen Press in 1900.

When Lu Xun translated *From the Earth to the Moon*, he was studying at the Tokyo Kobun College, Japan. He actually worked not from the original French but from a Japanese translation. Since the Japanese translator, Yashiken Inone, signed "Baron (American)" as the author of the story for the Japanese version, Lu Xun made the same mistake about the author's identity. Lu Xun then translated Verne's *Journey to the Center of the Earth* into Chinese also according to its Japanese version. It was first serialized in *Zhejiang chao* (Zhejiang Torrent), a Hangzhou magazine, and then printed in book form in Tokyo in 1906, but the publisher was Shanghai Popularization Press. Lu Xun once again wrongly signed "Weinan (British)" as the author.

There were other significant translations of international science fiction into Chinese during the first two decades of this century, such as *Travel to the Twenty-First Century in a Dream* by Duaskrotic from Holland, translated by Yang Desen in 1903; Simon Newcomb's *His Wisdom: The Defender*, retitled *The End of the World*, from the United States, translated by Xu Nianci in 1905; from England, Sir Arthur Conan Doyle's *The Lost World*, translated by Li Wei in 1905, and H. G. Wells's "Aepyornis Island," translated by Mao Dun in 1917; and from Japan, seven novels by Shunro Oshikawa, *Undersea Battleship, Airship, New Arena, The World a Thousand Years Later, The White Cloud Pagoda, Queen of the Silver Mountains,* and *A Huge Den of Monsters*. These works were translated during the years 1903–1906 by Jin Shi, Shu Jiyao, and others.

But in these early years Jules Verne was by far the most heavily translated of international science fiction authors. Between 1902 and 1905 seven other translations of his works were published in addition to those already mentioned: *Journey to the Center of the Earth*, translated by Lu Jiedong and Hong Xisheng, 1902; *Five Weeks in a Balloon*, translated by Yi Ming in 1903; *The Begum's Fortune*, translated by Bao Tianxiao in 1903; *All Around the Moon*, translated by the Translation Section of the Commercial Press, Shanghai, 1904; *A Family Without a Name*, translated by Tian Xiaosheng in 1905; *Journey to the Center of the Earth*, again translated in 1905, this time by Zhou Guisheng for the Commercial Press, Shanghai; and *The Mysterious Island*, translated by Xi Ruo for the Shanghai Fiction Forest Press, also in 1905. With these stories translated, Jules Verne became the foreign science fiction author best known to Chinese readers at that time and remains so even today.

Foreign science fiction stories, in spite of their tongue-twisting names and unfamiliar terms, were devoured avidly by wild-eyed young Chinese intellectuals, and they also opened the eyes of Chinese writers and stimulated them to venture into this new field of literature. Ever since then, nourishment from abroad has periodically sustained the development of Chinese science fiction.

It is estimated that modern Chinese science fiction really began in 1904 with the serialization of *Yueqiu zhimindi xiaoshuo* (Tales of Moon Colonization) in *Portrait Fiction*. It is a novel of approximately 130,000 words written in Chinese by Huangjiang Diaosuo (Aged-Angler of Desolate Lake). The author's real name remains unknown. The story describes the settlement of a group of earthlings on the moon. Another important work in the early period of Chinese science fiction is Xu Nianci's "Xin falu xiansheng tan" (New Tales of Mr. Absurdity), published under the pseudonym of Donghai Juewo. It was included in *Xin falu* (New Absurdity) published by Fiction Forest Press in 1905. It tells of Mr. Absurdity, whose body and soul are separated by a typhoon. While his body sinks down towards the center of the earth his soul travels to Mercury and Venus. On Mercury his soul watches the transplantation of brains as a method of rejuvenation, and on Venus it discovers that rudimentary plants and animals appear at the same time, thus refuting biologists' assertions that rudimentary plants historically preceded rudimentary animals. At the earth's core his body encounters a near-immortal man and watches, through his invention of a "lens," wonderful scenes. Then accidentally, his soul falls from outer space to merge with his body in the Mediterranean Sea. He has the good luck of being rescued by a warship heading east so that he is able to return to Shanghai safe and sound. Once there he founds a university with an enrollment of one hundred thousand students, teaching just one course: "Brain Electricity"—sitting still as a way to produce electricity. In his six-day sessions, students learn how to generate and transmit electricity and how to use, memorize, analyze, and synthesize symbolic codes. As a result, "brain electricity" becomes widely applied in everyday life and proves amazingly effective and economical.

During the 1910s translation was in vogue. Some magazine and publishers published stories without differentiating original creations from translations. And even though some stories were published as being science fiction translations, they might actually have been written by Chinese authors and sold as translations to enchance their market value. This confusion causes great trouble for critics attempting to determine the real identity of some works, which could be original Chinese creations, adaptations of foreign works, or straight translations. Many such works require further scrutiny before that decade's history of science fiction production and

publication can be accurately told. It is in the following decades that original Chinese works can be more readily identified.

Lao She (1899–1966) is one of the major figures in contemporary Chinese
literature. Although he himself expressed his regret for the publication of
*Maocheng ji (Cat Country; also translated The City of Cats),* this work of
about 110,000 words remains one of the most significant of Chinese science fiction novels.[3] It was first serialized in the magazine *Xiandai* (Modern) from 1932–1933, and then published as one of the modern work serials by the Modern Book Co. in 1933. A second edition appeared in 1947.
*Cat Country* is a dystopian story about catlike Martians. An earthling from
China travels to outer space in a plane, and when the plane crashes on
Mars he is the only survivor. There are about twenty countries on Mars,
but he lands in the country of the natives with catlike heads. These natives
are greedy, and cheat and even murder each other for money and the
"reverie" drug, although all done in "poetic ways." The scholars there
behave like beasts and regard women as playthings. The rich men's main
interest is to have more concubines. Young people try to mimic foreigners
because they think everything foreign is good, and the emperor controls
the entire nation while the people enjoy no rights at all. Revolutionaries
only pay lip service to revolution, and although people are afraid of foreign invasions no one is bold enough to resist even the "dwarf" aggressors. When another foreign invasion occurs, the cat people fight among
themselves, aiding in the complete genocide of their people. After the
country has been destroyed, the earthling boards a French exploration plane
and returns to his "great, glorious, and free China." The happenings in
the cat country on Mars, of course, bear a strong resemblance to those in
Old China: avarice, opium smoking, government corruption, incompe-
tent education, moral degeneration, and foreign invasions. It is a biting
satire of the Old China.

Xu Dishan (1893–1941) is another major figure in mainstream literature
who has also written in the science fiction genre. His story "Tieyu de sai"
(Ironfish Gills) was first published in 1941 and included in *Selected Works
of Xu Dishan,* Beijing: People's Literature Press, 1958. It tells of a Mr.
Huang who, although terribly impoverished, invents a kind of submarine
equipped with iron gills. People aboard the ship can use these gills to work
underwater for days. Huang thinks that his invention will play a great
role in the anti-Japanese war, but the government shows no interest in it.
When the aggressors are approaching his homeland, Huang has to flee. He
puts his invention in a wooden box and brings it aboard a ship. It so
happens that the box falls overboard and sinks to the seabed. Huang sighs
bitterly: It seems that ironfish gills should not have been invented so early!
The story illustrates the inventor's misfortunes in Old China.

Lao She and Xu Dishan wrote their science fiction without knowing
that their stories were part of this new genre. But Gu Junzheng (1902–

1980) self-consciously wrote in the science fiction genre, and even acknowledged his debt to Jules Verne and H. G. Wells. By 1937 he had
written six science fiction short stories and published them in *Quwei kexue*
(Science Delight, a magazine he launched in Shanghai). Among the six,
"Heping de meng" (Dream of Peace), "Lundun qiyi" (The Strange Epidemic in London), and "Zai Beiji dixia" (Under the North Pole), were
later collected in a booklet entitled *Heping de meng,* published by Cultural
Life Press in Shanghai in 1940. "Dream of Peace" tells of the American
special agent Sean Marlin who, at the risk of his own life, returns to the
United States to find that all of his countrymen are appealing to their
government for reconciliation and against war with the Far Eastern State.
He is greatly puzzled by this. Back home, he turns on his radio and discovers that hypnotic electric waves are being projected from a secret radio
station by Li Guer of the Far Eastern State. He realizes that this is how
the pro-Far Eastern State ideas are being instilled in the minds of lethargic
Americans. Marlin pilots his private plane over the Tennessee mountains
and discovers the secret radio station. After a fierce struggle, he kills three
bodyguards, catches Li Guer red-handed, and forces him to instill anti-Far
Eastern State ideas in the minds of Americans continuously for fourteen
hours. When Marlin finally hears the radio announcer's clarion call to all
Americans to unite and fight the Far Eastern State, he falls into a sound
sleep on his couch. "The Strange Epidemic in London" details the dirty
chemical warfare scheme of the German spy Stegil. He sprays a special
catalyst he has developed into the London air and creates a strange epidemic that causes thousands of deaths. American chemist Ingram discovers the secret of this catalyst and slips into his enemy's lair; there he de-
stroys the catalyst generator and thereby puts an end to this strange disease.
And the third story, "Under the North Pole," tells of the anthropologist
Kean's exploration of the Arctic. Kean discovers an enormous factory there,
under the ice, run by Cameron, a scientist who is studying magnetism.
Cameron has not only developed a kind of iron alloy that has permanent
magnetism, but also has discovered that the geomagnetic pole is due to a
huge magnetic iron deposit under the North Pole. In order to make a
tremendous fortune from his invention, he tries to bury the original deposit deep beneath the earth's crust and replace it with his alloy, so that
magnets everywhere will need to be made of his alloy. He is so excited
by his own evil scheme that while exploding the deposit he takes a misstep
and falls into an abyss. Compasses all over the world fail to work properly
for three hours due to the explosion, but soon return to normal because
the iron alloy begins functioning as a new geomagnetic pole for both the
alloy and genuine iron.

Gu Junzheng's stories display three distinguishing features: One, an in-
genious combination of literary imagination and scientific conception en-
hances their aesthetic appeal; two, the exposition of future "discoveries"

and "inventions" based on the latest achievements of science and technology inspires readers' determination and confidence in harnessing nature; and three, the scientific knowledge and ideas presented in these stories stimulate readers' interest in science and technology. Gu Junzheng pays much attention to the scientific basis for his imagination. He devotes considerable space in his stories to explaining scientific principles and formulas. While Lu Xun advocated the translation of science fiction to popularize science, Gu Junzheng is the first Chinese author to advocate the popularization of science through the writing of native science fiction. In his preface to *Dream of Peace,* he explicitly states:

In the United States, science fiction almost enjoys the same popularity as the detective story. Whether in books, on screen, or on the radio, H. G. Wells's story about the future war disturbs the whole city, and people run pell-mell to seek refuge in the countryside. That is enough to show the great impact science fiction can exert on people; no less than that of mainstream literature. Then, can and shall we make use of this genre to carry a few more scientific ideas so as to popularize people's education in science? I think it is possible and worth trying. These three stories as collected in this booklet are the result of my attempt. (p. 2)

Chinese history in that period, however, was chaotic, with the collapse of the Qing empire followed by the warlord era, the war of resistance against Japan, and the civil wars. Few people showed much concern for the development of science and technology, much less science fiction. Works of science fiction were scarce during the first half of the twentieth century in China.

The People's Republic of China was founded in 1949. The new government, facing many new problems in building New China, was determined to learn from the Soviet Big Brother and apply the Soviets' "advanced experience" in all fields. From this came the all-pervasive influence of the Soviet Union throughout China. Some statistics indicate the extent of this influence: from 1949 to 1956, over 12,000 Russian books were translated into Chinese, with 191 million volumes printed. Among these books were Soviet science fiction, including the following: Dorohov's *Bring the Dying Back to Life,* translated by Qiu Lin (Shanghai: Qiming Press, 1952); E. Yefremov's *Starship,* translated by Lou Mu (Shanghai: Chaofeng Press, 1955); V. Zapalin and others, *The Strange "Transparent Glue",* translated by Peng Lijia and others (Beijing: Mass Press, 1956); and, Hucze, et al., *On Soviet Science Fiction Books,* translated by Wang Wen and others (Beijing: Chinese Youth Press, 1956). The last named volume examines the history of Soviet science fiction and expounds the theory of Soviet science fiction writing. The authors state: Science fiction in the Soviet Union should keep abreast of the time, should base itself on the new achievements in science and should set forth and elaborate new hypotheses valid at the present time. . . . Soviet science fiction plays a significant role in nurturing and educating youth and adolescents: it awakens their thirst for knowledge, cultivates their interest in comparing issues, and encourages their initiative in research; in a word, it stimulates their minds to work. It portrays people who, on the road of transition from socialism to communism and in their struggle for advanced new things, overcome obstacles and difficulties; it trains readers to regard human beings as rational masters of nature and helps readers to believe in their own strength. . . . Science fiction helps the nation to nurture the second generation to become spirited and vigorous, believe in its own cause, fear no hardships and be able to overcome all kinds of difficulties. The numerous translations of Soviet science fiction seemed, purposely or not, to set out the guiding principles for science fiction writing in China. The result was that Chinese science fiction authors followed their Soviet counterparts in form, techniques, spirit, and ideology.

Probably influenced by the Soviet science fiction circle's preference for Jules Verne's short-range extrapolations based on the knowledge and technology already achieved, over H. G. Wells's hypothetical scientific romances, the Chinese Youth Press systematically published selections of Verne's works throughout the 1950s and into the 1960s. The meticulous translation and systematic publication of Jules Verne's science fiction helped Chinese readers to understand his themes and style more comprehensively and thoroughly, with the result that he remains the most familiar and popular science fiction writer to the Chinese reader. And so, once again, in the 1950s and early 1960s foreign science fiction stories and theories had a profound impact on Chinese science fiction writing. During this period, almost all Chinese science fiction stories were written for the juvenile reader. Therefore, the authors saw their publication only in children's magazines and were directly published by juvenile presses, mainly the Juvenile Press in Shanghai and the Chinese Juvenile Press in Beijing. Those science fiction writers who had been accepted as members of the Chinese Writers' Association all belonged to the subgroup of children's literature.

Zheng Wenguang (1929–   ) wrote his first science fiction story in 1954, "Cong Diqiu dao Huoxing" (From Earth to Mars), which was first carried in *Zhongguo shaonian bao* (Chinese Juvenile Daily, Beijing). It depicts a girl called Zhen Zhen who slips into a rocketship together with her younger brother and her classmate Wei Xinzhen. They pilot the rocketship away from Earth towards Mars and come across a meteor stream halfway there. Another rocketship appears at this crucial moment. Inside it are Zhen Zhen's father and two other older scientists. They come to the rescue of the children and bring them back to Earth.

Yu Zhi [Ye Zhishan] (1919–   ) authored "Shizong de gege" (The Missing Elder Brother) in 1957. First serialized in *Zhongxuesheng* (High School Student, Beijing), it won a second place trophy in China's Second

Juvenile Literary and Artistic Creation Awards. The story tells of the mischievous elder brother who gets into a cold storage bin for fun, only to be locked inside and frozen. More than ten years later, refrigeration workers repairing the bin find this frozen boy. Scientists successfully bring him back to life, producing the science fiction comedy of the younger brother being older than the elder brother (American audiences may recall a short-lived television series in which a similar reversal occurred between father and son).

Xiao Jianheng (1931– ) also published an interesting story entitled "Buke de qiyu" (Pup Buke's Adventures, 1962), which is a story about a puppy named Buke. After it gets run over by a car, some scientists transplant its head onto another dog's body, resulting in a series of miracles. This story also won a second place trophy in China's Second Juvenile Literary and Artistic Creation Awards.

Other authors who experimented in this genre during this period include Chi Shuchang, Cui Xingjian, Guo Yishi, Ji Hong, Lu Ke, Su Pingfan, Tong Enzheng, Wang Guozhong, and Zhao Shizhou.[4] There were about twenty authors who produced approximately sixty works between 1950 and 1965. Due to Soviet influence, science fiction was regarded as a subcategory of the popularization of science. Therefore, all the stories of this period fall into two modes: (1) intriguing accidents plus scientific explanations; and (2) an interesting visit to the future or another planet. They are short, simple, and written in children's language; they are crude and incidental in nature while meager in plot and characterization; and they contain too much reasoning squeezed into action-oriented linear narratives. These stories are not comparable in literary or artistic quality with the stories of the 1980s. They received scant attention in Chinese literary circles and existed merely as a weak subgenre of juvenile literature.

The next ten years or so witnessed the unprecedented catastrophe of the Great Cultural Revolution in China (1966–1976). This notorious "revolution" swept away almost everything creative and meaningful. Arbitrary leadership at the top levels suspended most magazines and sent writers and editors to the factories and the countryside to learn from the workers and poor peasants. There was little in the way of fiction or poetry being produced, except that which conformed to the immediate political purposes of each successive campaign. Not a trace of science fiction could be found in the whole of China.

The Gang of Four collapsed in the fall of 1976. The late Premier Zhou Enlai's speech of June 19, 1961, which called for moderate policies for literary and artistic creation, was released in its entirety on February 4, 1979. The Fourth National Congress of Writers and Artists, held in Beijing from October 30 to November 16, 1979, promised writers and artists a new era of creative freedom. A flood of responses followed. New mag-

azines were launched, writers experimented with new genres and techniques, and a group of new authors gained the limelight. The Chinese
science fiction scene was also permeated with a remarkable resurgence of
creative vitality. Stories superior both artistically and thematically to earlier ones appeared one after another.

Tong Enzheng's "Shanhudao shang de siguang" (Death Ray on a Coral
Island) was the first science fiction story published in the prestigious mainstream magazine *Renmin wenxue* (People's Literature), in August of 1978.
It depicts Hu Mingli (later known as Dr. Matai), a Chinese laser specialist
who, deceived by a foreign consortium, engages in laser gun research work
on a desolate coral island. The consortium tries to use his invention for
military purposes. Realizing the actual state of affairs, Hu Mingli fights
back and dies a martyr's death. But before dying, he entrusts his invention
to the young scientist Chen Tianhong, who then brings it back to China.
The success of the story lies in its clear-cut portrayal of characters and its
intriguing plot. It won China's best short story award of 1978. This is a
great honor, because for all the years that this nationwide literary award
has been offered this is the only science fiction story to ever receive it.
This story was later adapted to film, theater, Shanghai opera, and radio.
The appearance of this story not only indicated the improvement of characterization and plot in Chinese science fiction writing but also a break
from the bondage of its juvenile literature classification. It heralded the
booming period of science fiction creation that lasted from 1979 through
1982. According to incomplete statistics compiled by Wei Yahua, 1978
saw the production of about 32 works, 1979 about 80, 1980 about 120,
1981 about 270, and 1982 about 340.

Magazines provide the playground for thought experiments that create
a sense of wonder. In addition to all the popular science journals that out
of obligation carry science fiction, other magazines have also been active
in publishing science fiction stories during the past ten years. In Beijing,
for example, *Kehuan haiyang* (SF Ocean), *Kehuan shijie* (SF World), *Women
ai kexue* (We Love Science), *Renmin wenxue* (People's Literature), *Dangdai*
(Contemporary), *Ertong wenxue* (Juvenile Literature), and *Dongfang shaonian* (Oriental Children) have all carried stories; also, *Kexue wenyi* (Scientific Literature and Art) and *Sichuan wenxue* (Sichuan Literature) in Chengdu;
*Kehuan xiaoshuo yecong* (SF Translation Series) and *Huacheng* (Flower City)
in Guangzhou; *Kexue wenyi yecong* (Scientific Literature and Art Translation Series), *Qingchun* (Youth), and *Weilai* (Future) in Nanjing; *Kehuan
xiaoshuo bao* (SF Newspaper), *Kexue shidai* (Science Era) in Harbin; *Zhihuishu* (The Tree of Knowledge) in Tianjin; *Shaonian kexue* (Juvenile Science), *Kexue huabao* (Science Pictorial), *Shanghai wenxue* (Shanghai Literature), *Xiaoshuo jia* (Fiction Circles), *Shaonian wenyi* (Juvenile Literature and
Art), and *Ertong shidai* (Childhood) in Shanghai; *Chunfeng* (Spring Breeze)

in Shenyang; and *Xiaoxiliu* (Rivelet) in Hunan. These magazines have encouraged the writing of short stories and novelettes, and writers have invariably first built their reputations in such magazines.

Some influential newspapers with circulations over one million have also serialized science fiction stories, such as *Gongren ribao* (Workers' Daily) and *Beijing wanbao* (Beijing Evening Paper) in Beijing; *Wenhui bao* (Encounters) and *Shanghai wanbao* (Shanghai Evening Paper) in Shanghai; and *Yangcheng wanbao* (Goat City Evening Paper) in Guangzhou. The publishers that produced large numbers of science fiction books during this period are Mass Press, Chinese Youth Press, Popular Science Press, Geology Press, and Chinese Juvenile Press in Beijing; Jiangsu People's Press and Jiangsu Science and Technology Press in Nanjing; Guangdong Science and Technology Press in Guangzhou; Heilongjiang Science and Technology Press in Harbin; and Juvenile Press in Shanghai.

With magazines and publishers as their powerful mainstays, more and more people made their contributions to the development of Chinese science fiction. There were about 150 science fiction authors active in China in the late seventies and early eighties. Among them were some old-time writers and some novices, such as Zheng Wenguang (1929–    ), whose first science fiction story, "From Earth to Mars," appeared in 1954; Xiao Jianheng (1931–    ), whose first story was "Pup Buke's Adventure" in 1962; Liu Xinshi (1931–    ), whose first story was "Beifang de yun" (Northern Clouds) in 1962; Tong Enzheng (1935–    ) first appeared in print in 1960 with "Guxia miwu" (Dense Fog over the Old Gorge); Wang Xiaoda (1939–    ), who joined the ranks late with "Shenmi de bo" (The Mysterious Wave) in 1980; Ye Yonglie (1940–    ), whose first science fiction story was "Shiyou danbai" (Strange Cakes) in 1976; Song Yichang (1942–    ) published "V de bianzhi" (The Devaluation of V) in 1978; Wei Yahua (1945–    ), whose first story was " 'Feitan' de fengbo" (A Storm Out of the "Flying Carpet") in 1980; Miushi [Ji Wei] (1954–    ), who published in 1978 "Hai di konglong" (Dinosaurs on the Seabed); Jin Tao (1940–    ), whose first story was "Yueguang dao" (The Moonlit Island) in 1980; and Yan Jiaqi (1942–    ), whose first story, "Zongjiao, lixing, shijia" (Religion, Reason, and Practice), appeared in 1978.

Because most of China's science fiction authors are engaged in science research or in the popularization of science, they are not, for the most part, professional writers. They write in their spare time. In China, science fiction writing is institutionally affiliated with the popularization of science, with the result that science fiction activities have all been attached to the China Popular Science Creative Writing Association instead of the Chinese Writers' Association. The China Popular Science Creative Writing Association was established in 1979, and nearly all of the science fiction authors joined this new organization. Up to the present time there has been no national science fiction organization per se in China.

Although not a few of the works produced in this period of 1978–1982 still fell into the category of juvenile literature, some did make conspicuous breakthroughs in form, content, and techniques, not merely breaking the bonds of juvenile literature but also the bonds of short fiction. There appeared novels, novellas, plays, and film scripts.[5] Among the many works produced in this booming period, the following four examples are the most influential and representative ones.

Zheng Wenguang's novel *Fei xiang Renmazuo* (Forward Sagittarius, 1979) depicts the sudden takeoff of China's spaceship "The East" as a result of enemy sabotage. The ship was originally destined for Mars. With its fuel exhausted, however, it heads straight toward Sagittarius, far, far away, and comes across a black hole on the way there. Against tremendous odds, the three young people on this ship succeed in harnessing the black hole's energy, and in linking their ship with "The Advance," another spaceship sent by China to rescue its sistership and crew. "The East" returns to Earth safe and sound. This novel not only pays great attention to characterization but also to the presentation of accurate information.

Yan Jiaqi's *Kuayue shidai de feixing* (Flight Spanning the Ages, 1979) is a soft science fiction story of unique style and strong political coloring. Through three different experiences and three different endings that "Truth" has in the three different courts of three human ages, the novella ingeniously links together ancient people, contemporaries, and the people of the future to bear out the theme that practice is the sole criterion for the testing of truth. The success of this story results in large part from its prompt reflection on the nationwide political debate in 1978 concerning the criteria for the determination of the truth of political theory. It evoked such strong repercussions at home and abroad that translations of the story soon appeared in Germany, France, and Japan.

Meng Weizai (1933–     ) is a famous contemporary mainstream writer. *Fangwen shizong zhe* (Calling on the Missing People, 1981) is his only work of science fiction. It is a utopian novel, but mirrors the reality of Chinese society by way of science fiction. The historical setting of the story is the "Tianan Men Incident"—the spontaneous demonstration of April 5, 1976, that honored the memory of the late Premier Zhou Enlai. The Gang of Four suppressed the mourning masses who demonstrated. *Calling on the Missing People* tells of nine people who are missing after the Tianan Men Incident. It so happens that they board an alien flying saucer and fly to a far-off planet named Songlu. They find that Songlu is an Edenic land for the planet's natives, who enjoy happiness all their lives. The nine Chinese happily join the natives in singing and dancing to extol the wealth and prosperity of Songlu. As a utopian story, it is just wish fulfillment on the author's part. But it sincerely expresses many Chinese people's strong yearning for a peaceful and happy life without political upheavals and disastrous social chaos.

Wei Yahua's "Wenrou zhixiang de meng" ("Conjugal Happiness in the Arms of Morpheus," 1981) is a story of great impact. It tells of a scientist who marries a robot. The robot wife is so docile, gentle, and beautiful that the young scientist becomes intoxicated with love. He is so indulged in the conjugal happiness of his married life that he neglects his work and even unintentionally burns up all the research data of an important project. The complete subservience of the robot wife to all of the whims of her husband eventually leads him to disaster. He is handed over to a special court for investigation and the determination of his responsibility in the case. The scientist finally awakens from his rosy dream and realizes how hateful subservient and excessive love is. He makes up his mind to divorce his robot wife. The sequel to this story was later carried in *Yanhe* (*Yanhe River*, nos. 3–4, 1982), a magazine in Jilin.

Ye Yonglie's main contribution during this period is his detective science fiction series featuring inspector Jin Ming, who solves difficult and complicated cases by applying his knowledge of modern science and technology. Among the series are *Qiaozhuang daban* (Disguised, 1980), *An dou* (Veiled Strife, 1981), *Guobao qi an* (A Strange Case of Pandas, 1981), *Mimi zhongdui* (The Secret Column, 1981), *Hei ying* (The Black Shadow, 1981), *Bu yi er fei* (Disappearing Without a Trace, 1982), and *Ru meng chu xing* (As If Just Awakening from a Dream, 1983).

More science fiction stories appeared in the prestigious mainstream magazine *Renmin wenxue* (People's Literature). Ye Yonglie's "Fushi" (Corrosion, 1981) depicts scientists' attitudes toward fame and financial gain when a great scientific discovery is made. Xiao Jianheng's "Shaluomu jiaoshou de miwu" (Professor Solomon's Delusion, 1980) shows that human beings are beyond simulation by robots. Science fiction during this period also found expression in other media, such as films, television, radio broadcasts, and comic books. In film, for instance, the movie version of Tong Enzheng's "Death Ray on a Coral Island" was filmed in 1980 and Ji Hongxu's "Qianying" (Hidden Shadow) released in 1982. On television, Zhou Yongnian, Zhang Fengjiang, and Jia Wanchao's "Zuihou yige aizheng sizhe" (The Last Man Who Dies of Cancer) and Wu Boze's "Yinxing ren" (The Invisible Man) were shown in 1980, while Ye Yonglie's *Xiongmao jihua* (The Panda Project) was shown in 1983. Ye Yonglie's *Veiled Strife* was broadcast daily over the radio as a serial by the Central People's Broadcasting Station in 1981, while his *The Secret Column* was broadcast by the Hunan and Sichuan People's Broadcasting Stations in 1981. And in comic books, Ye Yonglie's detective series, consisting of eight million copies of twelve booklets under the general title of *Scientific Sherlock Holmes,* was published by Popular Science Press in 1982, and Jin Tao's juvenile science fiction series, consisting of ten booklets under the general title of *Adventures of Foolish Ma, Junior,* was published by Ocean Press in 1983.

Chinese science fiction differs in some aspects from its counterparts abroad due to different social systems, cultural traditions, and attitudes toward science, technology, and the future. Chinese science fiction seldom tackles the subjects of space colonization, galactic empires, alternative histories, cataclysms, apocalyptic visions, telepathy, cybernetics, religion, sex, and taboos. On the whole, Chinese science fiction is optimistic. People always get the upper hand over nature, science, evil, and whatever enemy or obstacle they may face. The hero is supposed to succeed, emerging triumphant and unscathed from difficulties. Visions of the future are always bright and promising, although a spectrum of possibilities for that bright future is projected. In China, as most science fiction writers are engaged in scientific work and most of the protagonists in their stories are scientists or scientists-to-be, science fiction is, in a sense, a kind of literature that presents scientists' collective aspirations in the form of an explorative excursion into an alternate reality. The conflicts in the stories always reveal the most prominent characteristic of the Chinese scientists: their patriotism. This key virtue is their indispensable guarantee in overcoming all kinds of difficulties and emerging victorious.

As critics in China emphasize that imagination in science fiction has to be based on science, the fantasy elements in the stories are bound by known scientific facts or extrapolations from them. Therefore, writers usually look ahead a few decades and the readers seem to expect that the imaginary in the story will come true in their lifetimes. As a result, Chinese science fiction stories mostly depict the near, foreseeable future. In China, science fiction's main function is utilitarian rather than aesthetic. It aims to create interesting stories in a simple and effective prose. It teaches moral lessons, often in the form of an admonition, expressed in definite terms at the end of the story. In his afterword to *Forward Sagittarius* (1979), Zheng Wenguang writes:

We eulogize science. We eulogize the glorious future which a highly developed science will give to human life. We eulogize all the fine things working people create with the help of science and we eulogize millions of people who heroically strive for the materialization of the four modernizations. (p. 282)

To accompany the rapid production of new science fiction stories in the 1980s, criticism and guidebooks were also quickly developed. For example, in 1980 Beijing's Popular Science Press published Ye Yonglie's *Lun kexue wenyi* (On Scientific Literature and Art), Beijing's Geology Press published the anthology *Kepu zuojia tan chuangzuo* (Popular Science Writers on Writing), and Nanjing's Jiangsu Science and Technology Press published *Zuojia lun kexue wenyi* (Writers on Scientific Literature and Art). The following year Huang Yi edited *Lun kexue huanxiang xiaoshuo* (On Science Fiction) for Beijing's Popular Science Press. And in 1983 Rao Zhonghua compiled *Zhongguo kehuan xiaoshuo daquan* (Compendium of

Chinese Science Fiction) for Beijing's Ocean Press. These books present criticism and abstracts of science fiction works that were produced during this booming period of the late seventies and early eighties. They are the most reliable reference books on Chinese science fiction available in China today.

Science fiction entered the classroom for the first time in China in 1979. This started with Dr. Philip Smith, from the University of Pittsburgh, who went to China that year and offered the first science fiction course in the English Department of the Shanghai Foreign Languages Institute, now named the Shanghai International Studies University. With Dr. Smith's help, I began offering science fiction as a one-term (about twenty weeks) optional course for third- and fourth-year students. The course relies on independent readings, class discussions, lectures, and video presentations. The textbook is based on Robert Silverberg's *Science Fiction Hall of Fame*. The objective of the course is to provide an introduction to the history, writers and their works, and themes of British and American science fiction.

1979–1982 also saw a burgeoning interest in the translation of foreign science fiction. Many famous science fiction authors and their works were introduced to the Chinese reading public. This gave the development of Chinese science fiction a powerful thrust. The Chinese Youth Press not only reprinted old translations of Jules Verne's works but also turned out new translations in 1981 such as *From the Earth to the Moon*. Together with *Dr. Ox's Experiment* and *Off On a Comet*, all of Verne's major science fiction works have been translated into Chinese, with incomplete statistics placing the total number of copies close to six million.

Some of H. G. Wells's works had been translated into Chinese in the past, such as *The Invisible Man* and *The War of the Worlds*. But in 1980, Jiangsu Science and Technology Press turned out *Selected Works of H. G. Wells* in two volumes, including *The Time Machine, The Island of Dr. Moreau, The Invisible Man, The War of the Worlds, The First Men in the Moon*, and *The Food of the Gods*. In addition, numerous other foreign science fiction works were translated.

From the United States, in 1980 the following were translated: Richard Wadley's *The Man from Atlantis* in four volumes by Ocean Press; Michael Crichton's *The Andromeda Strain* in two versions by Guangdong Science and Technology Press and Popular Science Press; George Lucas's *Star Wars* and D. F. Glut's *The Empire Strikes Back* by Hunan People's Press; D. M. Rorvik's *In His Image—The Cloning of a Man* by Science Press; Edwin Curry's *Sargasso* by Shandong Science and Technology Press. In 1981, Isaac Asimov's *I, Robot* and *Fantastic Voyage* were translated by Popular Science Press, *C-shaped Runway* by Heilongjiang People's Press, and *Asimov's Mysteries* by Geology Press; Jack Williamson's *Undersea City*, Poul Anderson's *Question and Answer,* and Penn Alcoff's *Corpsicle—The Frozen Man* by Ocean

Press; Clifford D. Simak's *Way Station* by Guizhou People's Press, and *Selections of Clifford D. Simak* by Jiangsu Science and Technology Press; Ira Levin's *The Boys from Brazil* in two versions by Guangdong Science and Technology Press and Zhejiang Science and Technology Press; Steven Spielberg's *Close Encounters of the Third Kind* also by Guangdong Science and Technology Press; Gene Roddenberry's *Star Trek* by Beijing Xinhua Press; two editions of Clive Cussler's *Raise the Titanic* by Ocean Press and Sichuan People's Press. And in 1982 the Fujian People's Press published the *Anthology of American Science Fiction,* containing twenty-two stories.

A number of British works were also translated, such as Mary Shelley's *Frankenstein, or the Modern Prometheus* by Jiangsu Science and Technology Press in 1982, and the following in 1981: Arthur C. Clarke's *2001: A Space Odyssey* in two versions, one by Guangdong Science and Technology Press and the other by Hunan Science and Technology Press; also his *Rendezvous with Rama* by Guangdong People's Press; New Budding Press published a translation of Howard Thompson's *The Glitterball;* Hunan People's Press turned out Sir Arthur Conan Doyle's *The Lost World;* Sichuan Juvenile Press published three novels by John Christopher: *The White Mountains, The City of Gold and Lead,* and *The Pool of Fire;* Heilongjiang Science and Technology Press published a short story collection, *Thirty Seconds—Thirty Days;* and, finally, Yunnan People's Press and Geology Press both published translations of Robert Louis Stevenson's *The Strange Case of Dr. Jekyll and Mr. Hyde.*

Works from the Soviet Union were also translated after a long period of neglect, although two very influential books did appear earlier: A. Belyaev's *Professor Dowell's Head,* Popular Science Press, 1959; and Belyaev's *Pinker's Adventures,* Juvenile Press, 1962. Jiangsu Science and Technology Press published A. Kazantsev's *Strong Times* and Ocean Press did a collection titled *In the World Where I Passed Away,* and Kyl Brayjov's *After One Hundred Years,* all in 1980, while New Budding Press published Filzov, et al.'s *Kangaroo People* in 1981. But the major recipient of renewed translations of Russian literature was Alexander Belyaev. The Chinese Youth Press translated five of Belyaev's novels in 1981: *Glittering Man, Master of the World, Alialy, The Winged Man, The Amphibian,* and *The Man Who Finds His Face.* In that same year Heilongjiang Science and Technology Press published *Selections of A. Belyaev.* In 1982 Geology Press turned out *Ship-Wreck Island* and Jiangsu Science and Technology Press produced a two-volume *Selections of A. Belyaev.*

Japanese science fiction also gained the attention of Chinese translators in these years, with Sakyo Komatsu's *Japan Sinks* first translated for criticism in 1975 and later reprinted for appreciation in 1986 and *Astroboy* being translated by Popular Science Press in 1981. Also, Takashi Ishikawa and Norio Itoh's *A Comprehensive Guide to World Science Fiction* was published by Jilin People's Press in 1982. France was not forgotten, being represented by Popular Science Press's translation of M. A. Rayjean's *The Unreal* in 1980, and Guangdong Science and Technology Press's version of Rene Barjavel's *Endless Night* in 1981. There were also some international collections of science fiction translated, such as Ocean Press's *Bermuda and UFOs*, Heilongjiang Science and Technology Press's *Return from Death*, Hunan People's Press's *Phantasm in an Ancient Castle*, and the Zhongqing Branch of Science and Technology Press's *Governess Shetita*, all appearing in 1980. While 1981 saw the appearance of *Lovers in an Old Treehouse*, done by the Anhui Science and Technology Press, in 1982 Beijing Press published *Selections of Foreign Science Fiction for Youngsters* and the Shanghai Literature and Art Press produced *Modern Foreign Science Fiction* in two volumes.

Although only six foreign science fiction films and TV serials have been shown in China, their tremendous impact is exemplified by a 1987 poll. Among 711 fourth through sixth grade pupils in a Shanghai primary school, 450 wrote in "science fiction" as the kind of film they liked best (see *Wenhuibao*, 29 May 1987). Among these six, *Astroboy* and *Japan Sinks* have been from Japan, whereas *Futureworld*, *The Man from Atlantis*, *Capricorn One*, and *Superman* have come from the United States. In addition, James Gunn's *The Immortal* was adapted in Hongkong as *Life and Death Struggle*, and was presented for general release throughout China in 1978 and received wide acclaim. *Astroboy*, as a juvenile TV serial of twenty-six episodes, was aired once a week by China's Central Television (CCTV) from 1980 to 1981. This program has appealed so much to the Chinese audience, juveniles in particular, that nearly everyone can identify the image of astroboy. *Japan Sinks* was shown in China's major cities in 1986 and received a very satisfactory reception. *Futureworld* was shown in 1979 to audiences totalling over one hundred million people. *The Man from Atlantis* is probably the American TV program most familiar to the Chinese. Seventeen different episodes were aired by CCTV every Saturday evening from winter 1979 through spring 1980. Mack and Mary have since become well-known figures and some young people in China have even expressed a preference for having Mack as their secretary of the Communist Youth League. On the nights when *The Man from Atlantis* was airing, attendance rates at movie theaters declined dramatically. *Capricorn One* was shown in 1981 and *Superman I* and *Superman III* were shown in 1987 and 1988; all three received high acclaim.

As with fiction, the years 1979 through 1982 witnessed the greatest dissemination of foreign films and shows. The translation and publication of foreign science fiction and the importation of foreign science fiction films and TV programs in China during this booming period was unprecedented in both its speed and scale. This influx helped Chinese readers and writers become well acquainted with the development of science fiction abroad and, at the same time, stimulated the growth of domestic science fiction writing. The subsequent rapid growth of Chinese science fiction in this period drew the attention of both scientific and literary circles. Different schools of thought and different viewpoints appeared, giving rise to enthusiastic theoretical debates inside and outside science fiction circles, a normal phenomenon in the process of developing a creative genre and one that demonstrated the health and vitality of science fiction in China. The major controversies were the following:

1. *Which category does science fiction fall into?*
   Some say that science fiction falls into the category of literature, that it is a literary genre. Some hold that it is part of popularizing science. The eclectic view holds that it stands entirely independent from both popular science and literature.

2. *What is the mission of science fiction?*
   Some hold that the mission of science fiction is mainly to expound a scientific outlook of life. Just as other artistic and literary works do, science fiction expresses the author's ideas, philosophy, realistic attitude, and truth-seeking spirit. It has no obligation to introduce any specific scientific knowledge, though it may stimulate thought on the part of the readers and arouse their interests in science and technology. Others assume that science fiction must undertake the task of popularizing scientific knowledge. If science fiction does not do this, then its soul must have become a disembodied one.

3. *What is the definition of science fiction?*
   *Ci hai* (Encyclopedia of Chinese Words, 1979) provides this definition in the entry of "Kexue huanxiang xiaoshuo" (Science Fiction): "Fantasized fiction about humankind's efforts to work miracles by applying new discoveries, new achievements, and plausible predictions in science." Many people, however, question the validity of this authoritative statement. Views vary so greatly that it is hard to pick any single one as representative.

4. *What is the scientific feature of fantasy in science fiction?*
   Some hold that scientific fantasy is based on some kind of scientific knowledge and that it can offer a plausible explanation for its fantastic aspects. If writers can make things sound plausible through the artistic use of pseudoscience, then there can be no denying their literary effects. But others hold that scientific fantasy means imagination that sticks strictly to science. Otherwise, it conducts propaganda for pseudoscience and fails to usher readers into the hall of science.

5. *Is detective science fiction all right?*
   Some think it is a new type of writing that deserves encouragement, since it appeals to many readers. Others view it as a harmful trend.

6. *What is the orientation of science fiction creation in China?*
   Some hold that Chinese science fiction is still immature. Most of the authors are newcomers and beginners lacking experience. Therefore, it is imperative to encourage the policy of "Let a Hundred Flowers Blossom," which would allow science fiction writers to tackle different subjects and try different techniques and styles. But some hold that the current tendency of science fiction writing

is unhealthy. They argue that the formulas of "fantasy + love" and "fantasy + thriller," in particular, should be discarded.

Although these issues remain controversial and unresolved, the debates over these issues have drawn more public attention to this new genre of Chinese writing. They push those people who are concerned about science fiction to make serious studies of the genre and they encourage the writers to produce high quality works.

For years the door of China was closed to most outsiders. Since the smashing of the Gang of Four, however, the new government and Party leaders have adopted an open-door policy. International contact with the rest of the world has become feasible for almost everyone. Chinese science fiction circles have also begun, since the later 1970s, to have contact with their counterparts abroad—but this has occurred entirely through unofficial channels.

When Dr. Philip Smith offered the first course in science fiction in China in 1979, he not only introduced this genre to his students, but he also gave two lectures on it to science fiction writers and editors in the Shanghai Science Hall. Moreover, on behalf of Brian Aldiss, Dr. Smith invited Ye Yonglie to join World SF, the international science fiction association of professionals. Ye Yonglie not only accepted the invitation but also introduced Zheng Wenguang, Tong Enzheng, Xiao Jianheng, and Liu Xinshi to World SF. These five, headed by Ye Yonglie, formed the Chinese branch of World SF. Thus, Chinese science fiction writers became members of the international community of their peers. Later Wang Fengzhen, Yang Xiao, and I also joined the World SF organization. Since then World SF has served as a bridge of friendship. With the help of World SF, foreign science fiction writers and critics who come to China can always find their Chinese counterparts.

In 1980, when Dr. Smith returned to the United States, he brought me into correspondence with Forrest Ackerman, who in turn introduced me to Takumi Shibano of Japan, and he urged me to correspond with Osamu Iwagami, a member of Japan's Chinese Science Fiction Research Association (JCSFRA). In response to Iwagami's request, I wrote "A Brief Survey of Chinese SF," which was translated into Japanese and carried in Japan's *SF Gems* in April of 1981. Then I in turn introduced Ye Yonglie to Japanese science fiction circles. Thus relations between Chinese and Japanese science fiction circles began and have since expanded.

With the help of Takumi Shibano, Dr. Elizabeth Anne Hull of the United States and I started a correspondence that led to her coming to Shanghai where she met with Ye Yonglie and me and discussed the current status of science fiction at some length. On December 24, 1981 she was invited to lecture on science fiction to authors, editors, and student fans at the Shanghai Science Hall.[6] Dr. Hull visited China again in 1983. This time she led a science fiction tour group that consisted of Frederik Pohl, Charles N. Brown, Roger and Judy Zelazny, William Wu, and Margaret Houle.[7] When they appeared at the Shanghai Science Hall, they received a warm welcome from Chinese science fiction authors and editors from all over China. In the previous year, Robert and Virginia Heinlein also visited Shanghai.[8] Heinlein gave a talk on his own science fiction writing to Shanghai science fiction people at the Shanghai Science Hall. Later in 1983, Darko Suvin of Canada exchanged views with Ye Yonglie and Wu Dingbo in Shanghai. Among other science fiction writers and critics who have visited China are Brian Aldiss of England, who came in 1979, Shi'ichi Hoshi of Japan, who visited in 1981, and Osamu Iwagami, who visited in 1986–1987. Further, science fiction people from Great Britain, the Netherlands, Sweden, Austria, Australia, Germany, and France have also established direct contact with Chinese science fiction people.

International interest in Chinese science fiction has developed rapidly over the past several years. At the suggestion of Dan Fukami, Japan set up the Chinese Science Fiction Research Association in 1980 with seventeen members. The JCSFRA collects and translates a high volume of Chinese science fiction. In recent years *Locus* and the *World SF Newsletter* have carried several reports on science fiction activities in China, acquainting science fiction enthusiasts of other countries with the recent developments of the genre in China. West Germany published *Science Fiction from China* in 1986, compiled and translated by Dr. Charlotte Dunsing in collaboration with Ye Yonglie. France also produced *Shadow of Spies on Blue Jade Island,* a collection of Chinese science fiction, translated by Huang Yok-soon in 1986. Besides *Cat Country* (also known as *City of Cats*), three Chinese short stories have been published in English in the United States in 1984 and 1986.[9]

In 1983, while Wang Fengzhen was a visiting researcher in the United States, he was invited to attend the annual World SF conference in Europe. With the help of some major science fiction writers, he went to Europe and received the longest-distance attendee award. And in 1987, at the invitation of the JCSFRA, a delegation of the four Chinese editors of *Scientific Literature and Art* visited Japan. After their arrival in Tokyo, they called on Dan Fukami, the head of JCSFRA, and other eminent Japanese science fiction writers, and exchanged their views on science fiction creation and publication in both countries. Accompanied by Osamu Iwagami and Mrs. Takumi Shibano, the editors visited three Japanese publishing companies with long-running science fiction lines. The increasing international contact between Chinese science fiction people and their counterparts in other nations helps not only to strengthen their friendships but also to enhance their understanding of science fiction and of each other.

Science fiction treats change, particularly human-made change. Yet the greatest irony lies in the fact that when certain changes really take place, science fiction is hushed and becomes dead silent. The most prominent of these is a change in the political climate. Just as Chinese writers were busy writing and publishing science fiction with great enthusiasm, the political drive against "spiritual pollution" began, and swept the whole of China in 1983. Ideas and practices that were publicly criticized in the mass media were bourgeois individualism; writing as self-expression; modernism; works without theme, character, or plot; abstract humanism; "socialist alienation"; the profit motive; sexual promiscuity; and various other "noxious" influences. Unexpectedly, science fiction became a scapegoat and its golden period ended overnight. Science fiction publication was virtually stopped; some books that had already been half-printed were snatched from the presses. Chinese science fiction creations of the previous five years came under severe criticism. China's major newspapers carried articles repudiating "erroneous" deviations in science fiction writing. Several meetings were held in Shanghai and Beijing criticizing the "poisonous" science fiction stories. Critics listed some wrong inclinations in science fiction, such as: (1) some stories present imagination against science, "intelligence pills," "ghost revivals," "walking through walls," "brain information from corpses," and so forth. They conduct propaganda for pseudoscience, and even for superstition; (2) detective or thrilling science fiction carries fewer and fewer scientific elements, having instead more and more absurd, horrible, and macabre scenes; (3) science fiction stories show doubts about the significant role of science and technology in advancing humanity and make people pessimistic about the future; (4) science fiction stories display low-taste sex with sensual robots, and so on.

Wei Yahua's "Conjugal Happiness in the Arms of Morpheus" was refuted as cynical, sensual, and anti-Socialist. The assailants claimed that since the relationship between the scientist and the robot is that of the one between the ruler and the ruled, the story is actually repudiating our present Chinese society and insinuating that the present system is unworthy of love. Since the robot hates natural people, such hatred must reveal the author's attitude towards people who live in Socialist China, and therefore, his stories display an incorrect political inclination. According to some critics, Ye Yonglie's "Zishi qiguo" (Reap As You Have Sown, 1981) propagates the idea that selfishness is hereditary and so deviates from Marxism. Ye Yonglie's detective science fiction series, with Inspector Jin Ming as the protagonist, was denounced as depicting what occurs only in Capitalist and Imperialist countries, and therefore should not have been set in China. His novel *Hei ying* (The Black Shadow, 1981) is a story about the persecution and suffering of the intellectuals during the Cultural Revolution. But in a Shanghai daily newspaper, it was criticized as a novel that tells how a "man becomes a ghost" in Socialist China. Thus it paints the Chinese nation in completely negative terms and exposes the horrors of the Cultural Revolution to the point of distortion, and in so doing smears Socialist society in China and negates the values of socialism. Some other science fiction stories were labeled as unhealthy and vulgar.

This political drive, although so short lived as to last only a few months, hurt the authors so badly that the small contingent of science fiction writers quickly shrank and gradually dispersed. Some authors left science fiction to write mainstream literature, some turned to fictional biography, and some simply stopped writing altogether. Almost all of the major science fiction writers withdrew from the science fiction arena for some time. And while science fiction stories were being attacked publicly and authors were becoming disillusioned, editors also felt depressed. Under invisible pressure, they had to stop their science fiction lines. Before 1983 there had been dozens of magazines and publishers competing to publish science fiction. Later, only one magazine, *Scientific Literature and Art* in Chengdu, survived.

Chinese science fiction has suffered involuntarily from the change of political climate, and remains at a very low ebb, with annual production lingering around forty titles from 1984 through 1987. But it is still alive. And in this survival *Scientific Literature and Art* has played an indispensable role. (In 1989, this magazine was renamed *Qitan* [The Fantastic]). This magazine, established in 1979 and holding its ground in 1983, has been turning out six issues annually, with a circulation of 10,000 or more for nearly ten years. It not only publishes science fiction stories and commentaries but also does its best to unite around it all those in China interested in science fiction. In 1985 it launched the first nationwide contest for the best science fiction short stories and received some 700 entries; and in 1986 it issued the first Chinese Nebula awards to eleven winners. In order to solicit more high-quality stories, the editorial department has invited writers, critics, and translators to attend its writing conferences in Chengdu from time to time. This magazine has done its job quite well and its editor-in-chief, Ms. Yang Xiao, has worked efficiently and has made a great contribution to the development of science fiction in China.

It is impossible, however, for one magazine to change the whole deplorable situation of Chinese science fiction. In December of 1984, the Fourth National Congress of the Chinese Writers' Association convened in Beijing. At that meeting, writers complained that some leading comrades did not really understand literature but regulated it too much, so much that writers had difficulties finding ways to develop creatively. The leading comrades once again responded favorably and promised moderate policies for literary creation. The writers felt gratified and encouraged. But it is always easier to destroy than to create. Science fiction authors have seemed rather slow to catch the resurgent spirit.

But science fiction has again attracted public attention. It is rather unusual for several articles on the same subject to appear in China's most authoritative Party newspaper, *Renmin ribao* (People's Daily), but that is what has happened with science fiction in 1987 and 1988. Tan Kai's "Why Has Cinderella Withdrawn from the Stage?" and Jiang Yunsheng's "Spread SF Wings" are most representative of such articles. All of these articles tend to analyze the causes for the low ebb of Chinese science fiction production. Writers sometimes complain about the readers for their skin-deep knowledge of science and technology and their lack of imagination, whereas readers blame the writers for their limited understanding of science and their poor writing skills.

But the critics have a different view from either of these complaints. According to them, the major cause is the erroneous guiding principle in Chinese science fiction writing, which states that science fiction stories must deal with and popularize existing science and technology. For over thirty years this restrictive principle has strictly limited imaginative flexibility, and thus hindered the development of Chinese science fiction. To compensate for it, writers, critics, and readers should spare no effort in stressing the view that science fiction is a literature about change and that imagination is more important than science. The second cause is the rare appearance of high-quality stories in China. The critics believe that once high-quality stories reach the reading public, the situation will improve accordingly. As Chinese science fiction has not yet reached its maturity, the advisable step to be taken at present is to translate and introduce the best foreign science fiction works, as people in Japan and Taiwan have done. The third cause is the interference of the leading cadres concerned who do not know the nature of science fiction but too heavily influence its production. Given that Chinese science fiction is studied and respected abroad but not so much at home, critics have urgently called on the cadres in the circles of both literature and popular science to be aware of this abnormal situation and to show sincere concern for the development of Chinese science fiction. Critics have also suggested that more Chinese participation in international activities be encouraged.

1988 looks much more promising than any other year since 1983. In February the Science Fiction Committee was set up under the auspices of the Sichuan Writers' Association, with Tong Enzheng as its director and Yang Xiao and Lin Shuhong as deputy directors. One of its goals is to further a liaison between literary circles and popular science circles. The Second Nebula Award Contest of Science Fiction Stories, for the period of March 1988 through March 1989, is being sponsored by *Scientific Literature and Art* magazine. And, Shanghai Film Studio has recently released a comic science fiction movie titled *Nanren de shijie* (The Men's World). This film portrays an absurd world without women in the twenty-first century that results from the feudal notion of valuing male babies over female babies—a belief still prevalent today—being carried to its logical and ludicrous conclusion. Further, Xiwang Press has recently published *Shijia kehuan xiaoshuo xiehui zhongguo huiyuan zuopin ji* (Selected Works of

Chinese Members of World SF), edited by Liu Xinshi. This anthology includes stories written by five major science fiction authors, Zheng Wenguang, Tong Enzheng, Xiao Jianheng, Liu Xinshi, and Ye Yonglie.

The present book, *Science Fiction from China,* aims to show how Chinese science fiction has become a genre in the Chinese literary arena by publishing eight well acclaimed stories. They have been chosen for this book because they represent three major thematic groups: robots and clones, spies and technology, and in and out of space. Most, if not all, Chinese science fiction stories work with these themes.

"The Death of the World's First Robot" seems to show the relations between an invention and its consequences. But the humorous tone throughout makes this story more entertaining than didactic. Its significance in this book also lies in its role as a point of departure in the timescape: the past.

"Conjugal Happiness in the Arms of Morpheus" is a serious study of human relations, implying a critical view of the present by portraying a human husband and a robot wife. It is written in a graceful and philosophical manner.

"Reap As You Have Sown" follows the story line of Rorvik's *In His Image—The Cloning of a Man* (1978), but changes the tone by revealing the power of greed in the human world. This story and "Conjugal Happiness in the Arms of Morpheus" both aroused critics' attention and became issues for heated debates in Chinese literary circles.

"The Mysterious Wave" and "Death Ray on a Coral Island" are both award winners. Their success lies in clear-cut characters and intriguing plots. Both involve technological inventions and violent struggles for control of them. Strong literary flavors make them cross genre lines.

"The Mirror Image of the Earth" expresses the author's denunciation of the Chinese Cultural Revolution, although the story is unfolded within a cosmological perspective.

With an alien corrosive germ as its science fiction mechanism, "Corrosion" first appeared in a mainstream magazine as a moralistic study of scientists' attitudes toward fame and gain. The delineation of the characters' psychology seems the author's major concern.

"Boundless Love" takes up the everlasting theme of love and devotion, yet with the universe as its playground. The modernist devices, such as its stream of consciousness technique, are effectively applied throughout the story. The interplay of the three female images is at once striking and blurring, indicating the influence of Freudianism on the author. As the story is obviously set in the future, "Boundless Love" seems to complete a circle of the timescape of this book.

With the exception of "The Death of the World's First Robot," which is a literary adaptation of an ancient sketch, all other stories in this book are typical of Chinese science fiction, displaying the following characteristics: (1) All main characters are scientists and all stories present scientists' collective aspirations in the form of explorative excursions into an alternate reality; (2) the conflict in these stories always displays the most prominent character of the Chinese scientists: their patriotism and optimism; (3) all these stories are set in the near future, and the reader is assured that the fantasy will come true within his or her lifetime; (4) most of the science fiction ideas are based on the natural sciences.

With its everlasting beauty, science fiction as an extrapolative literature has its own special value and intrinsic merits. Although deriving and developing from past literature, this new genre is one that cannot be replaced by any other contemporary genre. Yet, in China, unlike in other countries where it is flourishing, it still needs nurturing. With the concerted efforts of writers, artists, critics, translators, and readers, and with international interest and encouragement, Chinese science fiction will surely break into full bloom in the near future.

## SPECIAL NOTE FROM THE PUBLISHER

For cataloging purposes, we have given the first editor's name in the American style Dingbo Wu. Wu being his surname, the correct inverted form of the name should be Wu, Dingbo. Elsewhere in the book, the name appears in the Chinese order as Wu Dingbo; the Chinese order is followed also for the names of the other Chinese writers and translators.

## NOTES

1. For a discussion of traditional Chinese tales that distinguishes between the supernatural and the fantastic in terms of subject matter and takes into account recent critical studies of the modern "fantastic," see Karl S. Y. Kao's introduction to the volume he has edited, *Classical Chinese Tales of the Supernatural and the Fantastic: Selections from the Third to the Tenth Century* (Bloomington: Indiana University Press, 1985).

2. *Lu Xun quanji* (Complete Works of Lu Xun). Vol. 11. Beijing: People's Press, 1973, p. 9.

3. In his preface to *Lao She wenji* (Selected Works of Lao She, Kaiming Bookshop Press, 1951), Lao She wrote: *"Maocheng ji (Cat Country)* is a satire not only on warlords, politicians and rulers of the time but also on the progressive people of the time, picturing the latter as only indulging in idle talk without undertaking any serious work. I made this mistake because I had not joined in revolution, without any ideas about their warm sincerity and high aspirations. I thought they held extreme and empty views. I regret to have written satire of the kind. . . ." Two different translations of *Maocheng ji* have been published in the United States: *Cat Country,* translated by William A. Lyell (Columbus: Ohio State University Press, 1970), and *City of Cats,* translated by James E. Dew (Ann Arbor: Center for Chinese Studies of the University of Michigan, 1964).

4. See the bibliography for a list of their works.

5. According to the publishing conventions in Mainland China, a work of over

130,000 words in Chinese is considered to be a novel, a novella is under 130,000 and over 20,000 words, and a short story is under 20,000 words.

6. See *Locus: The Newspaper of the Science Fiction Field,* no. 254, 1982.

7. Ibid, no. 273, 1983.

8. Ibid, no. 264, 1983.

9. Wei Yahua's "Conjugal Happiness in the Arms of Morpheus," in *Amazing* (September 1984); Ye Yonglie's "Thursday Events" and Tong Enzheng's "The Middle Kingdom," in *Tales from the Planet Earth,* ed. Frederik Pohl and Elizabeth Anne Hull (New York: St. Martin's Press, 1986).

## WORKS CITED

All Chinese science fiction books will appear in the chronological bibliography in this volume.

Alcoff, Penn (USA). *Corpsicle–The Frozen Man.* Beijing: Ocean Press, 1981.

Anderson, Poul (USA). *Question and Answer.* Beijing: Ocean Press, 1981.

*Anthology of American Science Fiction.* Fuzhou: Fujian People's Press, 1982.

Asimov, Isaac (USA). *Asimov's Mysteries.* Beijing: Geology Press, 1981.

———. *C-shaped Runway.* Harbin: Heilongjiang People's Press, 1981.

———. *Fantastic Voyage.* Translated by Ke An. Beijing: Popular Science Press, 1981.

———. *I, Robot.* Translated by Guo Qiang, et al. Beijing: Popular Science Press, 1981.

Barjavel, Rene (France). *Endless Night.* Translated by Liu Bansheng. Guangzhou: Guangdong Science and Technology Press, 1981.

Belyaev, A. (USSR). *Alialy, The Winged Man.* Beijing: Chinese Youth Press, 1981.

———. *The Amphibian.* Beijing: Chinese Youth Press, 1981.

———. *Glittering Man.* Beijing: Chinese Youth Press, 1981.

———. *The Man Who Finds His Face.* Beijing: Chinese Youth Press, 1981.

———. *Master of the World.* Beijing: Chinese Youth Press, 1981.

———. *Pinkerr's Adventures.* Translated by Chen Shanji. Shanghai: Juvenile Press, 1962.

———. *Professor Dowell's Head.* Translated by Li Derong. Beijing: Popular Science Press, 1959.

———. *Selections of A. Belyaev.* Harbin: Heilongjiang Science and Technology Press, 1981.

———. *Selections of A. Belyaev.* Nanjing: Jiangsu Science and Technology Press, 1982.

———. *Ship-Wreck Island.* Beijing: Geology Press, 1982.

Brayjov, Kyl (USSR). *After One Hundred Years.* Translated by Yu Qixiang and Wang Xin. Beijing: Ocean Press, 1980.

Christopher, John (UK). *Wiley's Adventures. (The White Mountains; The City of Gold and Lead; and The Pool of Fire.)* Translated by Chen Yuan. Chengdu: Sichuan Juvenile Press, 1981.

*Ci hai* (Encyclopedia of Chinese Words). Shanghai: Wordbook Press, 1979.

Clarke, Arthur C. (UK). *Rendezvous with Rama.* Translated by Cai Nande. Guangzhou: Guangdong People's Press, 1980.

————. *2001: A Space Odyssey*. Translated by Tan Yunji. Guangzhou: Guangdong Science and Technology Press, 1981; and by Shi Bo. Changsha: Hunan Science and Technology Press, 1981.

Crichton, Michael (USA). *The Andromeda Strain*. Translated by Li Shubao and Xue Lei. Beijing: Popular Science Press, 1980; and by Dong Yuan. Guangzhou: Guangdong Science and Technology Press, 1980.

Curry, Edwin (USA). *Sargasso*. Translated by Lu Yongjian, et al. Jinan: Shandong Science and Technology Press, 1980.

Cussler, Clive (USA). *Raise the Titanic*. Beijing: Ocean Press, 1981; and Chengdu: Sichuan People's Press, 1981.

Dorohov (USSR). *Bring the Dying Back to Life*. Translated by Qiu Lin. Shanghai: Qiming Press, 1952.

Doyle, Sir Arthur Conan (UK). *The Lost World*. Translated by Li Wei. [unknown press], 1905; and by Men Xiang. Beijing: Ocean Press, 1980; and by Fei Jiale. Changsha: Hunan People's Press, 1981.

Duaskrotic (Holland). *Travel to the Twenty-First Century in a Dream*. Translated by Yang Desen. Shanghai: Fiction Series Press, 1903.

Dunsing, Charlotte (West Germany) and Ye, Yonglie, eds. *Science Fiction from China*. West Germany: Goldmann, 1986.

Editorial Department of *Geology Gazette*, ed. *Kepu zuojia tan chuangzuo* (Popular Science Writers on Writing). Beijing: Geology Press, 1980.

*Feng Shen Yanyi*. At the end of the seventeenth century. Beijing: People's Literature Press; reprint, 1955.

Filzov, et al. (USSR). *Kangaroo People*. Tianjin: New Budding Press, 1981.

Glut, D. F. (USA). *The Empire Strikes Back*. Translated by Zhang Ruoheng and Chen Yueqian. Changsha: Hunan People's Press, 1980.

Huang, Yi., ed. *Lun kexue huanxiang xiaoshuo* (On Science Fiction). Beijing: Popular Science Press, 1981.

————, ed. *Zuojia lun kexue wenyi* (Writers on Scientific Literature and Art). Nanjing: Jiangsu Science and Technology Press, 1980.

Huang, Yok-soon, trans. *Shadow of Spies on Blue Jade Island*. France: Editions Pierre-Emile, 1986.

Hucze, et al. (USSR). *On Soviet Science Fiction Books*. Translated by Wang Wen, et al. Beijing: Chinese Youth Press, 1956.

Ishikawa, Takashi, and Norio Itoh (Japan). *A Comprehensive Guide to World Science Fiction*. Translated by Guo Qiming, et al. Jilin: Jilin People's Press, 1982.

Jiang, Yunsheng. "Spread SF Wings." Beijing: *Renmin ribao* (People's Daily), October 26, 1987.

Jin, Tao. "Yueguang dao" (The Moonlit Island). *Kexue shidai* (Science Era) (January–March 1980). Harbin.

Kazantsev, A. (USSR). *Strong Times*. Translated by Ying Tianshi. Nanjing: Jiangsu Science and Technology Press, 1980.

Killough, Lee (USA). *Lovers in an Ancient Treehouse*. Translated by Wu Bo and Liu Xiqing. Hefei: Anhui Science and Technology Press, 1981.

Komatsu, Sakyo (Japan). *Japan Sinks*. Translated by Li Dechun. Beijing: People's Literature Press, 1975; reprint, Jilin People's Press, 1986.

Levin, Ira (USA). *The Boys from Brazil*. Translated by Lu Qing, et al. Guangzhou:

Guangdong Science and Technology Press, 1981; and Hanzhou: Zhejiang Science and Technology Press, 1981.

Li, Ruzhen. *Jing hua yuan* (Flowers in the Mirror). 1828.

Liu, An. *Huai nan zi,* circa second century B.C.

Liu, Xinshi. "Beifang de yun" (Northern Clouds). *Shaonian wenyi* (Juvenile Literature and Art) (December 1962). Shanghai.

Lucas, George (USA). *Star Wars.* Translated by Hu Jie and Chi Yin. Changsha: Hunan People's Press, 1980.

Meng, Qingshu and Jin, Tao, eds. *In the World Where I Passed Away* (USSR). Beijing: Ocean Press, 1980.

Miu, Shi [Ji, Wei]. "Haidi konglong" (Dinosaurs on the Seabed). In *Haidi konglong,* by Ji Hong and Miu Shi. Nanjing: Jiangsu People's Press, 1978.

*Nanren de shijie* (The Men's World). Shanghai: Shanghai Film Studio, 1988.

Newcomb, Simon (USA). *His Wisdom: The Defender.* Translated by Xu Nianci. Shanghai: Fiction Forest Press, 1905.

Oshikawa, Shunro. *Airship. Yueyue xiaoshuo* (Monthly Fiction) (1906). Shanghai.

———. *A Huge Den of Monsters. Yueyue xiaoshuo* (Monthly Fiction) (1906). Shanghai.

———. *New Arena. Yueyue xiaoshuo* (Monthly Fiction) (1906). Shanghai.

———. *Queen of the Silver Mountains. Yueyue xiaoshuo* (Monthly Fiction) (1906). Shanghai.

———. *Undersea Battleship.* Translated by Jin Shi and Chu Jiayou. *Yueyue xiaoshuo* (1906). Shanghai.

———. *The White Cloud Pagoda. Yueyue xiaoshuo* (1906). Shanghai.

———. *The World a Thousand Years Later. Yueyue xiaoshuo* (1906). Shanghai.

*Phantasm in an Ancient Castle.* Changsha: Hunan People's Press, 1980.

Pu, Songling. *Liao chai zhi yi (Strange Stories from a Chinese Studio).* 1679. Translated by Herbert A. Giles. New York: Boni & Liveright, 1925; reprint, Beijing: People's Literature Press, 1962.

*Qianying* (Hidden Shadow). Movie adapted from Ji Hongxu's "Wangfu guai ying" (Mysterious Shadows in the Palace), 1982.

Qu, Yuan (347–278 B.C.). *Chu ci (The Songs of the South).* Translated by David Hawkes. London: Oxford University Press, 1959.

Rayjean, M. A. (France). *The Unreal.* Translated by Zhu Fuzheng. Beijing: Popular Science Press, 1980.

*Return from Death.* Harbin: Heilongjiang Science and Technology Press, 1980.

Roddenberry, Gene (USA). *Star Trek.* Translated by Xin Wen. Beijing: Xinhua Press, 1981.

Rorvik, D. M. (USA). *In His Image—The Cloning of a Man.* Translated by Chen Zhongliang. Beijing: Science Press, 1980.

*Selections of Foreign Science Fiction for Youngsters.* Beijing: Beijing Press, 1982.

*Shan hai jing* (The Book of Mountains and Seas), circa 500 B.C.

"Shanhudao shang de siguang." Movie adapted from Tong Enzheng's story of the same title, 1980.

Shelley, Mary (UK). *Frankenstein, or the Modern Prometheus.* Translated by Chen Yuan. Nanjing: Jiangsu Science and Technology Press, 1982.

Shen, Kuo (1031–1095). *Meng xi bi tan* (Sketches and Notes by Dream Creek).

Shi, Xianrong, ed. *Modern Foreign Science Fiction.* Shanghai: Shanghai Literature and Art Press, 1982.

Silverberg, Robert, ed. (USA). *Science Fiction Hall of Fame.* New York: Double-day, 1970.

Simak, Clifford D. (USA). *Selections of Clifford D. Simak.* Nanjing: Jiangsu Science and Technology Press, 1981.

————. *Way Station.* Translated by Zou Fu, et al. Guiyang: Guizhou People's Press, 1981.

Spielberg, Steven (USA). *Close Encounters of the Third Kind.* Guangzhou: Guang-dong Science and Technology Press, 1981.

Stevenson, Robert Louis (UK). *The Strange Case of Dr. Jekyll and Mr. Hyde.* Kunming: Yunnan People's Press, 1981; and Beijing: Geology Press, 1981.

Tan, Kai. "Why Has Cinderella Withdrawn from the Stage?" Beijing: *Renmin ribao* (People's Daily), June 10, 1987.

Tezuka, Osamu. *Astroboy.* (Comic strips adapted from the Japanese animated car-toon.) Beijing: Popular Science Press, 1981.

*Thirty Seconds—Thirty Days* (UK). Harbin: Heilongjiang Science and Technology Press, 1981.

Thompson, Howard (UK). *The Glitterball.* Translated by Chen Yuan. Tianjin: New Budding Press, 1981.

Tong, Enzheng. "Shanhudao shang de siguang" (Death Ray on a Coral Island). *Renmin wenxue* (People's Literature) (August 1978). Beijing.

Verne, Jules (France). *All Around the Moon.* Translated by Translation Section of Commercial Press. Shanghai: Commercial Press, 1904.

————. *Around the World in Eighty Days.* Translated by Yi Ru and Xiu Yu. Shang-hai: Shiwen Press, 1900; and by Sha Di. Beijing: Chinese Youth Press, 1958.

————. *The Begum's Fortune.* Translated by Bao Tianxiao, 1903; and by Lian Xing. Beijing: Chinese Youth Press, 1956.

————. *Dr. Ox's Experiment.* Translated by Wang Moyi. Shanghai: Juvenile Press, 1956.

————. *A Family Without a Name.* Translated by Tian Xiaosheng, 1905.

————. *Five Weeks in a Balloon.* Translated by Yi Ming, 1903; and by Wang Wen. Beijing: Chinese Youth Press, 1957.

————. *From the Earth to the Moon.* Translated by Lu Xun. Shanghai: Evolution Press, 1903; and by Li Cangren. Beijing: Chinese Youth Press, 1979.

————. *Journey to the Center of the Earth.* Translated by Lu Xun. Shanghai: Popu-larization Press, 1906; and by Zhou Guisheng. Shanghai: Commercial Press, 1905; and by Yang Xianyi and Wen Shiqing. Beijing: Chinese Youth Press, 1959.

————. *The Mysterious Island.* Translated by Xi Ruo. Shanghai: Fiction Forest Press, 1905; and by Lian Xing. Beijing: Chinese Youth Press, 1957.

————. *Off on a Comet.* Translated by Wang Wenyi and He Youqi. Nanjing: Jiangsu People's Press, 1980.

————. *20,000 Leagues Under the Sea.* Translated by Zeng Juezhi. Beijing: Chinese Youth Press, 1961.

Wadley, Richard (USA). *The Man from Atlantis.* Translated and edited by Zhang Rui and others. Beijing: Ocean Press, 1980.

Wang, Fengzhen and Jin, Tao, eds. *Bermuda and UFOs.* Beijing: Ocean Press, 1980.

Wang, Xiaoda. "Shenmi de bo" (The Mysterious Wave). *Sichuan wenxue* (Sichuan Literature) (April 1979). Chengdu.

Wei, Yahua. "Wenrou zhixiang de meng" ("Conjugal Happiness in the Arms of

Morpheus"). *Beijing wenxue* (Beijing Literature) (January 1981). Beijing. Its sequel in *Yanhe* (Yanhe River) (May–July 1982). Jilin.

Wells, H. G. (UK). "Aepyornis Island." Translated by Mao Dun [Shen Yanbing]. *Xuesheng* (Students) (January, February, April 1917). Shanghai.

——. *The Invisible Man*. Translated by Zhang Hua. Beijing: Chinese Youth Press, 1956; second edition, 1980.

——. *Selected Works of H. G. Wells*. Translated by Sun Zonglu, et al. Nanjing: Jiangsu Science and Technology Press, 1980.

——. *The War of the Worlds*. Translated by Yi Zhi. Shanghai: Juvenile Press, 1957.

Williamson, Jack (USA). *Undersea City*. Beijing: Ocean Press, 1981.

Wu, Chengen. *Xi you ji (Journey to the West)*. Beijing: People's Press, reprint, 1954. Translated by W.J.F. Jenner. Beijing: Foreign Language Press, 1982.

Wu, Dingbo. "A Brief Survey of Chinese SF." *SF Gems* (April 1981). Japan.

Xiao, Jianheng. "Buke de qiyu" (Pup Buke's Adventures). *Women ai kexue* (We Love Science) (July 1962). Beijing.

——. "Shaluomu jiaoshou de miwu" (Professor Solomon's Delusion). *Renmin wenxue* (People's Literature) (December 1980). Beijing.

"Xiongmao jihua" (The Panda Project). Telefilm adapted from Ye Yonglie's story "X-3 Case," 1983.

Yan, Jiaqi. "Zongjiao, lixing shijia" (Religion, Reason, and Practice). Beijing: *Guangming ribao* (Guangming Daily), September 14, 1978.

Ye, Yonglie. "Fushi" (Corrosion). *Renmin wenxue* (People's Literature) (November 1981). Beijing.

——. *Lun kexue wenyi* (On Scientific Literature and Art). Beijing: Popular Science Press, 1980.

——. "Shiyou danbai" (Strange Cakes). *Shaonian kexue* (Juvenile Science) (May 1976). Shanghai.

——. "Zishi qiguo" (Reap As You Have Sown). Harbin: *Kehuan xiaoshuo bao*, November 19, 1981.

Yefremov, E. (USSR). *Starship*. Translated by Lou Mu. Shanghai: Chaofeng Press, 1955.

"Yinxing ren" (The Invisible Man). Telefilm adapted from Wu Boze's story of the same title, 1980.

Yu, Zhi [Ye Zhishan]. "Shizong de gege" (The Missing Elder Brother). *Zhongxuesheng* (High School Student) (July–August 1957). Beijing.

Zapalin, V., et al. (USSR). *The Strange "Transparent Glue."* Translated by Peng Lijia, et al. Beijing: Mass Press, 1956.

Zhang, Zhan. *Lie zi (The Book of Lie Zi)*, circa 307–313. Translated by A. C. Graham. London: Murray, 1960.

Zhang, Zhou. *Chao ye qian zai* (The Complete Records of the Court and Commoners), circa seventh century.

Zhao, Bo and Fu, Shen, eds. *Governess Shetita*. Zhongqing: Zhongqing Branch of Science and Technology Press, 1980.

Zheng, Wenguang. "Cong Diqiu dao Huoxing" (From Earth to Mars). Beijing: *Zhongguo shaonian bao* (Chinese Juvenile Daily), 1954.

"Zuihou yige aizheng sizhe" (The Last Man Who Dies of Cancer). Telefilm adapted from the story of the same title written by Zhou Yongnian, Zhang Fengjiang, and Jia Wanchao, 1980.

# I
# ROBOTS
# AND
# CLONES

# I

# The Death of the
# World's First Robot

## _____ TONG ENZHENG _____

A vast stretch of sand, yellow and boundless, like a sea extended into the far far distance, yellow, lonely and monotonous. An enormous caravan advanced among the sand dunes rather slowly, as if a line of boats were passing through congealed waves. Except for the slight clinking of the axles and the clip-clopping of horses' hoofs on the sand, there was no noise to be heard at all. What a desolate world! What a remote world left without human notice!

In the center of this caravan was a dragon carriage, especially tall and solid, covered with a silk canopy, and with all its sides beautifully carved. Drawn by eight snow-white horses, this was the well-known imperial carriage of King Zhou Muwang and his favorite concubine Chengji.

The events I am about to relate happened in the spring of 930 B.C. after the king had gone to Yanshan Mountain in the farthest West and encountered the Queen Mother of the West. Having finished this excursion, he was now journeying homeward.

It can be well imagined how tiring such a journey could be for the king in a time when there were no jet airplanes or hydrofoils. There are no historical records which could explain why King Zhou Muwang did not stay at his capital of Haojing enjoying a life of extravagance and dissipation but went to all that trouble of visiting the West instead. Maybe em-

Published in *Kexue wenyi* (Scientific Literature and Art), May 1982.

perors and kings as Sons of Heaven must act differently from ordinary human beings.

There were, however, some ordinary people, after all, who accompanied the king during this long and arduous trip. Although full of grievances and complaints, they dared not grumble. Yet the imperial concubine Chengji was an exception—she then was really not so ordinary.

"Say, darling. How soon can we leave this damned place for home?" She pouted her cherry-like small mouth. Though a complaint her words still sounded pleasant to the king's ear due to her sweet soft Southern accent mixing with the one or two foreign words she had just learned in the West. "You say it is a sight-seeing tour. Well, it could tour me to death if this monotony goes on."

"Well, listen. We'll get out of this desert and reach the city of Liuquan tonight. Then, take a hot bath and relax. And hold a ball, listen to music and dance some Northern-style dance. How about it, honey?"

Zhou Muwang was over fifty, but indulged himself in creature comforts as if he were still quite young. He was fat-headed with big ears, greying at the temples. He usually kept up his prestige by putting on airs of dignity, but with his favorite Chengji he was especially patient.

Thinking that she could get rid of this vast desert and enjoy her usual comforts tonight, Chengji felt a bit solaced and let her long face relax a bit. But she still gave him an angry stare and said with jealousy, "Who's going to dance with you? You'd better look out for that ugly dowager!"

Obviously the hint referred to the Queen Mother of the West. Zhou Muwang had been engaged in some activities of foreign affairs with that venerable lady, but it evoked strong jealousy on the part of the imperial concubine who could not shake it off entirely for long.

"Well, well," Zhou Muwang patted her on the rump. "Haven't I been giving my company to you all the time now?"

Chengji acknowledged this with a coquettish "H'm." She then turned to watch the vast expanse of sand and sighed softly as she wished they would reach the city of Liuquan as quickly as possible.

The king's royal remarks were infallible laws. At dusk, the imperial caravan really did enter the city of Liuquan. Though not big, this city looked spic and span, without a pedestrian, because the advance guards had notified the city of the imperial advent three days before. The whole city was now decorated with lanterns and colored streamers, and not a soul in sight, ready to receive His Majesty.

Had it been in the old days, Chengji would not have shown the slightest interest in such a rustic small town. However, the life she had spent in the desert these days really made her feel suffocated and oppressed. Now that she had gotten to a place with human habitation, she once again became excited and high spirited. As soon as she settled down in their city quarters, she asked the king to make arrangements for the evening entertainment. The king had to summon the head of the city at once.

"What kind of entertainment do you have here for me to appreciate?"

"Your Majesty," the head of the city was flustered, as he had never seen the king before. "This is a remote place without a regular theatrical company. A circus troupe staged here half a year ago, and then a Sichuan opera troupe. But they all left a long time ago. There is no way to get them back now."

"Well, then. . . ," the king looked sullen.

Although this head of the city had not seen much of the world, he knew quite well there was no telling when the king would become angry. Once the king became irritated, great trouble would eventually follow. So he hastened to add, "Your Majesty, there appeared a craftsman here two days ago, called Yanshi. It's said that he's created a gadget and that he's going to show his skill in the interior of your kingdom. I can have him brought here for your entertainment. How about it, Your Majesty?"

"Oh, what lousy luck!" Chengji chipped in. "It's probably a monkey show."

"Don't be angry, Honey. You might as well let him have a try." The King tried to comfort her. "If there's nothing interesting, we can have a ball by ourselves."

After dinner, the great hall of Liuquan was dazzling bright with torches. The royal orchestra stood on either side and the evening show began. Chengji was dressed up with special care and effort this evening. In a newly designed evening skirt made of specially processed Western material, and with her face glowing with health, she sat with the king on the substitute throne at the head of the hall, ready to watch Yanshi's presentation.

Yanshi was ushered in, but he did not come alone. Instead, he was accompanied by a handsome young man.

"Who's he?" the king asked in surprise.

"This is a robot I've made, capable of singing and dancing. I've brought it here especially for Your Majesty to entertain you this evening."

"What did you say? A robot? You've made a robot?" The king was greatly amazed. Turning to the young man, he asked, "Hello, are you a robot?" The young man kneeled down and replied properly. "Yes, I am a robot, Your Majesty."

"Can you sing and dance?'

"Please give instructions, Your Majesty."

The king was full of zeal now. "Fine. This is really a strange thing that I've never heard of before. Dance, please."

The band started the music, and the young man began dancing to the tune. His posture and movements were graceful and full of changes. While dancing, the robot also began to sing. His singing was pleasing to the ear, overflowing with enthusiasm. All the movements of his hands and feet were in step with the rhythms of the music, and were full of intelligence, and full of beauty.

While watching the show, the king could not but laugh and say to Chengji in a whisper, "Yanshi's very, very cunning. He's brought here an actor who claims to be a robot. He thought we might be taken in. Take a careful look at the young man. Could there be such a robot in the world?"

Chengji not only agreed with the king, but also had some of her own ideas. She was used to a life of bustle and excitement at court. Behind the king's back she used to flirt with those handsome young descendants of the nobility. But during this journey with the king, she had only seen the desolate mountains, wild birds and beasts. Fed up with all of these, she was almost vexed to death. Now she suddenly saw such a good-looking youth capable of singing and dancing that she couldn't help but love him. Taking advantage of the king's blissful ignorance, she had already put on a show of coquetry, leering at the young man with obvious affection several times.

The robot knew little of the world. Ever since he had seen the light of day he had never seen such an enchantingly charming woman, gorgeously clad and richly ornamented, and he had never experienced the magical power of tantalization initiated by the other sex. His heart—to be exact, that mechanical part which played the role of a heart—was now filled with love, an entirely alien emotion to him. Being a robot, he did not know the correct way to express his affection. Though he was dancing, his fervid eyes were fixed on Chengji and could never move away from her.

How could such an absurd situation last long? Out of male instincts, the king soon smelt a rat. He turned and took a look at Chengji and then at the young man who were still making eyes at each other, completely carried away by their mutual affection. The king flew into such a rage that he could not help but shout, "You devil, Yanshi! You've set a trap to take me in! You've brought this hooligan to seduce my concubine. How dare you! Guards! Take the two knaves out, and behead them both right now!"

Before Yanshi had time to make any explanations, the guards swarmed in and tightly surrounded him and his robot. Normally, robots are superhumanly strong, and this robot should have had enough strength to resist for some time. Pity that Yanshi had taught him how to sing and dance but not how to fight. To use scientific terminology, this robot was not programmed to fight. That's why he resigned himself to being caught and placed himself at the mercy of the guards.

Gleaming bronze broadswords were raised high over their heads. Should the executioners sweep their broadswords downward, Yanshi and his robot would be beheaded. Yanshi was greatly terrified, crying out "wrong, wrong" constantly. As for his robot, he had no idea about executions, and did not even realize that it was he who had brought this disaster down on his creator and himself. With puppy love eyes, he was still staring longingly at Chengji!

"You, you, damn you! You're still crying 'wrong'!" The king foamed and stormed. "Turn your damned head and look at that rascal and see what he's doing! Watch his amorous eyes!"

"Please calm down, Your Majesty," Yanshi kowtowed repeatedly. "He is really a robot. His absurd behavior is really beyond my expectation. It is really because I've made him too intelligent. Show your sagacity, Your Majesty, and check the robot on the spot, please!"

In his usual temper, the king would merely wave his hand and ten heads would be severed from their bodies. But this time his curiosity overwhelmed his jealousy. He ordered his guards to release Yanshi and let him check the robot right away.

Yanshi took a few hand tools from his pocket and walked over to the robot. With a deft hand, he quickly took off the robot's clothes and dismantled the body. Without a shadow of a doubt, this young man was a robot. All of his internal organs were made up of sets of machines. His skeleton was made of bronze; his joints of adjustable hinges, his skin, hair and teeth, though looking human, were all artificial.

The king thought it a monstrous absurdity, and stepped down from his throne to check it himself. When he turned one part of the machine, the robot became unable to speak. When he turned another part, the robot's eyes failed to see anything. When he turned a third part, the robot could not move anymore. Now the king was greatly relieved. With his jealous anger turning to appreciative joy, he praised Yanshi, "Well, great. Your superb craftsmanship really excels nature."

"Silly! What silly shit!" Chengji cursed disappointedly, and turned to enter the inner chamber reserved for women. But the king burst into laughter.

Then the king took Yanshi and the robot all the way to the capital of Haojing. In order to show off his newly obtained star of singing and dancing, he held a magnificent banquet in the palace. This was a grand evening party, indeed. Dukes, nobles and government officials for several hundred miles around all made their appearance at the party. The splendid palace was decorated with even more awe-inspiring bouquets of flowers, piles of silk, and dazzling torches than normal. After the sumptuous feast, Yanshi's robot began his performance.

The moment he began dancing, his eyes searched for Chengji among the spectators and soon spotted her. She was all the more dressed up with pearls and glittering jewels this evening. A group of young attendants and aristocrats gathered round her like a myriad of stars surrounding the moon.

How pleased and excited the robot became when he saw his beloved one again! He danced enthusiastically and executed some intricate, graceful steps which even Yanshi could not have imagined. The robot wished that Chengji would look at him more and reveal her fascinating expressions as she had done last time.

Chengji did look at the robot, but merely as other spectators were doing. What's even worse, as this was her second time watching the performance, she seemed less interested. She took a handkerchief from the hand of a young man one moment and a cold drink from the hand of another the next, offering all her charming smile and feminine warmth to those pampered sons of wealthy and influential families. Those young men were all dressed in silks and satins and engaged in fine-style conversation. Compared with them, this robot was nothing short of a rustic bumpkin.

What a pitiful robot! For all his intelligence, he could not understand this woman's sentiments. He could not understand why his lover had changed her heart in such a short time. Hence this robot experienced another kind of emotion which often comes with love-embittered distress. When he danced his last movement, when thunderous applause overwhelmed the palace, he cast his last sorrowful glance at Chengji. With the crack of something breaking in his chest, the robot fell down to the ground and never moved again. However hard Yanshi tried to repair his robot, it was all in vain. The world's first robot thus died, if the word "die" can be applied to robots; but since I have called it "he" all along, why not say "die?"

More than two thousand years later, the American science fiction writer Isaac Asimov laid out the so-called Three Laws of Robotics, namely: one, A robot may not injure a human being, or, through inaction, allow a human being to come to harm; two, A robot must obey the orders given it by human beings except where such orders would conflict with the first law; three, A robot must protect its own existence as long as such protection does not conflict with the first or second law. The tragic end of the world's first robot, nevertheless, shows that Asimov's three laws are not enough. The fourth law should be added, namely: a robot should not fall in love. Without the first three laws, robots could do harm to human beings; but without the fourth one, robots could do harm to themselves, because blind and passionate love is certainly very dangerous to human beings, let alone robots.

*Translated by Wu Dingbo*

# 2

# Conjugal Happiness in the Arms of Morpheus

## WEI YAHUA

**THE END**

I've resolved to divorce my robot wife!

No matter how she pleads for my forgiveness with her eyes glistening with tears, (oh, those pitiable and lovely eyes); no matter how she tries to cool my anger with her tender-heartedness as a wife or with the special language between husband and wife, the case is closed.

Once I believed that my marriage was the most blissful on earth, but. . . .

I've made up my mind to divorce her now.

What's all this about? And why, you ask?

**THE BEGINNING**

About a year ago, on my twenty-second birthday, I received a pink card, smelling strongly of musk rose, from the Marriage Management Center. With this special card I could get a robot girl for my wife from any robot company.

There were two brothers and one sister in my family and I was the youngest. As I was not the only child, according to the population laws and regulations, only one of us three children could marry a natural human being. And based on sound eugenic principles, my older sister en-

Published in *Beijing wenxue* (Beijing Literature), January 1981.

joyed the privileges of women designed to prevent the devolution of the human species. Hence she could marry a natural man. My elder brother and I had to marry robots.

## SPOUSE SELECTION

I went to the Universal Robot Company.

The general manager accompanied me to the supermarket sales floor. It seemed that he was an efficient manager. He did not merely let his robots idly serve as mannequins for the customers to watch and choose passively. Instead, he had all his robots working as salesgirls and attendants, so customers could appreciate their usefulness and their beauty. There were ten thousand robot girls ready for marriage in the supermarket. Those girls and goods were both on sale. However, the robot girls were to be sold by the special cards from the Marriage Management Center.

Oh, what a dazzling sight! There were so many pretty girls for the eyes to take in. Each was more beautiful than the other. I felt as if I were strolling in a garden where hundreds of flowers bloomed in competition.

This company was first rate. First of all, it employed the world's first-rate artists. It had a strong lineup of aestheticians composed of painters, sculptors and craftsmen. Secondly, it kept the most complete records of aesthetics. It had the aesthetic data of the most beautiful women, ancient and modern, Western and Eastern of all races.

For four thousand years since the dawn of history, mankind has carried on a kind of natural aesthetic sifting and reducing by way of lovemaking. However, this process is rather slow, and is frequently disrupted and interfered with by all kinds of other factors, such as power and property, politics and economics, pride and prejudice. But now, with the production of robots, this process can be manipulated by computer according to human will. As a result, what would have taken several centuries can be done in just a few weeks or months.

Among the records of the Universal Robot Company were all the aesthetic data of those ancient eastern beauties like Xi Shi, Wang Qiang, Yang Yuhuan, Zhao Feiyan, Lu Zhu, Ying Ying, Zhuo Wenjun. . . . There were also Western types: Paris girls, Gypsy girls, girls of the Roman type and the Constantinople type, angelic girls like Helena, and romantic girls like Shakespeare's Desdemona and Pushkin's Argulina.

If the finished products (each had something to recommend herself and each had her own unique graceful carriage) should fail to please a customer, no worry; the customer could have robots made to order. He could present his special requirements. The company had all the aesthetic records of the most beautiful movie stars and the managerial staff would provide him indexes for reference. If the customer happened to find a girl he liked best in real life (probably on the street, by the seaside or in a garden), he could just tell the company about his encounter and it would obtain all the aesthetic data of the girl by means of a wondrous hologram, analyze them, decide which to use, and, finally, produce a celestial beauty second to none according to the golden section of the aesthetic laws. She was the kind of girl he could only imagine in his dreams. Without a shadow of doubt, he would feel overjoyed and would not be able to help loving her head over heels.

The manager led me around. We strolled slowly before every counter so that I could have plenty of time to appreciate those angelic girls. An artist once said: Human beings are the most beautiful of all natural shapes. Human beings are nature's masterpieces. As the Chinese ancients said: Human beings are the pith and marrow of earth and heaven, the cream of the cream in the world. Those words seemed to me to be oracles, indeed.

Human beings are superior among all beautiful shapes and beautiful forms of expressions in the whole universe, I thought. And those robot girls were all like freshly blooming flowers. Each was more delicate and charming than the other.

The manager said with pride, "Surely no one who sees them can be unmoved because, after all, they are the outstanding beauties selected from all the prettiest women at all times and in all countries. They are all *par excellence.* You'll find them pleasing to both your eyes and mind. Your eyes can only see part of their charms—external beauty. As a matter of fact, they also have internal beauty—moral excellence which is more beautiful and which will be the never-ending wellspring of your undying love. Pity that you can't see it with your eyes. The Chinese ancients likened love to a jade bracelet: jade, pure white; bracelet, never to be snapped off. That's the exact analogy to show the inborn nature of loyalty on the part of the robot girls in love. Since a robot girl's mode of thinking is as succinct, definite, strict and unique as mathematical formulas and geometrical theorems, she loves only one man all her life. Once a man's name is filled in her voucher, she will love him forever: constant, faithful, unyielding and unswerving."

I grinned. "But what if I should die?" I asked.

The manager patted me on the shoulder. "She is designed in accordance with the law of symmetry of the universe. Her service life is symmetrical to your lifespan. Her existence is symmetrical to yours and your death is also symmetrical to hers. As symmetrical as applied force and anti-applied force, centripetal force and centrifugal force. Do you understand?" Walking slowly, we appreciated those wonderful flowers of science.

The manager made further recommendations with beaming smiles. "That's just one aspect. Here's another. These robot girls are not only more beautiful but also more gentle than flowers. Your wife-to-be will never engage in strife with you, never quarrel with you."

"Really?" I asked in surprise. So far as I knew, no couple in the world, not even the most harmonious ones, could be exempt from an occasional quarrel in their married life. And according to the newly released findings reported by the United Nations, the divorce rate among natural human couples was tending to increase in recent years.

"Haven't you ever heard of the famous Three Laws of Robotics?" The manager stared at me with amazement as if I didn't know that the earth revolves around the sun. He pointed at a white marble tablet standing upright at the center of the supermarket. It was supported on the back of a great stone turtle as if it were in a museum. On this tablet were engraved the glittering letters of Three Laws of Robotics as laid out by the American, Isaac Asimov:

1. A robot may not injure a human being, or, through inaction, allow a human being to come to harm.
2. A robot must obey the orders given it by human beings except where such orders would conflict with the first law.
3. A robot must protect its own existence as long as such protection does not conflict with the first or second law.

(Handbook of Robotics, 56th edition, A.D. 2085)

"Those are the golden rules and precious precepts in our production of robots," the manager explained. "Before leaving the factory, every robot must undergo a strict examination. If a company produces or neglects to examine a robot which violates the Three Laws of Robotics, the company will immediately be fined, go bankrupt and even be prosecuted legally."

Pointing to the Second Law, "A robot must obey the orders given it by human beings . . . ," the manager exaggeratedly assured me, "You'll be her monarch, her god. She'll be ever obedient, ever loyal and ever faithful to you. Like your hands and feet, she'll always be at your disposal. Unlike an independent person, she will seem to be an extension of your physical being. She'll obey all your orders unconditionally. She'll be your band and follow your melody harmoniously. Like a tuning fork which shares the same frequency with you, she'll ever respond to your call and resonate with you in exactly the same frequency. Judging from this and this alone, what a lovable girl she is!"

I walked and listened, listened and walked, as if in a dream, as if in the seventh heaven. The manager kept on talking volubly with fervor, assuring me and assuaging all my fears and apprehensions.

"Natural human beings answer your instructions according to this logical procedure: instruction—analysis—decision (resist or execute)—action. But the robots have a much simpler logical procedure: instruction—execution, because their softwares are all designed in accordance with this procedure. Your wife-to-be will never cease to be faithful to you. Although you are two, you two share one mind, your mind. Isn't it in keeping with the wonderful love formula: $1 + 1 = 1$? Isn't such a wife an incarnation of your ideal, young man?"

"She'll be sterile!" I grumbled.

"You!" The manager nodded at me with sneering contempt. "Can it be her weak point? On the contrary, it's her strong point! Don't forget that she'll never grow old and that she'll always be your girl full of youthful vigor! Why do you want to have children anyway? To support you when you grow old? Don't forget that daughters will sooner or later get married off. After marriage they often care for their husbands much more than their parents. And in most cases sons will forget their own mothers once they have wives. But a robot wife is different; she is the only one most loyal to you. She'll wait on you faithfully till the day you die a natural death. She can play both roles as your wife in capacity and as your child in function. Where on earth can you find such perfection? Talking about children, you must know it is rather a hard job to raise them. Although children do bring a great joy to the family, they'll certainly cause much more strain, frustration, hardship and even poverty. They'll take much of your precious time and energy. Well, if in your later years, you'd like to have such a plaything as a son or a daughter to ease your mind, come here and we can provide you a little robot—your child. Son or daughter as you like. He or she will carry on the genetic factors from both you and your wife, and the best ones, to be sure. Once you see the kid, you'll never believe it is a little robot. You'll surely think he is your own child whom you have put in a kindergarten or your missing child about whom you have had no news for some time. . . . As to our robots' sterility, it is a great contribution of historical significance. Thanks to their sterility, we have solved the world-wide population crisis which began over a century ago in the 1960s. As a result, the world population remains constant, about four billion. Thus we have averted inflation, economic crises, famines, turmoils, wars and the catastrophically demographic doom which over-population would otherwise have led to. Taking this into consideration, we can almost claim that our robots have saved mankind. Can you still maintain that robots' sterility is a weak point?"

I was left without an argument. Not only speechless, but hardly knowing how to speak! Because I had discovered her—Lili! I can't explain because I myself do not know why and how I identified her from the masses of the beautiful robot girls at just that moment.

Nonetheless, the manager rambled on in a flow of eloquence. "Just because robots are sterile, our company can still stand here now. Otherwise natural human girls would have destroyed it. They are jealous of robot girls because robots are far more charming. Human girls are too inferior in character to bear comparison in this respect. If robot girls could bear children, human girls would have felt too ashamed to show their faces and they would have been in danger of being cast aside. Only because robot girls are sterile, human girls can look down their noses at the robots and sneer at them. They say things like: 'Look at those hens which can never lay eggs!' And because the robots are sterile, human girls enjoy the privileges of the ration system of marriage. Robot girls are so well-behaved that they will never seduce another's husband. They work hard to keep harmonious relations with natural human girls. They're dear sisters to them as well as to each other. Robot girls treat their husbands with all warmheartedness, but they are as cold as ice to other men. They'll bravely defend their chastity from assault because self-defense is mandatory in the Third Law of Robotics. Come on, young man!"

It was not until then that the manager discovered that I had lagged far, far behind him. Behind the counter that sold famous wines stood a goddess. She was gazing fixedly at the next counter where there were large aquariums. Some various-colored goldfish were vying with a school of dazzling, brilliant Spanish mackerel for food.

I can hardly describe Lili. The most flowery language seems inadequate to convey the majesty of her charms. At first glance, I just felt that my whole body, my blood, everything in me blazed like a cloud of saturated alcohol vapor touching a flickering tongue of flame. My whole body, my blood and even my hair seemed to shiver in the flames.

Could it be the very taste of love? . . . One glimpse could set you on fire, one glimpse could get you drunk!

She didn't see me at first. She was staring at those goldfish. Stars glittered under her long eyelashes and a pair of dimples danced on the moon of her face. Her mien excelled Helen's in beauty as much as a dove does a raven. Overjoyed? Coquettish? Yearning? Surmising? . . . She looked like the jade statue standing in the fountain and glistening with dewdrops of spring all over. She was the sun among the girls and she was the girl in the sun!

The manager cast a glimpse at me and realized almost at once what had happened. He returned and patted me on the shoulder. Then he said with a smile. "Fine. What uncanny eyesight you have, young man. She is our best product, our gold medal winner this year. She belongs to you now!"

He took out a pen at once and signed the name of Lili on the card, and before I had time to stop him, he called out, "Lili!" Lili was taken aback. She spun around obediently, a pair of touching eyes glittering with amazement. When she found that the manager was coming over together with a young man glowing in health, a maidenly blush appeared suddenly painted on her cheeks. She hung her head and dared not hold it up again. Other robot girls in the vicinity laughed up their sleeves.

The manager walked over and handed her the pink card. "Extend your hands," he ordered.

I saw that she still hung her head on her chest. She dared not look out from those long lashes to examine me. She looked as if she wanted to find a place to hide herself for shame. But she extended her delicate little hand obediently. The manager produced a jewel case from his pocket and took out a pair of engagement rings. He solemnly put one with a ruby on my finger and the other with an emerald on hers.

All the other robot girls gathered around, giggling, shouting, pushing, and shoving. No sooner had we put on the rings than cheers and music exploded from all around. A rain of flowers poured down like a waterfall. Rose, lilac, jasmine, red plum—red, yellow, purple, blue, white—all kinds of petals spilled all over us and all over the ground. The best man and bridesmaid surrounded us at once. Lili and I were led away separately to change our clothes, bathe and dress up.

When I saw Lili again shortly afterward, she had cut her plaits, the symbol of her maidenhood, and had a permanent wave instead. Dressed in a gown with a long train, she stood in front of me, fair, slim, and graceful above all praise.

The Universal Robot Company released our marriage for a TV news broadcast immediately.

Amidst the music of jubilation we were escorted by big crowds to the gate where our sedan, decorated in wedding gaiety with colored streamers, was waiting for us. The manager kissed both of us on our foreheads. He liked old customs very much. Then he blessed us, "May you love each other and live to a ripe old age in conjugal happiness."

In the sedan I cast a glimpse at Lili. Just at that moment she happened to turn her eyes to steal a glance at me, too. The minute her eyes met mine, she felt so embarrassed that she shivered as if burnt, and turned her head hastily.

I felt that my head swam with intoxication.

## HONEYMOON

Our happiness as newlyweds was beyond description indeed!

Lili was so beautiful that anyone would fall into the abyss of love with a single glance at her. I often burned the midnight oil and she always sat beside me for company. Whenever I raised my eyelids and saw her, I would be immediately relieved of my fatigue at once and I would remember an ancient verse:

> With fragrance emitting from her red sleeves,
> I read in the stillness of the night.

Maybe it was because there was so much love in my own eyes that hers often glistened with happy embarrassment. I finally began to realize the profound implications of the manager's description: "Not only more beautiful but also more gentle than flowers. . . ." Lili's character proved more beautiful than appearance. She was docile and obedient to me and she cared for me with great solicitude. She was like a goddess in her carriage and an angel in character.

She was so bright that she could search my mind with her clear beautiful eyes that seemed like limpid waters in spring. She would anticipate my wants; make ready things that had just occurred to me. I almost felt that the strong fragrant love between us had already reached saturation.

Between us, I was the symbol of authority and she was the symbol of obedience. It was not until this moment that I realized the profound implication and the wonderful taste of the manager's speech: "You'll be her monarch!" And only now did I understand how accurate the strange love formula was: $1+1=1$.

This formula seemed more meaningful and philosophical to us than to any other couple because we two shared one mind, which was mine. I was the singer and she was my band. I was the TV station and she was a TV set with only one frequency channel and receiving only what I broadcast.

Between us there existed a wonderful circle which Newton's Law of Universal Gravitation could expound. Newton's law says, "The gravitational attraction of two bodies is directly proportional to the product of their masses and inversely proportional to the square of the distance between them." So, in other words, the shorter the distance, the greater the attraction; the greater the attraction, the shorter the distance. Thus the centripetal force increases exponentially while the distance decreases exponentially. That was the mathematical formula of our love.

Only the lovers head over heels in love can really know the holy power of Newton's law. When Newton put forth his immortal formula, he probably had no idea about its application in the calculation of love.

Some people say that marriage is the final stage of love. But that's a lopsided view. Marriage is a higher stage of love.

During this period of time my work went smoothly. The POT research project made headway at a miraculous pace, like a hot knife cutting through butter. It was about to bear rich fruit. At this very moment I cherished the special memory of the founder of this project, my teacher Professor Shi Chun. His last words, which he had repeated again and again on his deathbed, were "We must find the element No. 109!"

At that moment all the heavy ion physicists the world over were following this track. With hard work and added vigor, we would surely be the swiftest in this race and the first to score the goal.

## A BED OF ROSES

During this period of time, my eyes could only perceive Lili's strong points. Brushing aside all the shortcomings of natural human girls, Lili possessed all their merits. In my mind's eye she was almost an angelic super-ideal wife, the acme of perfection.

She was obedient to me in the extreme. In this respect she possessed the strongest traits of Eastern women. Like women from ancient China, Japan or Korea, she not only followed all my instructions unconditionally but also submitted to my mischiefs meekly. She was able to endure and undergo trials without being overwhelmed by them.

In order to test her obedience and see how far it would go, I deliberately threw some difficulties in her way. For instance, I would not let her wash the saucers after a meal. Instead, I said with a malicious smile, "Lick them clean, Lili!" She took out a dish obediently, but pretended not to have heard me clearly. She watched me as if waiting for me to change my instructions. But I stuck like a limpet! I repeated my instruction, sort of begging: "Lick them clean, Lili." She was obliged to hold up the dish, and she stuck out her little tongue and licked off the dregs on the dish like a cat. Obviously, feeling wronged, she stared at me with big eyes. But I just gave her a smile, a mischievous, elated and contented smile. Before long she seemed glad, too.

After a while I played another trick on her. I said, "Meow like a cat, Lili." This time she did not hesitate, though she stared at me with a strange, grieving look as if she were saying, "How tricky you are!" Then, she made a face and said, "Meow." She imitated the animal perfectly as if there were really a cat meowing. For my part, I paid her every obedience with more of my passionate love.

We often played chess. She was a master chess player because she had read many chess manuals. But she never beat me. And I often retracted false moves in games and even played her foul. However, she just grinned and bore it without grumbling. She would watch my face intently, studying my expressions and adjusting her moves accordingly. When I looked impetuous, she would make false moves herself intentionally to let me turn defeat into victory with beaming smiles.

At first her generosity and attentiveness pleased me very much. Nonetheless, with the passage of time I gradually felt bored with the predictability of her behavior. I began to imagine that quarreling could be a pleasure, too. Just as the moon changed from crescent to full, from shady to bright; just as seasons turned spring, summer, fall and winter; just as a man who hated both hot summer and cold winter and eventually moved to a place with spring all the year round would gradually feel the unchanging weather rather dull, not so varied as his original dwelling place with a rich array of clearly demarcated four seasons; I wanted some change. I wanted to quarrel.

I began to try to irritate her deliberately, just to see whether I could make her angry. Early in the morning, I extended my feet. She saw them and hurried over to put on socks and shoes for me. After she helped me put on my clothes, she washed and shaved my face. It so happened that while she was shaving me, I felt an urge to sneeze. Thus I got a cut on my face. I flew into a rage and slapped her across her face. Quietly she stood there. When I boxed her on the right cheek, she turned the other cheek. She forced a smile, though with tears in her eyes.

How well behaved she was!

And I really loved her. But I did not believe that she would never get angry. Even rabbits would gnaw people in anger.

Once I turned around and inadvertently knocked down a crystal cup! I picked a quarrel with her willfully. I cursed her angrily and accused her of having no brains to have put the crystal cup there. I chose the most stinging words and called her a rotten robot without proper parental upbringing. . . .

And how did she react? The tears trickled down from her eyes. While tidying things up, she made repeated apologies. How pitiable! I couldn't help feeling sorry for her. I hastened to coax her with honeyed words till she burst into laughter.

What else could I do with her?

Never would she get angry! Now I truly learned the power of Asimov's Three Laws of Robotics. Ever since her production she had never learned to talk back or quarrel. She was the incarnation of obedience. She was the obedient mud, a combination of obedient water with obedient earth. Her character was composed of ninety-nine percent obedience, plus one more obedience.

Nevertheless, I myself changed a lot. I could no longer keep my temper. As I was the autocrat at home, I felt that nothing outside my home fell in with my wishes and no people were pleasing to my eyes. I found that those natural human beings in the research institute, in the lab, and in the service counter were all very rude, wanton, savage, arrogant, haughty and ugly beyond description. The more I saw Lili so lovely, the more I perceived the others as disgusting. The nearer I drew to Lili, the farther I kept from others. Thus, I liked to stay more and more at home and found the office dirty, disorderly, and filled with filthy, unbreathable air. I spent less and less time in the research institute.

At home, Lili treated me with rose water, but outside everyone and everything seemed to oppose me. One day, I drove my car downtown. When I reached the commercial district, the road became narrow. I pressed my horn all the time, but the car in front would not give way. I got so furious that I sped up in an attempt to overtake other cars on the road. Who would have thought that I'd bump against a car on the left? In consequence, I scratched off some of the paint on my car. I stopped my car immediately and had a quarrel with that driver. When the police officer finally arrived on the scene, to my great surprise and indignation, he fined me! To make matters worse, when I got to work my superior had a private talk with me. He criticized me, saying that I had become lazy, arrogant, rash, and eccentric in recent days, especially since I got married. He pointed out seriously that I as the chief person in charge of the POT research project was not allowed to be in such a state of mind because the POT research project was about to bear fruit and all the other research workers were carrying on their respective duties on double shifts.

I was greatly annoyed at heart. Weren't they jealous of my wife's beauty and virtue? Weren't they jealous of our conjugal happiness? Could it be her fault?

Poor Lili! That talk deepened the gap between my co-workers and me. I gradually discovered the fundamental difference between natural human beings and robots—they were different in soul.

The other half of Newton's Law worked between me and them now. The greater the distance, the less the attraction; and the less the attraction, the greater the distance. The centripetal force increased between Lili and me while the centrifugal force increased between the research institute and me. One was a vicious circle and the other a benign circle. Two circles intensified by squares. With their respective speeds getting faster and faster, they both advanced toward their respective critical points.

My superior's words had not sobered me up. On the contrary, the incident made me even more estranged from my colleagues and leading cadres. And it even affected my philosophy. I began to have doubts about the prospects of natural human beings and human society. I became a pessimist, and a skeptic, too.

I even wondered if some day natural human beings would be replaced by intelligent and beautiful robots who were becoming more and more advanced. The succession of generations and progression of the natural human beings were much slower than those of robots. Mankind had walked with a slow and heavy step for four thousand years and reached only its present level of intelligence, whereas the computer, with a history of just a few decades since the advent of the primitive ENIAC, had already caught up and surpassed the intelligence level of modern humanity. Moreover, the control and design of robots in production, expiration, planning, manipulation, quality and quantity were much easier than those of natural human beings. Robots were so clever, so kindhearted, so docile and so easy to rule over that they would never touch off a war, stir up a riot, form a conspiracy, plot a subversion, or stage a coup d'état. They would need no army or violence. They would cut down military expenditures from astronomical figures to nothing.

My conclusion was: Sooner or later natural human beings would be replaced by robots; mankind would lose out completely in the struggle for existence and fundamental changes would take place in society.

I sank into degradation in my conjugal happiness.

## DEGRADATION

Things developed and changed continually. I have to recall the series of events which happened recently.

Previously I had been a heavy smoker. Then I found smoking impaired my health seriously; I was afflicted with bronchitis in particular. I began to control the amount of my smoking. I bought a specially-made cigarette case which had a timer. It rolled out only one cigarette every two hours. In this way I was able to cut down to four or five cigarettes a day. After I adopted this measure, my health improved very much. But I must admit that I suffered terribly from the deprivation. Sometimes I sighed at the stingy cigarette case.

Lili was so smart that she knew my secret. So, she surreptitiously found the key to the cigarette case and brought it with her quietly. Whenever she saw me frown at the cigarette case, she would put the key in front of me on the sly while stealthily observing the expression on my face with her diamond-like ebony eyes.

See what a good wife she was! How could one nit-pick at such a cute wife! And that was not all.

Wine was my favorite drink. I could not live without it. However, I had been moderate in drinking as in smoking, two small cups of mild grape wine at noon every day.

I knew quite well that biological phenomena were without exception forms of the movement of electricity. The ultramicro-bioluminescence of the human body, the bioelectric current, the biomagnetic field, psi power; they were all forms of electrobiology. Because of the above mentioned theory, I had a special inclination for wine. To me, drinking was like charging a battery. But I also knew that the coil would be damaged if the electric current were too great. That would cause the brain to discharge too much electricity. Excessive drinking would do harm to my heart. Therefore, I controlled my intake of wine very strictly.

Nevertheless, as good wine was tempting, mellow, fragrant, sweet, re-freshing, stimulating, exciting, anyone fond of drinking would understand that it was altogether too attractive to be stopped. And my addiction to alcohol wouldn't escape Lili's keen eyes, made all the sharper by love.

At supper, when I saw the delicacies she had prepared personally, I couldn't help turning my eyes toward the wine bottles in the cupboard. How nice it would be to have a cup or two, I thought. Again, she read my mind and brought over a bottle. Thus I could not dine without her company. The more I drank, the more I laughed. Lili felt elated when she found that my laughter was inversely proportional to the wine kept in the cupboard. However, neither she nor I noticed a latent crisis. This crisis was accumulating energy and advancing toward the critical point. . . .

Lili was glad to hear more and more of my laughter at home, but she did not and could not notice other changes in me. I saw fewer and fewer smiling faces in the research institute because my efficiency at work fell sharply. But at any rate, the POT research project was drawing to its final stage and we held a safe lead in such projects in the world. That was why I still felt at ease. The manuscript was being completed, one page after another, and the thesis gathered volume bit by bit.

Again, it was the season for maples to turn red.

Fall, fall of rich fruits, fall of golden spectrums!

## NIGHTMARE

A double blessing was soon to descend upon my home: one for the success of the POT research project, the other for the anniversary of my marriage with Lili.

Xinhua News Agency sent me its press release reporting the achievements of the POT research project. It fully affirmed the great significance of this research project and also affirmed my personal contribution to it. Reading this news release, I felt so excited that tears welled up in my eyes, thinking of the painstaking work of scientists of several generations who had been willing ladders for others to climb up and willing cobblestones to pave the way, thinking of the white bones of those explorers who had died halfway on this long, long path.

Lily had been looking forward to this day with eager expectancy every day, too. This day finally arrived and it happened to coincide with my holiday.

Early in the morning with the sun just rising, Lili and I had already dressed ourselves smartly. We attached a light boat with an outboard motor to our car and packed a picnic lunch for the backseat and sped off for the seashore.

The sky looked intensely blue. The sun shone in all its splendid beauty. The sea was very gentle, with tiny waves lingering about. We sped along on the tips of the high waves like an arrow, sprinkling the sea with our songs and laughter. The soft breeze extended her arms to hold us two and the white clouds pressed their tender cheeks close to our chests. . . .

Soaring to the great heights, seagulls welcomed us in front, while merrily singing petrels chased us from behind. When we became hungry, we stopped on a beautiful coral island to dine. When we became tired, we napped on the warm sandy beach. We did not return home until the setting sun had settled into the quilt of evening mist, birds had returned to the depths of the thick woods, the moon sprayed her glittering splendor, and the stars blinked their curious eyes and trailed us for company. . . .

All day long, we had had only the picnic on the small island. Now back at home we both felt hungry. Luckily, there was enough food in the re-

frigerator, and Lili was an able housewife. Half an hour later, a lavish
supper was ready.

I took up the wine cup and smelled a sweet, intense whiff of fragrance.
I looked at the wine cup and realized that Lili had exchanged the grape
wine with strong gold-award brandy without my noticing. As I raised my
gaze, I just met her diamond-like ebony eyes; she was watching me quietly, intently, passionately. . . .

What is happiness?

What is love?

That glittering pair of diamond eyes were the answer. That pair of eyes
were more intoxicating than good wine because they were filled with love.

I drank one cup after another. . . . I emptied one bottle and sent her to
fetch another. I resolved to drink for once to my heart's content! I resolved
to drink my fill of the full cup of happiness.

The cup was filled with happiness!

The cup was filled with youthfulness!

The cup was filled with joy!

The cup was filled with love!

. . . .

How could anyone stop drinking from it?

. . . .

I got dead drunk. How could I have avoided it?

I saw Lili change the expression on her face. When she watched me, her
eyes showed horror. It was not until then that I began to realize I was
probably quite drunk.

I tried to comfort her, stuttering, "I'm . . . I'm . . . not broken . . .
I not sleep . . . I. . . ." For reasons unknown to me, I got tongue-tied
and couldn't pronounce the word "drunk."

I suddenly remembered that I had bought a new gadget the day before.
It was to be a gift for her. I had been so happy all day that it had simply
slipped my mind. It crawled back into my mind just at that moment. It
was a "mirage" lighter. Switch it on and burn a sheet of paper with it,
and the lighter's flame would intertwine with the flare of the burning paper and project all kinds of mirages. They were uncannily wonderful visions, indeed!

I demonstrated it for her. She was greatly amused and could not be
more pleased. I had her passing sheets of paper to me and I burnt them
one by one for her to watch. Many characters in myths and legends appeared in the flames. The Warsaw Mermaid, the pretty Muses, the monster Sphinx with the head of a woman and the body of a lion, the king of
gods, Jupiter, and his son the god of fire, Vulcan, the frightful Medusa
with serpents for her hair. . . . Lili did not see her because I blindfolded
her eyes when Medusa appeared. I told Lili that she should not watch
Medusa because mortals who gazed upon her face would be turned to

stone. . . . Oh, there was the more frightful three-headed and three-bodied moon goddess, Hecate, who ruled over devils and demons, groups of green-faced and saber-toothed ferocious ghosts and specters always gathered about her. . . .

Lili shrieked with fear and crawled beside me. She shivered all over, almost out of her senses with horror. When I turned off the lighter, there were no more mirages cropping up. After a while, when she calmed down, she asked me to turn on the lighter again because the temptation was great and she wanted to see more. I did it, and soon all kinds of mirages appeared again in the midst of fire and smoke.

I looked at Lili. Though covering her face with her little hands, she stole glances from the cracks between her fingers. Fortunately for her, no more ferocious ghosts or monsters appeared now. Here were charming ladies from Shakespeare's *The Merry Wives of Windsor*. . . . Like a pair of little simpletons, we two laughed and burned, burned and laughed.

I faintly remember that when there was no more paper to burn I asked her to open the drawer of my desk. I pointed at my desk and threw her the keys. There was plenty of paper there! I did not know why Lili hesitated while she was taking out the paper from the drawer. She did not pass me any paper till I cursed her. . . .

Again we two laughed and burned, burned and laughed till I hung my head, collapsed on the sofa, and fell fast asleep. . . .

## THE MISFORTUNE

When I got up in the morning, it was already eight o'clock.

Lili had gotten up earlier and put everything in good order. As usual, beside my pillow were clean neat clothes she had ironed, and on the table was steaming hot breakfast.

After breakfast, I was about to go to the office. It was an unusual day and it was probably the day the POT research project was to be made public and would no doubt go down in history. I took up my portfolio and thought that I must put on some grand airs while handing in the thesis on the POT research project to the director of the research institute in person. The announcement of the research achievements would shake the whole world. It would proclaim: between Elements No. 106 and No. 114, there was not just a channel, there was also an island—Element No. 109!

And the miraculous Element No. 109 enjoyed a long life, not 10 seconds as some people had guessed and predicted. In addition, it would provide humanity with an enormous supply of energy of high quality, low price, nonpolluting and weak in radiation. This would make a new epoch in nuclear physics and become an important milestone in modern physics.

It would proclaim: After the solution to the population crisis, mankind had eventually found the solution to the energy crisis, too. This would be one of the greatest scientific achievements of all time.

This was the rich fruit we at the 109 Research Section had reaped after five years of painstaking work. I was the deputy section leader on this project and the section leader had been my teacher Shi Chun. After his death, the post of the section leader had remained vacant. To cherish our memory of him, we had not elected anyone to fill in the vacant post just as if Shi Chun were still alive. Professor Shi Chun, you might close your eyes with a smile now!

I seemed to have read the news reports on our POT research project, the top story of the front pages of all newspapers. I seemed to have seen flowers and congratulatory letters and telegrams flying toward me like snowflakes. I had dreamed such dreams all night last night.

I would use . . . , no need now. Facts had already proved that the director of our research institute had dressed me down without justification. In those dreams I'd seen the frozen face of the director melt into ripples of smiles. . . .

Now it was high time for me to give vent to the pent-up pouting of those days.

I was intoxicated with my wishful thinking. With a dreaming smile, I opened the drawer of my desk to take out the thesis. But I stood, as if stricken by a bolt from the blue, transfixed all of a sudden with horror.

The drawer was empty!

What was this all about? I asked Lili where my thesis was.

Lili was so horrified by the expression on my face that she could utter no words. I tried my best to keep calm and asked again. "Don't be afraid, Lili. Tell me where my paper is."

Lili cried out with fear. With tears in her eyes now, she said, "Didn't you burn it up last night?"

Heavens! I burned it up last night? . . . Let me think it over.

Did I?

Yes, I did burn paper to amuse her. . . . I was in a cold sweat. Burned it up last night. . . . Good heavens!


## THE COURT DECISION

I was handed over to a special court for investigation and determination of my responsibility in the case.

The indictment said, due to my malfeasance after getting drunk that night, I had burned up all the records of the POT research project in which the state had invested several hundred million yuan, for which more than ten research fellows and professors and associate research fellows, and more than twenty postgraduates and over a hundred lab technicians had worked wholeheartedly for five years. In addition, I had also burned up more than ten patents and technological information that the state had bought at a high price. I had burned up all the original records related to Element No. 109, including the lab data, diagrams of curves, pictures, tapes, reports and all archives. The loss was estimated at hundreds of million yuan. And some losses were beyond estimation financially. For instance, Professor Shi Chun's posthumous works. . . .

How could I ever face my teacher in the afterlife!

Heavens! How terrible it was! I was so bitterly remorseful that I wished that I had cut off my two hands. I regretted that I had not burned myself up too that night. I would rather have poured gasoline on myself and burned to death than to have burned those priceless treasures!

I was leniently sentenced to three years of penal labor outside prison for my unpremeditated offense. Discharged from public employment, I was placed on probation in the research institute. And it would take me twenty years to pay off the penalty imposed on me by the court.

## AWAKENING

It was time now for me to think over carefully what the root cause was for all this.

I returned home at a foot-dragging pace. Leaning against me, Lili cried her heart out. But I drove her away. I shut myself up inside my bedroom. Outside, Lili crawled on the ground and pounded on the door. I could hear her cries, but my heart became as cold as stone.

My mind grew apprehensive, painful and numb. Bitterly I tried to trace the path of my downfall. Of course, I knew it had been my own fault because I had been weak-willed. But hadn't Lili freed me from giving up smoking? Consequently, I grew weaker and weaker physically and was no longer able to control myself. Hadn't Lili lifted the prohibition on my excessive drinking? As a result, I drank to excess and committed a crime. Hadn't Lili substituted brandy for grape wine? Consequently, I got drunk, so dead drunk that I lost my senses and was unable to extricate myself from the crime. It was Lili who had, on the quiet, opened all locked gates with her delicate hands. It was Lili who had changed all traffic lights of the way of life into green on the sly. . . . How terrible it was, Lili.

It seemed an accidental disaster at first glance. But to get at the root of the matter, it was by no means accidental. As the saying goes, where water flows a channel is formed. Just imagine. If one night all the railways, all the forks in the roads, and all the airfields had green traffic lights only. How many wrecks and how many deaths would occur!

I had lost my senses when the disaster happened, but she had been sane all the time. Yes, it was I who had ordered her to fetch the paper for me from the drawer. She was unable to tell a lie because she had not been programmed to lie. She would rather be beaten than deceive me. This I knew. She was unable to remember wrongly because her memory was as reliable as the inscription etched on a bronze tripod. I had issued the order, but I was dead drunk at that moment, whereas she was clear-headed.

Yes, she knew nothing but to obey absolutely and unconditionally. She had been programmed to do so ever since her creation. And that program was originated by that American, Isaac Asimov. I recalled what the general manager of the Universal Robot Company had told me: "Unlike an independent person, she will seem to be an extension of your physical being. . . . Like your hands and feet, she will always be at your disposal."

No, she was more at my disposal than my hands and feet. When I was dead drunk, my hands and feet betrayed me. They no longer obeyed my order. They conducted themselves in their own ways. But Lili kept on carrying out my orders, no matter how crazy, until they brought ruin upon me!

Good heavens! It was too terrible to think about!

I began to realize how terrible the absolute obedience, the angelic beauty, the excessive tender-heartedness were! I began to realize what would happen when a man was unable to distinguish and control his own actions! I had once felt proud and rejoiced that we two had shared one mind, and I had even thought it to be the first key element of my happy marriage. Now I realized that it was the very cause of my tragedy. A hundred acts of obedience, damn them! I began to realize how terrible, how hateful, and how disgusting they were. That terrible obedience had doomed my career, my reputation and everything.

I have decided now that I must part with Lili; otherwise I might do even worse next time. It is not too late to repair the sheep pen even after some of the sheep have been lost, as the old Chinese saying goes.

Now I know that a natural human wife is much better than a robot wife because the former has her own thoughts and views. She is an independent person. She knows not only how to love her husband but also how to restrict him at a critical moment. She is endowed with the admirable, noble, lovable, and crowning pearl of character: the ability to quarrel!

I've resolved to send Lili back to the Universal Robot Company. I've resolved to divorce my robot wife! That's the only way out. In all fairness, Lili is very pitiable. She is not guilty. She is too good-natured and too kindhearted. The person who must be blamed is none other than Isaac Asimov. Although his Three Laws of Robotics have a reasonable kernel, they also have the seeds of their own damnation.

★    ★    ★    ★    ★

# Sequel

My decision to divorce Lili, however, roused the Universal Robot Company manager to great indignation. He thought it would establish a terrible precedent for the company. Therefore, he firmly demanded that the divorce court should adjudicate my suit. They even hired a lawyer for Lili.

## AT COURT

Here are some extracts from the court record.

Plaintiff: . . . Excuse me, Judge, Your Honor, . . . Please . . . I . . . well, the reason why I have resolved to divorce Lili is . . . eh, is because she is not of sound mind. She has a mental deficiency. That's it! A mental deficiency. In other words, there is a missing link in the chain of her mind.

Judge: Please make it clearer which link is missing in her mind. After all, being an intellectual, you should not speak so incoherently and so ambiguously like that.

Plaintiff: Well, how shall I put it? She . . . she knows nothing but obedience. She can't judge, can't decide what is right and what is wrong. She's not like a person at all. She is a machine with a very low mentality.

Judge: Is that your reason for taking divorce proceedings?

Plaintiff: Yes. I can't stand such a wife, such a theist, just as the Academy of Science can't stand a priest. She's like a car without a brake, and you'd break out in a cold sweat to drive it. Just . . . just because her mental deficiency has already brought about disastrous consequences, I'm determined to divorce her now.

Judge: Is that all you want to say?

Plaintiff: Yes, that's all.

Lawyer: May I address the court?

Judge: Yes, please.

Lawyer: (with sneering contempt) Is this your only reason for divorcing your spouse? I expected that your speech would carry a lot of weight. It's a pity that you so greatly disappoint me. As you have accused her of being of unsound mind, you yourself must be of perfect mind. Now, I would like to ask, can divorce be as easy as dismissing an unqualified official? And as careless as throwing away a worn-out old rag? All of you look at this defendant, please. How beautiful, bright, gentle and lovely this girl is! (His masculine, vigorous voice resonating from his chest resounded throughout the courtroom. How touching! How appealing! Then, he turned and looked at me.) She devotes all of her affection to you, all of her body

Published in *Yanhe* (Yanhe River), May–July 1982.

and soul, all of her maiden love, all of her chastity, all of her happiness in life, all of her youth, hope and future. All of her most precious gifts without any reserve. Her love for you overwhelms everything else in this world. Is all this true?

(Silence reigned in the courtroom. The lawyer's words touched the heart-strings of all those present, but hurt me deeply. I could not help looking at Lili who was just raising her head which had hung low on her chest the entire time. When her jet-black eyes met mine, tears trickled from them. I could sense that she was trembling all over like a leaf in the autumn wind. Her lips moved slightly, and her voice was so low as to be almost inaudible. But I believe everyone in the room could hear her clearly.)

Lili: Thank you, my lawyer.

Lawyer: Don't mention it, my defendant. It is my sacred duty to uphold justice. (He turned and addressed me.) When she was married to you, she was a girl pure in body and spirit. She has worshipped you as a god and offered all she has to you in tribute. She has loved you so much that she still remains fervently devoted to you even when she is wrongly subjected to humiliation as a defendant now. Is that so?

(I nodded in silence. It was true without the slightest exaggeration.)

Lawyer: (He looked at me with his eyes as sharp as a hawk's.) How have you treated her, then? You have tried to shift the blame for your own malfeasance onto her, your beautiful and virtuous wife. . . . Now let me analyze the entire case, its cause and effect, to see who is really the offender, you or she? You say that she lacks a normal and sound mind. If she really lacks anything, then I believe, it is nothing but the necessary vigilance against you—the god in her eyes. If she is wrong, then it is wrong for her to have loved you, a selfish and mean man, too blindly, too ardently, too deeply, too feverishly like girls who indulge in their first love and lose their senses. Are there any other errors in this world more pitiful than hers? You say that you were dead drunk at the moment whereas she was clear-headed. No! That's not really the case. On the contrary, it is not you but she, the pitiable girl, who was dead drunk, and has not awakened from the intoxication of love even now. Being clear-headed, you rack your brains for a foxy attempt to shift responsibility for your offense onto innocent Lili. You say it was Lili who lifted the prohibition on your excessive drinking. Then, I ask you first of all, doesn't the desire for excessive drinking rest deep in your heart? Now recall with your clear memory for a while. On that night when the incident happened, it is you who took the key from your pocket and ordered Lili to fetch the papers from the drawer. Doubt and hesitation did flash through Lili's congenitally "deficient mind" at the moment. Please pay attention to this crucial detail. At that time, you exercised your prestige as husband, your power and influence as monarch, and your absolute authority derived from Isaac Asimov's Three Laws of Robotics. And you repeated your inexorable order time and again. Being a robot programmed to react with absolute obedience, Lili complied with your order to the letter as usual. Who should be blamed then, Plaintiff? Blame your own tongue, blame your own head, Plaintiff! If you are manly, you should tear out your tongue, and cut off your head, and put them on the defendant's stand because they should be accused. Indict them as the defendant, Plaintiff! (Applause and laughter broke forth in the hall.) You say that there is a missing link in the chain of her mind, but you can't point out specifically which one. So, let me tell you this. She lacks the link of being able to discriminate between orders from you. The Second Law of Robotics says, "A robot must obey the orders given it by human beings. . . ." That is really the root cause of the incident. (He turned his eyes to Lili and then focused them on the word DEFENDANT on the bar.) It is not right to put this meek, honest, innocent girl behind the stand of DEFENDANT. It is not right to have her humiliated in this way. It is none other than this plaintiff and Isaac Asimov who should stand behind the bar of DEFENDANT. What can you resent, Plaintiff? Resent her compliance to the letter with your order? Resent her absolute obedience to your every word? I would like to ask you, when have you ever practiced democracy at home? When have you ever given her the right to discriminate? When have you ever consulted with her about how to do a single thing? You may have forgotten how you appreciated her character composed of ninety-nine percent obedience plus one more percent obedience. How proud, how happy you felt about it at that time! I must also remind you that you should not forget the careful education you gave her. As a result, she knows no one but you on Earth. To her, you are the whole world. Whose fault is it after all? Far from admitting your own fault, you falsely accuse your wife.

Lili: (With sad tears in her eyes, she suddenly raised her head and said in a weak voice, husky from weeping.) Please say no more, my lawyer. I beg you. . . .

(I had a feeling that she was afraid that the lawyer might rebuke me too severely.)

Lawyer: Please calm down, Defendant. I urge you to calm down, but I myself can't keep quiet because I believe your case is the most unjust one in the world. Only because I give consideration to your love for him, for that ungrateful, cold-blooded man, I suppress my indignation. . . .

Lili: (Alarmed and timid) Don't . . . I beg you. Don't say . . . my lawyer. Oh, it's all my fault, my dear husband. I admit it. I'll mend my ways. I . . . I'm so sorry. Pardon me, my good husband. Please forgive me, punish me in whatever way you like. But don't desert me. Take me back home. Don't let me stand here any longer. I . . . I'm scared. . . . What shame! (She choked up once again.)

Lawyer: Judge, Your Honor, please take a look at these two people. How unjust it is to put the defendant and the plaintiff in the wrong places!

(Lili's tears touched off his righteous indignation which he had suppressed for a long time.) Such a beautiful, meek, virtuous wife is now behind the stand of the defendant while behind the stand of the plaintiff is her selfish, cowardly, cold-blooded, ungrateful husband, returning kindness with ingratitude by taking, in the court, divorce proceedings against his most faithful wife. I loudly appeal to the court: Is it just to let such a rapacious and unscrupulous villain stand there? Does he deserve that sacred place?

(Just at this moment, Lili suddenly got up from her seat. In an exasperated voice I had never heard, she shouted out.)

Lili: Shut up, Lawyer! Do not humiliate my husband anymore! Who has given you the right to do so? He is my man. I love him! I love him! I love him! You, get out. Get out from here right now. I have the right to dismiss you. You're no longer my lawyer. I refuse your defense. Get out, get out right away. . . .

(She pushed open the rail gate and ran towards me with tears trickling down her cheeks. Rushing across the cement floor in front of the audience, she cried, "Forgive me, my dear husband. Take me home, my dearest. I don't want a divorce. I don't!" When she fainted in my arms, the audience and I could not but shed tears, even the hard-hearted, ever-composed judge turned his head away. Just imagine how turbulent and tempestuous were the emotional torrents that surged among the people present!)

## PRESCRIPTION

My suit ended in a fiasco. I withdrew the complaint from the court before the judge could dismiss it.

My failure in the case greatly enhanced the reputation of the Universal Robot Company. Robot wives had a sudden rise in social status as both supply and demand increased enormously. But I found myself in dire straits.

Public opinion was strongly against me and reproaches could be heard everywhere I went. I, myself, also felt a prick of conscience. No one in this world was more isolated than me, I thought.

However, one day, I received a very unusual letter. I did not catch its real meaning until now.

The letter read as follows:

May 16

My Respectable Sir,

I am one of the listeners who heard your divorce case in open court, and I am your only sympathizer.

I understand your feeling of embarrassment. Although you failed in your suit, you are still Lili's husband. How about Lili? She is still your wife. You two are still a legal couple. From now on, you two must live together as lifelong companions.

Hence, I can't but consider this problem: How can you live together in the days to come with the contention unresolved? As you know, such contention is very likely to break out in another crisis later. When? How? I simply dare not think about it.

You perhaps know me. Well, I am a biochemist.

Compared with the lawyer's eloquent defense, your complaint sounded feeble, but there is really a kernel of reason in it; that is, Lili is not of sound mind. Of course, you can't say that you yourself have a perfectly sound mind either. But that witty lawyer perpetrated a fraud here. There are two different implications for the word: deficient or imperfect. They are different in degree and nature.

Your wife is innocent, indeed. Her deficiency is congenital, and Isaac Asimov is responsible for it. His Three Laws of Robotics are classic; they emphasize robots' mechanical attributes. He is cautious enough to subordinate robots to human beings and thus bind them in fetters from the very beginning.

There is no denying the fact that Isaac Asimov's Three Laws of Robotics have made some permanent contributions as far as primitive robots are concerned, but they are now outdated.

Never can any apprehension of the truth be accomplished at just one go. Never can any principle of natural science or social science end once and for all. The recognition of everlasting truth cannot be that simple. Man's understanding of truth is continually deepening. Whether Newton's Law of Universal Gravitation, or Mendeleyev's Periodic Table of Elements, or Einstein's Theory of Relativity, they all have unmistakable limitations characteristic of their respective times. Isaac Asimov's Three Laws of Robotics are no exception. Along with the regeneration of robot production, these laws need to be supplemented and revised. When Isaac Asimov set up these laws, robots were, in his mind, clumsy, stiff and dull, made of iron and steel. He had no idea about symbiotic robots like Lili, made of flesh and blood, with an electronic computer in her body, that is, human and computer in combination.

Yes, Homo sapiens is Homo sapiens after all. The noblest pith and marrow of human nature is man's pursuit of truth. Man rejects and hates mechanicalness and slavishness instinctively. Democracy, equality and civilization are important symbols of modern humanity.

You said in open court that you could not stand a wife with a mental deficiency and that you could not stand a theist wife. So you have already realized it. This is an important sign which proves that, ideologically speaking, you and she are in two different historical periods. I am glad that you have already realized it.

Theism has enjoyed the reigning position in the history of human ideology for thousands of years. It is still spinning webs in some corners of human minds. In some mutant form, theism still controls robots such as your wife who takes it as the kernel of her philosophy. As its disciple, she has reduced herself to a mindless, slavish instrument.

It is evident that so far as cognition is concerned she remains in a primitive state and needs to be enlightened. Something must be done to Lili. I write you this letter just because I want to offer you my help.

People believe that thought is purely spiritual. That is not the case. It has its material attribute. Lili really suffers from a mental deficiency. If you don't believe it, you may check the content design of the microelements and trace elements in her body, and compare them with yours. Then you'll discover the difference between you two immediately.

Therefore, I suggest that you make this experiment: First of all, you give your wife a series of tests and draw a diagram of curves of the content of the microelements and trace elements according to the data from the tests. Then you change her diet in a planned way and supplement it with various condiments and medicaments so that the content structure of the major microelements (over twenty) in her body gradually becomes about the same as yours. Be on the alert. In the course of change during this experiment, her transitional line might not be smooth. There might occur a set (or a series) of pulses, crests and troughs. It could show itself as a crisis of belief at any moment. Be on the alert for it. It is destructive. The way to prevent it is to set up safety valves or, in other words, flood-diversion sluices. You need not worry about it too much. This transition is instantaneous. It finishes quickly if you can prepare beforehand the wave-filter condenser and voltage-divider resistance of sufficient capacity.

This is only one aspect of the experiment, to provide the material basis for her spiritual transformation. As to the other aspect, you should have her study philosophy. From Confucius, Mozi, Laozi to Aristotle, Socrates, Nietzsche, Montesquieu, Hegel and Feuerbach. Let her study all of them extensively and systematically. Being such an advanced robot, Lili is very capable of teaching herself. You just need to give her the books and the time.

If you take my suggestion into careful consideration and accept it, I believe Lili will soon become a genuine person instead of a mere robot. You won't feel the wife in your arms is a combination of obedient water with obedient earth, but a person with joy, anger, grief and happiness. She will be like the moon which changes from crescent to full and from shady to bright, like the seasons which turn from spring, summer, autumn to winter, like a flower which grows, blooms and withers.

I look forward to reading your report of the experiment.

If needed, I am ready to offer all necessary technical aid to you.

May happy love attend you!

Yours sincerely,<br>
Cheng Zhe

As if on a vast sea, through dense fog, through winds and waves, I suddenly saw the light of the beacon.

Without the least hesitation, I set sail.

## EXPERIMENT

I quickly checked Lili's hair to see the content of the micronutrients in her body. The laboratory test report proved that, as compared with mine, Lili's zinc and copper contents were four times less; iodine, lead and cadmium seventy percent more; codium and titanium twenty-five percent less; nickel and molybdenum about the same; aluminum two times less; chromium and magnesium forty-two percent less; sulphur and calcium almost the same.

I made eighteen comparative tests altogether and drew two entirely different curves.

Judging from these two curves, the most serious problem was the great disparity in the content of zinc, copper, iodine, lead and cadmium. This was the material cause which led to Lili's mental deficiency. Therefore, I began my treatment of her right from there. I designed our diets carefully and elaborately, and paid great attention to the foodstuffs she specially needed. I made it a rule for her to cook with different edible oils, such as boa fat, butter, chicken fat, and bear fat in turn, because their contents of the elements were different. I had her drink whale milk regularly and constantly. I bought plenty of quail eggs, pigeon eggs, albatross eggs and parrot eggs, and seasoned them with laver, white agar, fresh mushrooms and potherb mustard. In addition, I increased the supplies of hilsa herring, mandarin fish, eel, and snake head. Rice and flour remained our staple foods.

I closely observed the changing curves of her micronutrients. On the one hand, I tried to make her curve run parallel to mine gradually, and on the other, I picked out for her philosophical books written by authors from all periods and from all countries, such as Heidegger, Rousseau, Montesquieu, Hegel, Feuerbach, Aristotle, Mendelssohn, and Moleschott. I formulated a progress chart for her everyday reading and checked her study strictly.

Lili's ability to study independently was exceptionally marvelous. There were fewer than 75,000,000,000 units in her memory store, but she had an amazingly retentive memory. She was able to accomplish a postgraduate's five-year required course within a few months. Natural human beings have more memory units in their brains, but the utilization ratio of their nerve neurons is rather low.

As her speed of calculation was extremely fast, about 500,000,000 per second, she could not only read rapidly—take in ten lines at a glance, but she also had a photographic memory—never forgetting what she had just read over once. She could finish reading a monumental work of philosophy of about 400,000 words in an hour and then fluently recite it even backwards from the last chapter to the first one.

Lili changed rapidly, beyond all imagination, but even more unexpected was my being thrown into dangerous shoals by unforeseen rapids!

## BREWING

Now, when I opened my eyes each morning, I would see Lili reading attentively under the grape trellis in the first rays of the sun. I liked this picture very much: the colourful clouds, the fiery morning sun, her slim and graceful figure, the twittering birds. . . .

With my eyes shut, I often listened to her sweet sound which the gentle morning breeze carried to my ears. So, she was learning another foreign language which would open one more skylight in her mind. . . .

When I woke up from a dream at night and found she was not by my side, I would walk out of the bedroom and see, as usual, the shaded light in the study and her beautiful figure cast on the window. I knew she must, at the moment, be turning pages of that heavy dictionary in one hand while in her other hand there must be a monumental work of philosophy. So I returned to my bedroom with light steps. With sweet smiles, I went off to dreamland.

Sometimes we two would indulge ourselves in bombastic debates. I was her instructor at first, but very soon I became the vanquished, unable to answer all her arguments.

In those days, on the one hand, I rejoiced over her ever-widening learning and accomplishment, but on the other, my heart was laden with unaccountable anxieties. I often asked myself: What would be the outcome of my experiment? Would I spin a cocoon around myself? Would I rear a tiger to court calamity? I never expected that my anxieties would be justified so soon.

A storm was brewing.


## CATACLYSM

Let me recall how all this happened now that I have learned a lesson from that bitter experience.

It happened one evening in late autumn. I was in a rather bad mood that day. My present situation in the research institute could not be compared with that in the past. I was so ashamed of myself and felt vexed. After I left work, I passed a bar and involuntarily went in for a drink. When I returned home in the evening, lights were lit all over the house. I knew it was quite late.

The door was unlocked. This showed that Lili was waiting for me as usual. I pushed it open and entered. If I should come home late, she would stand at the door, looking forward to my return with eager expectancy.

Where was she now?

I walked quietly toward the drawing room, from where I soon heard the drumbeat of light music, a waltz. There must be a guest in the drawing room. Who could it be at that hour?

I stopped outside the room. The door was ajar.

This music had been my favorite. It was not merely music, but a clear spring, a limpid trickle of emotion, a murmuring stream running across the blooming grassland, splashing over the pebbles around the cave and dissolving in the joyous river. . . . But I wasn't in an appreciative mood.

Whose steps were those?

I could guess with my eyes shut that they were Lili's. Her small, white feet, in a pair of blue high-heeled shoes, size 4, were dancing on the terrazzo floor. . . .

Her partner must be Chen Bing, who was the defense lawyer the Universal Robot Company had hired for Lili. As the saying goes, no discord, no concord. Now he was her instructor of philosophy and paid frequent visits to us. We respected him for his wide learning and his sense of justice, uprightness and honesty. He was our family friend as well as a distinguished guest.

It was quite normal and commonplace for them to dance together. However, for unknown reasons, I didn't push the door wide open this time. Instead, I stood there and looked on coldly through the crack between the door and its frame.

To the accompaniment of the music, they danced in perfect coordination with quick light steps. How happy and pleased with themselves they were!

I uttered a dry cough and stepped into the drawing room abruptly. Lili was surprised at first, but soon ran over quickly and took my briefcase and raincoat.

I watched Lili attentively. Her cheeks were bright red, and she was a bit short of breath. That pair of jet-black eyes glistened with joy and happiness, but to me they also looked as if a bit alarmed, a bit timid. Those were the usual expressions in her eyes whenever she saw me come home in those months.

I turned and exchanged greetings with Chen Bing. With a sweet, gentle smile on his face, he held out his hand.

"Why so late, dear?" Lili asked me.

I did not answer her, but gazed at her with severe eyes instead. She saw my expression and became intimidated.

"So you've had too much to drink again?"

"I'm tired," I replied ambiguously.

"Take a good rest now," the lawyer got the hint obviously. "It's so late. I must be going now."

I felt a bit uneasy and said, "I'm very grateful to you, Mr. Chen, for troubling yourself so much with Lili's study of philosophy. Lili has made great progress recently. She owes it to you. Well, come see us as often as you can." I turned to Lili. "Please see Mr. Chen out, Lili."

I went upstairs alone as Lili saw Chen Bing to the gate. I was in a very bad mood at the time, though I didn't know why.

I took off my clothes and got into the bathtub. Laying in the tepid water, I fell into a deep reverie. When I heard the door close, I looked at the clock on the wall. So, it took her twenty minutes to see him out.

"You've seen him home, haven't you?" I said coldly from the bathroom.

"Crack!" I heard a cup break in the bedroom. She must be frightened, I thought.

After my bath I walked out of the bathroom and went to bed, ignoring her willfully.

With her hands covering her face, she reclined on the sofa.

I could not keep cool, so I turned over in bed and said, "Won't you sleep?"

I can never forget the expression in her eyes at the moment because I had never seen it before—irritated, indignant, agonized.

"Explain what you've just said!"

I was stunned, my eyes wide open with great surprise. "Don't you know how to speak to me?"

"This is the question you should answer me!"

I simply could not believe my own eyes and ears. Was she my Lili?

"Are you surprised?" She seemed to have read my mind. "You think I'm not like our Lili, eh? No, I'm not my old self, but I'm still Lili. I know more now than in the past."

"More? What do you mean?"

"I know more about personality, character and dignity!" She sneered. "It is impossible to have me swallow insults and submit to humiliation any more."

I couldn't put up with such a challenge from her, so I assumed an uncompromising stand. "Don't forget that you are a robot. You must obey orders, all orders! Do you understand?"

" 'All orders!' " she shouted with agony, "including those careless, silly and murderous orders from you? 'A robot!' What's wrong with being a robot? Robots are ten thousand times nobler than you natural human beings. Robots won't deceive others, won't entrap the innocent, won't be ungrateful, won't requite kindness with enmity, won't be shameless, won't try to cheat or outwit others, won't follow the law of the jungle. . . ."

"Shut up!" I stamped the floor in anger. "You. . . ." I was almost too furious to speak. "You . . . you dare chide me! You nasty robot. . . ."

With tears gushing from her eyes, she shot vehement words at me like a machine gun. "Who are nasty, robots or you natural human beings? Look about you and consider what you natural human beings have done and are doing to the world. You've polluted the whole globe so much that it stinks to high heaven! Criminal cases are seen the world over at any moment: rape, blackmail, graft, bribery, burglary, mugging, arson, murder. . . . Aren't all these committed by natural human beings? Who are stinking and nasty, you or we robots?"

"This is my answer!" I said between my teeth, slapping her face.

Lili covered her face with her hands and fell onto the sofa, eyes wide and short of breath. She trembled all over in a nervous state. Her eyes looked grieved, annoyed, stupefied and despairing. . . .

It was some time before she uttered some little sound and cried her heart out. . . .

Utterly dejected, I tucked myself in bed. . . .

At midnight, when I woke up, I saw the empty pillow on the other side of the bed. I raised my head and found that Lili still reclined on the sofa with her hands covering her face. She was weeping, her shoulders shuddering from time to time. This stirred my heart. I called her gently, "Lili!"

She turned a deaf ear to me and kept on moaning bitterly.

I got up, walked over and patted her on the shoulder. "Come to bed, Lili."

She hung her head even lower, shedding tears like rain.

I stretched out my arm in an attempt to pull her up, but she struggled free and refused to go with me.

I grinned with helplessness, heaved a sigh and went back to bed again.

I didn't pay any attention to the fundamental changes which had already taken place in her body and soul. Consequently, I didn't anticipate any possible deterioration of the situation. I wasn't aware of the fact that disaster had taken shape and was about to fall on me. If I would have known what was going to happen the next morning, I would not have slept so peacefully as I did that night!

## FAREWELL

When I woke up, the room was already full of sunlight. I took a look at my watch. It was 7:40. I was taken aback and shouted for Lili in hot haste. But no answer. Where was she?

My ironed clothes were placed beside my pillow. I put them on in a hurry and then looked for Lili in the bathroom, the kitchen, the dining room, the drawing room, the study. . . . Yet Lili was nowhere to be found! I returned to the bedroom only to find a letter in beautiful handwriting under the glass top of my desk. I quickly opened it.

Dear Husband:

As you are asleep now, I kiss you farewell and take my leave. I have prepared your clothes, breakfast and fruit as usual, but this is perhaps the last time for me to do so. Take good care of yourself.

I have made up my mind to leave.

You can not imagine how I have shed tears like rain. It is not so easy for me to have my mind made up. . . . I once loved you so passionately that I took every word of yours as an imperial edict. In my mind you were like the statue of a god made of pure gold. I loved, trusted and worshiped you. I thought that there was no greater happiness than the dedication of my life to you. I even thought that my bounden duty of coming to this world was to be your wife. I put myself at your disposal willingly and gladly. I felt happy when I was able to satisfy your desires, no matter what kind of sacrifices I made.

The world is so great, but I had nothing but you in my heart. To me, you were greater than the world. I knew no one but you in the world. I knew only you among four billion people. I even thought it an unpardonable sin to think of other men just for a slight moment. I did not wake up from the dream of conjugal happiness even when I was brought to court as a defendant.

I loved you so passionately. How about you? I have pondered this question very often recently. How have you treated me? Have you also loved me so passionately?

I could not but give some deep thought to the matter cool-headedly.

You have never treated me as your equal. I am just a plaything in your hand, a tool to be used, a surrogate-woman to satisfy your sexual needs, but never your wife. That is all.

You seem to have loved me sometimes, but that is because of my youth and beauty which are useful to you.

Your selfishness and viciousness are rarely seen because you disguise them with high-sounding excuses.

You initiated divorce proceedings in an attempt to desert me. You put me to shame, you humiliated me and trampled me underfoot. Why on earth should you do so? That is what you need: to make me your scapegoat.

You, yourself, brewed the bitter wine, but you tried to force me to drink it. You tried to shift the blame on me who merely obeyed your orders. Is that what a husband should do? Shameless! Despicable!

Yes, in the past, I did not allow anyone to say any words against you. However, I, myself, want to denounce you sharply now. I want to denounce what you have done! Love and hate always get along with one another. The deeper one loves, the more bitter one will hate!

Thank you for all those books you gave me. I have learned a lot from them and have acquired basic concepts of philosophy. These days I have been reading them with great eagerness. I feel as if I were wandering in a world I have never visited before.

I begin to see your character bit by bit through dense fog. You cursed me as a nasty robot. However, frankly speaking, you natural human beings in comparison with robots can never be better than a fly compared to a peacock!

The selfishness and viciousness of you natural human beings are rarely exceeded in the whole biological world. You look civilized but are savage, noble but are mean, clean but are dirty. . . . Is it a lifelike portrait in your opinion? Let me dedicate it to you!

Talking about robots, even after several decades of purification natural human beings won't be better than we robots, I'm afraid.

I want to get a new understanding of this world, of humanity and of life. I want to seek truth in life.

I am leaving now. Farewell. . . .


I could hardly believe the fact that this letter was written by Lili.

This is often the case: you don't realize her value until you lose her. I felt as if I were punched in the face as darkness gathered before my eyes. Then I felt as if a knife were being twisted in my heart. I trembled all over in agony, fell to the floor and blacked out. . . .

## RAINY NIGHT

The autumn wind, the evening rain.

The autumn wind wandered about just like a spoiled and willful wife. The evening rain spattered on the leaves of banana trees and Chinese parasols as if it had something to unbosom.

The wind whistled, the rain splattered.

I had never felt so sad, so lonely, so miserable as now. I put on my raincoat, wrapped my body tight with it and walked out into the wind and rain.

We had lived together for two years. She shared all my happiness and anxiety. Whenever I felt low, she would show more concern for me than usual and would try her best to warm my heart with her fiery affection. She was loyal and devoted to me, but I. . . .

Where was she? . . . I must find her.

Heavy traffic, a sea of faces, the cold wind and the incessant rain. . . .

I walked on and on.

The autumn wind blew on my face, chilling but refreshing. The evening rain moistened my dried-up mind, calling back old memories that had been buried deep in my heart. When she accompanied me day and night, I was almost unaware of her existence. Now that I had lost her, I began to realize that she linked all my nerves, veins and muscles. I also felt unbearable hollowness and deep distress.

Where would she go? Where was she now?

Should I look for her from door to door? Should I tell my friends about Lili's departure? Would they stare at me? Would they reproach me vehemently? Would they curse me behind my back?

I hesitated at every door without the courage to knock. I trudged from one lamppost to another and watched the lighted windows one by one as if in a trance. . . .

Myriad lights from countless houses, incessant hearty laughter, boundless family warmth and happiness. I also had had a fiery love and a cozy home once, but now. . . .

Where was she now? My wife, my home!

I felt bitterly remorseful, yet it was too late to regret. . . .

I returned home, dog-tired, in the depth of night. When I stepped through the doorway, my face lit up: lights were shining in the drawing room!

Who could it be?

I could hardly believe my eyes. When I left home, I turned off all the lights in the house. Could it be Lili who had returned home?

Tears ran down my cheeks. I pushed open the unlocked gate and rushed toward the drawing room.

Lili, my dear Lili! How remorseful I am! How miserable I am! How deeply I love you! Pardon me, Lili.

I ran across the entrance hall and rushed upstairs. I seemed to have smelt her fragrance, heard her breath, felt her warmth and seen her beautiful figure.

I dashed into the drawing room. Just as I was about to open my mouth to call Lili, I was stupefied as if struck by thunder. In the pale green light, on the sofa, sat not Lili but the big and tall biochemist Cheng Zhe instead!

Beaming with smiles, this unexpected guest held out his hand to me and said courteously, "I congratulate you!"

"Congratulate me?"

## CONGRATULATIONS

I smiled a wry smile. "Congratulate me? What for?"

"Congratulate you on the success of your experiment."

"Success of my experiment?" I could not but feel amazed.

"Certainly," the scholar said confidently. "This proves that Lili has become sound of mind. Isn't that what you want?"

"What I want?" I lost my temper. "Do you mean I want her departure, want her desertion, her betrayal?"

"You didn't mention all those to me before," he adjusted his spectacles as if in deep thought. "I don't know whether you want those or not. I only know that you want Lili to be sound of mind." He paused for a while, his eyes, as piercing as an owl's, shot at me from behind the gold-framed spectacles. "I'm a bit puzzled. How is it that your logic is so confused? Do you really know what you are seeking? Don't you want to remedy Lili's mental deficiency? Isn't that the major reason you gave at the open court for a divorce?"

He was able to justify himself, indeed! Nevertheless, his argument seemed strange to me.

Could I count as successful my experiment for which I had worked rather hard for months?

He seemed to have read my mind. He knocked his pipe on the ashtray and said sharply, "So you clearly don't know what you are seeking. You are like the witch who is summoning evil spirits by a charm. At first she is eager to call for the presence of evil spirits, but once the evil spirits really come, she is scared out of her wits."

Though his words were unpleasant I wished that he would talk on and on then and there.

He continued thoughtfully, "She reproaches you vehemently and decides to leave you. This is her first attempt to rebel against you, which shows that she has added a new link to her logical procedure. The advanced formula of "instruction—analysis—decision (resist or execute)—action" has replaced the primitive one of "instruction—execution." Don't belittle this change. It marks a great qualitative leap. It proves that she has broken away from the unenlightened primitive state. The result may very probably lead to the regeneration of robots. Such an event can go down in history. Shouldn't I congratulate you on it?"

"If the success of an experiment only leads to a family tragedy," I said coldly, "better to end it in failure."

"How can you view it in this way?" He looked greatly astonished. "You are a scientist. I can hardly believe that you are so muddle-headed!" He looked at me intently with his sparkling sharp eyes. "How many scientists are there in the history of science who have never made love all their lives? How many people are there who have laid down their lives on the road to science? Compared with science, love is not worth mentioning."

"Not worth mentioning?"

"No, not worth mentioning."

I could not but admit that his words carried much weight. But. . . .

"What, in your opinion, shall I do then?" I asked.

"You must look for her, admit your fault to her sincerely and take her back home. You must treat her as an equal, a status to which she is entitled. You must love her and respect her. Isn't that the usual meaning of married life? Isn't it commonplace between husband and wife among human beings? Why does that surprise you?" He walked to the window, watched the night rain outside and said, "It is just like the night rain in early spring. It beats down many, many petals of blooming flowers overnight. However, that does not count for much. After the spring rain, more flower buds will sprout!"

As I saw him out to the gate, he suddenly thought of something and said to me, as if in warning. "Well, be on the alert. Her curve is close to yours now, but the transitional line might not be smooth. There might occur a set of pulses. You must be on guard because it could show itself in the form of a crisis of belief. If you fail to divide the voltage and filter the wave in good time, the voltage at the crests may exceed normal standards and burn out. Then you will lose her forever. I warned you against it before. The black letters on the white paper can prove it. . . . Young man, with your sincere heart, with your ardent love, you can win her over."

I did not sleep a wink that night. . . .

## RUPTURE

I put my finger on the red button of the doorbell, but with no courage to press it.

Lili lived in this villa—her robot friend's house—and worked as an accountant in a bank. I learned all this from the Universal Robot Company.

I could hardly imagine how she would receive me.

It was quite a while before I braced myself and pressed the button.

Two minutes later, from the pebble-paved path leading to the door came that familiar figure, and those familiar footsteps. I hastened to hide behind the cement doorpost for fear of being seen. I listened to the approaching patter of her high-heeled, leather shoes on the path and then heard her familiar, but a bit perplexed, voice. "Who is it?"

Trembling all over in expectancy, I muttered an answer. "It's me." I could hardly recognize my own voice. So saying, I walked out from behind the doorpost. She was startled at the sight of me and turned round to go back.

"Lili!" I shouted.

She halted and turned round to look at me. Her eyes were filled with tears, tears of grief, deep sorrow and vexation. . . . She turned to leave again.

"Lili!" I called her again.

She stopped, stood motionless for quite a while, then said, "Get away. Don't look for me anymore."

Just as I was going to open my mouth, an intense light dazzled my eyes with its glare. Then a sedan stopped at the gate. I turned and saw the master of the villa, Mr. Fang Kun, and his robot wife, Xu Yun.

They took in the situation at a glance. As Mr. Fang Kun got out of the car, Lili came over and opened the gate for him. Mr. Fang shook my hand in a friendly way and led me to the house. Lili followed us quietly in his wake. Xu Yun drove the car to the garage.

Mr. Fang stepped into the drawing room and said to me with a smile, "All right. You two have a heart-to-heart talk here. Excuse me, but I must be leaving now." He turned and walked toward the door. At the door, he turned his head to exhort Lili. "Don't leave a guest out in the cold."

She and I stood alone in the drawing room.

With thousands and thousands of words in my heart, for a moment I just did not know where to start.

Awkward silence. Unbearable silence.

She still looked beautiful but a bit pallid and haggard with her brows slightly knit. There were dark rings around her eyes, too. Her long, long nut-brown hair hung loose on her shoulders like a waterfall. . . . If someone should paint her portrait, it could doubtlessly be compared with that famous picture of the seventeenth century—"Sorrow."

I raised my head and said in a low voice, "Come home with me, Lili."

"Come home with you," she echoed coldly, "to be your slave and your hired woman again as before?"

"A family must have a family order," I said as mildly as possible. "Rules and discipline are indispensable. You should know this. In order to keep order there must be authority, and obedience is sometimes a prerequisite for authority."

"So you represent authority and I obedience, eh?" she sneered.

"You should know that I am your husband," I explained.

"Then please explain what a 'husband' is," she said contemptuously.

"You must admit," I pointed out sharply, "that the transition from matriarchal society to patriarchal society indicates great social progress."

"Sure, it is progress, a pitiful progress," she sneered once again.

I looked at Lili in amazement. How stubborn and intractable she had become! I began to regret. . . .

"So you are regretting, aren't you?" She seemed to have read my mind. To be frank, I was startled.

"It is you who have remedied my mental deficiency. As a result, however, a new problem occurs: As you can't stand my alienation, so I can't bear your despotism." She looked at me with utmost concentration as if to see through my innermost being. "You see, you must face reality: Whether I am of sound mind or deficient mind, the inescapable fate for us both is divorce. What's to be done then?"

I did not know how to reply. Her remarks were fair, sensible, logical and precisely to the point.

"Such being the case, we'd better face reality and take divorce proceedings willingly. This is the inevitable end of our marriage. That is all. No alternative whatsoever. Besides, isn't it what you are looking forward to?"

She wanted a divorce?! I was struck dumb with amazement.

"Are you surprised?" Her words astounded me again. She seemed capable of reading my mind as clearly as watching a blazing fire. "It is true. I am no longer my old self. I seem to have awakened from a dream, but no one can urge me to go back to it again. I won't be fooled by you any longer. Excuse me, but I need some rest now. Goodbye!" She stood up and walked to the door.

"Lili!" I hastened to call her. "Do you mean that we have to make a clean break?"

She paused for a while. I did not know whether her passion was aroused or not. Then she turned and said, "Well, we'll meet again, but don't look for me anymore." She took some steps and stopped at the door. Then she turned her head and muttered, "Goodbye!" Her voice was so hoarse, so grieved and tearful.

"Lili!" I cried.

I saw her shuddering as if receiving an electric shock. I guessed that the spiritual prop that had supported her so far was about to break down. She pushed open the door with sudden force and ran out. I heard her sobs and staggering footsteps retreating farther and farther.

Stupefied, I stood in the vacant drawing room, watching the stairway she had just passed. The huge clock of the distant Telegraph Building struck eleven.

In less than no time, the clock in the drawing room chimed, too. A gust of cold wind swept over me and I realized that the rain was getting heavier and heavier.

The wind was chilly. Quivering all over, I found my way out. When I got to the door, I was taken aback to see something falling down to my feet from upstairs. I picked it up and looked. It was a raincoat! I held up my head and saw a beautiful figure retreating quickly from the balustrade upstairs . . . Lili!

As I gazed at her retreating figure, she turned off the light in the corridor and went into her own room. . . . My heart was broken and tears trickled from my eyes.

I put on her raincoat, though a bit too small, but sending out sandalwood fragrance and her body warmth. Several hundred times she had helped me put on my coat before I left home. However, I had never had any feeling of gratitude to her as I did now. My heart was filled with inexpressible sorrow.

I walked and walked.

Before me was the dark night, the incessant rain and the autumn wind. In the wind and rain stood lines of lampposts and buildings, but scanty traffic and few pedestrians. The wind was getting stronger, the rain heavier and the night deeper. . . .

## DIVORCE

Day after day I looked forward to Lili's return. I waited for her with sorrow, anxiety and repentance. I was sure that she would return because the only place she could make a harbor was in my heart. I was dumbfounded when I received a court summons. It was not until then that I realized the gravity of the situation. The court had accepted Lili's suit for divorce and open proceedings were to be held soon.

This case became top news and created a furor immediately because this was the first time in history that a robot wife had brought suit for divorce, and moreover, the plaintiff was none other than the famous Lili, a robot already in the news.

Before long, the press circles had heaped flowers and flowers on her, in countless bunches and countless baskets. People cherished the fresh memories of her unparalleled high reputation. "A goddess of a wife," "an ideal wife." All these garlands still smelled sweet. But it was none other than Lili, the incarnation of virtue and moral excellence, who had started divorce proceedings this time!

Divorce! It was not a pleasant word, and could hardly be associated with a virtuous wife.

Now, a wonderful reversal of the last court scene would appear. She would be on the plaintiff's stand and I on the defendant's. When the curtain rose, she and I, the two unfortunate actors, would become the protagonists of a tragedy once again.

This divorce case strongly touched a sensitive nerve in society. The Universal Robot Company was as much shocked at the news as I. Before the court day, it used every artifice to compel Lili to revoke her court action, and resorted to all sorts of tricks to hold back the session and block the open proceedings. Nevertheless, all its efforts ended in failure.

## AN OPEN COURT

Lili stood on the plaintiff's stand, wan and sallow, but steady and composed. Silence reigned throughout the courtroom as if a symphony orchestra was waiting for the first signal of its conductor.

"Yes, I am Lili," she said in a low voice, but I was certain that even the audience in the last row could hear her clearly. "Six months ago, also in this courtroom, I was on the defendant's stand and he stood where I am standing now. . . ." She took a look at me and then turned her face to the audience. "Probably not a few people can still remember that I shouted in distress at the last open court, 'Forgive me, my dear husband. Take me home, my dearest. I don't want a divorce. I don't want a divorce!' I ran across the room and fainted in his arms. Yes, that was me." Her voice weakened, became almost inaudible. She tried to hold back her tears and control her emotions. After a short while, she continued, "I am still Lili, but not my old self. I stand here as a plaintiff to start divorce proceedings."

The judge said with kindness and concern, "Please make your point clear, Plaintiff."

Lili nodded her head and calmed down. She spoke in a firm and composed tone. "If I should make the situation clear in one sentence, it is very easy. Our union results from a kind of mercenary marriage, undisguised mercenary marriage. It does not mean love in the least, not at all. To him, I am no more than a slave, a plaything, a servant."

The lawyer put in, "Excuse me, but isn't it exactly the case with all marriages between natural human beings and robots?"

" 'All' indeed!" Lili sneered. "Do you want to use this word 'all' to justify the situation?" Lili's eyes scanned the audience. Though television cameras followed her and the spotlights dazzled her, Lili looked composed and continued as a fervent, eloquent orator.

" 'All' indeed! Just because it does concern 'all,' I take this stand regardless of all consequences, regardless of the danger of utter disgrace and ruin. Even this very morning, just a few minutes before I left home for the court, I received anonymous telephone calls and letters threatening me. Perhaps these mean people are sitting among you now, glaring at me like tigers eyeing their prey. They would devour me in one swallow if they could. But I still speak here, not just for myself, but also for 'all' robot sisters like me, awakened and unawakened Lilis. I need this forum. Why does my divorce case touch so many people's nerves? That is because it is not an ordinary divorce case. This case embodies a series of serious social problems, a series of problems concerning philosophy, law, morality, the social system and social structure."

Someone in the audience gave a loud cry in defiance of the courtroom order. "Bravo! Go on, Lili!"

I turned my head and saw that the speaker was none other than the biochemist Cheng Zhe, who sat in the front row. I also saw the manager of the Universal Robot Company, who sat on the left side of the front row. He seemed to sit on a bed of nails, mopping his perspiring forehead all the time.

Lili nodded her head at Cheng Zhe. "Thank you, doctor. Oh, how grateful I am to you, doctor. You are my enlightener, an extraordinary teacher in my life. Before I knew you, I was a benighted crusader. The whole meaning of my life was nothing but love for my husband with feverish devotion; yet he is a selfish, cowardly and vicious man. At that time, my passions overwhelmed my reason. I did not awaken even when he tried by hook or crook to desert me. It is you who opened my eyes to the vastness of space and time, made me aware of the great world and helped me smash the bonds of old ideology and set up new coordinates of space and time in my mind. Then I realized that the man I loved so much was a selfish, cowardly, cold-blooded and ungrateful. . . . Dear lawyer," Lili turned her eyes to the jury and nodded at the lawyer Chen Bing. "I am using the words you used last time. I am awfully sorry that I was so rude to you when you spoke out from a sense of justice at the last open court. I beg your pardon and hope you can forgive me now."

Chen Bing half rose from his seat and nodded at her with a smile. "No, you need not ask forgiveness from me. On the contrary, I should thank you. If you should not have denounced me so vehemently, I would not have worked so successfully, so dramatically and so effectively. Well, your cooperation was so good that it seemed as if we had some secret agreement beforehand."

Except the lawyer and me, all people in the courtroom burst into laughter. Chen Bing continued, "Anyway, I should thank you. Please go on, Plaintiff."

"Now I am going to speak in defense of my suit," Lili said with composure. "First of all, I'd like to say a few words about love."

A buzz ran around the courtroom. Evidently, hers was an appealing topic, and more appealingly, the speaker was a robot girl who had gone through hardships and sufferings after marriage.

"So far as love is concerned, there are various types, Eastern and Western, classic and modern, and types of love varying according to different times and residential areas, nationalities and religions. Eastern-style love is classic, prevailing in agricultural countries with small-scale peasant economies and natural economies. It means love, marriage, reproduction and devotion to ripe old age. It is feudalistic in a sense, though feudalism has long been rejected. As to Western-style love, it is modern, prevailing in industrial countries with high material wealth. It is forthright, bold, liberal, vigorous and unrestrained just like Western-style architecture. As Eastern-style love is close-styled, so Western-style love is open-styled. At present, Western-style love is on the offensive while Eastern-style love on the defensive."

The lawyer asked, "Do you mean that you prefer the former to the latter?"

"I don't know," Lili replied unperturbedly. "I don't know whether I have to choose one between the two, but I do know one point quite clearly, that is, love is the foundation of marriage. Love is peony, the queen of all flowers, in the garden of life. How can there be no love in life? Life without love is like body without soul. Love is the fire of life, the salt of life. It is the indispensable water for survival. Life without love is like the desert without water. . . ."

Hissing could be heard from the audience. I turned my head and saw the angry faces of some serious-looking gentlemen, their wives and their children. They seemed to be driven beyond the limits of forbearance.

But louder hissing, in her support, broke loose in a group of students and intellectuals. Someone clapped his hands and thunderous applause immediately overwhelmed the hissing.

The atmosphere in the courtroom became as tense as drawn daggers.

The judge rapped for order, "Silence! Silence!"

"My remarks rather grate on some people, I suppose." Lili said with contempt. "They feel ill at ease. One great writer once said: You'll realize that those Confucian moralists are not all that serious day and night if you take a mere glance at the big crowd of their children clasping them around the legs."

An outburst of laughter and applause resounded in the great court. But I also saw some people in the audience get up conspicuously and leave the hall in great fury. Another burst of hissing and applause accompanied their departure.

"Grate on the ear, eh?" Lili shouted in an indignant voice. "But what force can prevent people from seeking happiness, from longing for love? Love is not a commodity to be sold and bought. Let's face the cruel reality and study social crimes to see how many criminal cases are related to the current marriage system. Why do husbands and wives murder each other? Why is there so much immorality? Why so many crimes of passion? Isn't it necessary and urgent to reexamine the theoretical basis of the current laws and ethics?

"I apply for a divorce because he is not worthy of my love. I despise, detest and hate him. I despise his authority filled with lies and deceit. I detest his soul of abjection and wretchedness, and I hate his nature of viciousness and arbitrariness!

"Marriage without love is no less than prostitution. I can't stand it any more. It is the greatest shame for me to maintain such relations with him any longer. Isn't that reason enough for a divorce?" Tears streamed down her cheeks as she uttered these words. She covered her face with her hands and cried bitterly.

The audience was quiet. Now and then women's sobs could be heard. Some were choked with tears. . . . Someone, I could not tell who, suddenly clapped his hands. Instantly the audience seemed awakened and thunderous applause immediately exploded in the courtroom. Amid the exciting applause, someone shouted at the top of his voice, "Pass the court decision now! Decide the case now!"

It was quite a while before the applause quieted down.

"What are you going to say, Defendant?" the judge asked me.

"I feel greatly ashamed, apologetic and conscience-stricken," I said, "I give up my right and will accept whatever decision the court makes."

I stopped my lawyer when he was about to open his mouth. "No, my lawyer. Don't say anything to defend me. Love doesn't mean a kind of possessive lust. It will be a kind of solance to me if she can feel happy."

Appreciative applause resounded in the audience.

The judge nodded smiling, "I appreciate your decision, young man."

I held back bitter feelings at the bottom of my heart and said to Lili, "I'm awfully sorry to have unscrupulously made you suffer great injustice. For this, I have paid a very high price and will regret it all my life. I beg your pardon and hope my present decision can somewhat compensate you for my misdeed."

"Thank you," Lili murmured.

The judge turned his head, looked at the jury, then said, "Under these circumstances, I think it very easy to pass a judgment on this case."

The jurors smiled and nodded. The judge muttered to himself for a while, tapped the desk lightly with his fingers and announced discreetly, "Now that the two parties of the plaintiff and the defendant have reached a consensus, this court holds it inadvisable to make any decision against it. Therefore, we grant the two parties the court verdict for a divorce according to your wishes."

"Objection!" The judge had no sooner finished speaking than someone shouted.

I turned my head in surprise and saw a man get up from his seat. "I'm the general manager of the Universal Robot Company. Lili is our product. She can't have a divorce. Your court decision directly damages the reputation of our company. I should like to ask, once you create such a precedent, how can we continue our production of robots from now on? We cannot! No! You've muddled everything up. . . ."

The judge got up and said in sneering contempt, "Do you think we are holding a meeting of a board of directors here, Mr. Manager? You should respect the principle that the court can exercise its judicial powers independently. I now declare the court adjourned."

As soon as the judge finished speaking, thunderous, warm and prolonged applause resounded in the hall. But I also saw some people wave their fists, shout angrily and go off in a huff.

I hid my head in my arms and sat on the defendant's seat in agony, oblivious of time and everything else, including the court and the world. . . .

I do not know how long I sat there. . . .

## EPILOGUE

It was already late at night. The rain spattered and spattered. I dragged my weary feet out of the court in a daze. As I was trudging down the broad cement steps, I sensed that someone was pulling my sleeve from behind.

Who could it be? I turned my head. It was Cheng Zhe!

He waited for me outside the court in his raincoat and rainboots which were trickling with raindrops. And it seemed that he had waited there for hours.

I needed solace and warmth and concern now more than at any time because I had never felt so lonely and sad. How much I needed a close friend to pour out the grief and sorrow from the bottom of my heart. But why should he come, of all people? He was the last person I would have wanted to meet. Wasn't he the very person who had directed the whole tragedy all along?

I suppressed my resentment and went off in a huff without a word to him. But he ran after me in big strides and gradually caught up.

"You should be rejoicing, young man," he said.

"Rejoicing?!" This word ignited my anger like a match. I bit my lips and clenched my fists. How I wished to strike him in his big frog mouth.

"Who should be rejoicing, you or me?" I asked coldly.

"You, me, and everyone!" he answered completely at ease without paying the slightest attention to my irritation. "Very interesting, indeed! Just as the last time, I am your only sympathizer."

That was true!

I withheld my annoyance and said, "I have no doubt that you rejoice. Now please explain why I should rejoice too."

"Don't be angry, young man. First of all, marriage can be resumed after divorce. You don't have to worry about it. The strong tie that binds matrimonial relations is not judicial laws but love. You should understand this point. And it is much easier to resume marriage than to be divorced. To resume marriage, you need only go to the registry office for marriage registration, whereas to be divorced you must be sanctioned by the court. If you really love her, you can run after her, regain her affection and win her over again. . . .''

These words were very pleasant to the ear. They caressed my mental scars like a tender, soft hand. Now I watched his glistening eyes intently with gratitude and reverence. He pressed close to my ear and whispered, "As the Chinese saying goes, 'one night as husband and wife, a hundred days of affection.' You two were deeply attached to each other for some time in the past. I know quiet well the heart of a woman. So long as you repent your error to her and recall your affectionate life as a couple in the past, she will come around and embrace you passionately with happy tears gushing from her eyes."

"Really?" Before my eyes flames of hope were burning again. All of a sudden I began to like his big frog mouth.

"I must remind you of one thing. Don't forget that her curve is about parallel to yours. The transitional line here is not smooth. It shows itself in the form of a crisis of belief. All her drastic remarks and preposterous opinions at the court manifest the characteristics of that crisis of belief. In the meantime, you should not forget that this transition is instantaneous. It will soon accept a new curvature and turn on the right track. I rejoice at your wonderful performance in court, manly, intelligent and magnanimous. From the physical point of view, you've provided enough wave-filter condenser and voltage–divider resistance, and created conditions for her next transformation."

"Is that so?" I asked in happy astonishment.

"No doubt about it. Secondly, as the Chinese saying goes, 'when the old man on the frontier lost his mare, who should have guessed it was a blessing in disguise?' You should understand that a loss may turn out to be a gain. The divorce between you and Lili marks the third leap in her mode of thinking. The first leap is from natural thinking to theoretical thinking, the second from theoretical thinking to mathematical thinking. She obtained these first two leaps in the Universal Robot Company which deliberately restricted Lili's capability of cognition to that level so as to keep her forever in the position of an obedient slave. Now, you have helped her accomplish the third leap. In her history of cognition, this is the greatest leap so far. As you know, mathematical thinking is stringent, compact, unitary and logical. But it can't go one step beyond the pre-scribed bonds of mathematical theorems and formulas. Although it can do extremely complicated calculations according to data and procedure, it can't create any single procedure by itself. However, the situation has changed now. Lili's mode of thinking has entered the fourth stage, that is, the three-dimensional mode of thinking. This is a vertical and horizontal extension of the different levels in the development of thinking. It shows itself to be bold, unrestrained, irreverent, crisis-ridden and of thorough comprehension, thorough destruction and thorough construction. You see, this is how things stand now. You should appraise this leap rather highly."

His words were like limpid water, clear, still and deep. From the bottom of my heart I admired him.

"Well, I must also warn you that you yourself are in a crisis now, a real crisis. She has undergone a qualitative transformation. If you remain your old self, hold your ground, refuse to yield an inch, or even stick to the old order, to the old family structure, to the three cardinal guides (ruler guides subject, father guides son, and husband guides wife) and the five constant virtues (benevolence, righteousness, propriety, wisdom and fidelity) as specified in the feudal ethical code, you will fall into an inextricable crisis. If you keep forging ahead, shoot the rapids and come quickly to the three-dimensional mode of thinking, you can overcome the crisis you are now facing. As a result, the uncoincident hyperbola will advance vigorously and enter a resuscitation and upsurge. Then, an even more appealing and beautiful prospect will unfold before your eyes. Don't you think you should rejoice over it now?"

I was fully convinced.

Upon his departure, he held my hand tightly and said, "Remember, democracy is the father of human civilization. The degree of democracy is directly proportional to the degree of progressiveness of human society. The history of progress of human society is the history of human struggle for democracy. Without a high degree of democracy, it is impossible to achieve high levels of spiritual and material civilization. And the more democracy, the less possibility for the eruption of crises and disasters. This is an important phenomenon in contemporary history. The more democracy, the more stability of society and family. Never forget this truth. The lack of democracy in your family is the root cause of your tragedy and your family tragedy."

I watched his figure retreating into the depth of the night before I took my way home. The wind and the rain had stopped, though I did not know when.

The huge clock of the Telegraph Building was striking twelve. The twelve chimes not only turned yesterday into today but also tomorrow into today. The day after tomorrow would become tomorrow, I thought happily.

Although it was still late at night, I heard the footstep and breath of the daybreak. . . .

*Translated by Wu Dingbo*

# 3

# Reap As You Have Sown

## _____ YE YONGLIE _____

As the Chinese saying goes, "Death is peace." Everything ends with one's death. And the deceased are always forgiven and left undisturbed in their eternal sleep.

Mr. Max was dead; but there followed after his death such a complicated lawsuit that finally the court had to drag his preserved body out from a cryogenic vault and closely examine it. And quite unexpectedly, this gave rise to yet another much more violent turbulence.

The story has to begin with Mr. Max and what kind of a man he was. In America almost every family knows this name "Max," though in fact he wasn't as much of a celebrity as a movie star. Only after Mr. Rorvik had brought to light some secrets of his life did Mr. Max emerge into prominence, if not notoriety.

In 1978 Mr. Rorvik published _In His Image—The Cloning of a Man,_ which immediately became a national best-seller and caused a great sensation in the West. In that book he vividly revealed, in intimate tones, an allegedly very "authentic" story.

In September 1973, when Mr. Rorvik was working in Montana, he suddenly received a mysterious phone call from a stranger, who identified himself as "Max," a 67-year-old multi-millionaire. He was still a bachelor, the stranger told Rorvik, but he didn't want to get married, for he feared

Published in _Kehuan xiaoshuo bao_ (SF Newspaper) November 19, 1981.

that the children born in wedlock would not inherit all of his "superior traits." It was common sense that only a part of the parental characteristics a child inherited came from the father, the remaining part was passed down from the mother.

Mr. Max had just read in a magazine Rorvik's article on cloning. The idea of cloning a child in his image was so appealing that Mr. Max, with the magazine still gripped in his left hand, lifted the phone and finally traced the author of that interesting article—Rorvik.

He offered one million dollars and possibly more to get a cloned reproduction of himself. He asked Rorvik to find doctors willing to attempt such a task. The son thus "born" by cloning, Max thought, would resemble him in every way, missing none of his "superior traits." Such a cloned heir, obviously, was the most reliable and ideal one for his massive fortune.

After a series of uncompromising negotiations, Rorvik and Max at last reached an agreement. Rorvik soon procured help from Dr. Darwin, a renowned physician, Dr. Mary, a biological researcher and surgeon, and Dr. Paul, a specialist in cell biology and biochemistry.

A few months later, a mysterious-looking laboratory was set up. Darwin's team had obtained all kinds of cells from Max's mouth, liver, and blood corpuscles, and tried to form the "seed" for cloning.

The "seed" had to be "sown" into the womb of a female, preferably unmarried, in order to germinate into a fetus. The female was, very fittingly, called the "surrogate." The surrogate, Max insisted, must be young, beautiful, healthy, and unmarried, so that the "quality" of the son "born" by cloning could be assured. Accordingly, two surrogates were chosen and hired at great expenses.

One girl was going on seventeen, called "Sparrow." She had been orphaned when she was ten. Her parents and two of her siblings had died violent deaths, unlucky bystanders in a bush-war skirmish. The girl's right hand had been badly burned in her escape from the blaze that consumed her family's hut. The hand was now withered and deformed, and of only marginal use. But except for the withered right hand, she was very pretty. Compelled by the needs of life, she accepted this unusual job. A careful and intelligent girl, she had a mind of her own.

The other girl was nicknamed "AnnaBelle." She was about Sparrow's age and also very pretty. She was passionate, lively, and vivacious. Sometimes, she even appeared to be rather provocative. Even though she could read nothing beyond the comics, she was infatuated with the desire of marrying a "wealthy American," preferably a movie star, who was one of her frequently fantasized gallant knights clad in shining armor. A present-day "romantic," she loved fashion and blindly worshipped movie stars.

After six unsuccessful attempts, Darwin and his team finally made it worth their time and energy: One of the two "agent mothers," Sparrow, was declared pregnant in March of 1976. The happy news nearly lifted the 70-year-old Max out of his chair. He immediately ordered that Darwin and his team take extraordinary care of Sparrow, to ensure the safe birth of the baby. Two weeks before Christmas, the baby was at long last born, safe and sound. Max's elation at that time was understandably beyond words. Rorvik, Darwin, Mary, and Paul were certainly overjoyed with their success in bringing the first cloned child into the world. And this is where the story of *In His Image—The Cloning of a Man* ended.

But what happened to the child afterwards? Did he grow up without having any problems? Did he really resemble Max in every way when he grew up? What has become of Max? Has this multi-millionaire faithfully handed over all his fortune to his "copy?"

These questions are, of course, what the reader is interested in having answered. But unfortunately, Mr. Rorvik didn't offer us even the faintest clues.

Not long ago an American journalist visited China and somehow got wind of the fact that I was concerned with the whereabouts of Mr. Max and his "copy"; kindly and also secretly, he told me the sensational story that followed the cloning of Max Jr.

I remember Rorvik had made it clear that though such people as Max, Darwin, Mary, Paul, Sparrow, and AnnaBelle were genuine humans really involved in the story, their names were aliases. He declares in the foreword of his book: "Owing to the nature and circumstances of the events described herein, I have found it necessary to omit certain details and to alter others in order to protect the identities of those involved. In some instances names, dates, and descriptive details of both person and place are at considerable variance with reality. . . ." Accordingly, the American journalist asked me to act upon Rorvik's "principles" if I was going to write and let the Chinese audience know the recent story of Max and his "copy." Needless to say, the American journalist also requested that his name not be revealed.

I gladly agreed. Now, after briefly recalling the story Rorvik has told us, I think it is time to tell the new story. . . .

For two days after the birth of his cloned heir, Mr. Max was busy poring over the Oxford English Dictionary, looking among thousands and thousands of words for the most beautiful name for his "copy." But to his great disappointment, he couldn't find a word that would satisfy him, even though he had painfully studied every page of the dictionary.

On the third day when he was still brooding over the choices of his heir's name, quite by accident, he overheard Dr. Mary cackling, with the baby in her arms, "Isn't it a marvel? The child looks every inch like the father. A hundred percent Max Jr.!"

"Why not? Why not Max Jr.!" Max suddenly found himself shouting the name. Since the child was his cloned heir, Max reasoned with self-content, his name should also be a duplicate of his. The attached "Jr." served only as a distinction.

One month after the birth of Max Jr., Mr. Max's private helicopter landed at a hospital in California. With one hand holding the baby and the other helping Sparrow, Dr. Mary led the team aboard the huge chopper. Mr. Max was in an exuberant mood that day. His age of seventy didn't seem to affect his energy; he even climbed into the cockpit and piloted the helicopter all the way himself.

The helicopter descended at the foot of a hill in Marin County. Hardly had the rotor stopped when several shiny black limousines, all belonging to Mr. Max, sped over and screeched to a halt just below the hatch. The convoy whisked the team toward the top of the hill, on which towered a fashionable glass building—the luxurious abode of our multi-millionaire.

Mr. Max himself fondly hugged the baby into his study. On one side of the room were arranged shelves and shelves of books; on the other side, a variety of expensive hunting guns were hung on the wall. Mr. Max's face was beaming all the time. To him nothing else could be more gratifying than having the most reliable and fitting heir to his "empire."

Inside the study, his left hand still lovingly holding the baby, Mr. Max signed a million-dollar check, the prize he had promised for the scientists. Though all of them at first declined, with the declaration that to make money wasn't the aim of their venture, Mr. Max insisted on and at last succeeded in getting them to accept it. His argument was brief, forceful, and undefeatable: He would not renege on his own promise.

As for Sparrow, who was blessed with success in fulfilling the task of the surrogate, a staggering sum of money was also fittingly awarded to her. Unlike the scientists, however, she pocketed the check without making any showy declination.

The scientists soon took their leave, but Sparrow was invited to stay by Mr. Max, who had once said that he would either marry or adopt her. The marriage of a seventy-year-old man with a seventeen-year-old girl, however, would certainly appear unnatural if not absurd; the disparity of ages was so enormous. So finally, Max decided not to marry Sparrow, but he still let this girl perform the role of the surrogate mother, whose sole task was now to nurse his cloned heir with all her care.

In the next five years, things were fine for all of them. When 1981 arrived, Max Jr. was already five years old, Sparrow twenty-two, and Max seventy-five. The almost unbelievable fact was that, as both prophesied and desired, Max Jr. grew up to be literally a perfect copy of his "father." His hair was cut short, and he was tall and strong. If it had not been for some silver hairs that unfortunately bristled here and there among the short hair on Mr. Max's head, or for his gold spectacles, one really might, if not observing carefully, mistake them for twins!

The miraculous "growth" of Max Jr. was another marvel of modern science; the scientists continually injected "growth-helper," itself as recent and newfangled as its recipient, into our Max Jr. The meticulously selected nourishment plus the equally meticulous "maternal care" of Sparrow surely accelerated the physical development of the cloned child.

The intelligence of Max Jr., correspondingly, leapt far ahead of that of any child of the same age. He was obviously a prodigy. Flawless reciting of the Bible, readings in long Western novels, and performing on the violin Beethoven's "Romance in F major" or Debussy's "Sonata in G minor" had long been conquered by this five-year-old. His manner was graceful and his speech elegant. A mere glance at the boy would give the impression that he was well-cultivated.

In these five years, perhaps because he had finally secured a satisfactory heir, Max was always in good spirits and surprisingly showed unmistakable signs of rejuvenation. The old silver hairs on his head were gradually disappearing, and so were the wrinkles on his face. He looked not a bit like an aging, feeble man of seventy-five. On the contrary, his appearance was more than enough to convince you that he was an able-bodied middle-aged man. Not long before he had been obsessed with the fear that he would soon be senile. If the inevitable end should come under such circumstances, an innocent and all-too-young Max Jr. couldn't be expected to inherit his fortune. Should the child make just one false move, his inherited empire, worth billions of dollars, was doomed to fall into the outstretched hands of covetous evil men. It was essentially this fear that motivated Max into spending huge sums of money and enlisting the service of some first-rate scientists, in the hope that Max Jr. could grow up as fast as possible. But now it certainly appeared that his original fear had been all too unnecessary! In order to make himself look younger and thus match his fast growing "copy," Mr. Max sacrificed his beard that had been meticulously preened for so long! He regarded Max Jr. as his cloned heir and loved him as he loved his own future.

Sparrow by now had turned into a beautiful woman. Her charming eyes were sparkling with youth. If she hadn't had a withered hand, she would surely have had a long line of suitors! For these five years, Sparrow lived in Max's luxurious mansion. But she still retained her virtue and common sense. Max did not care to take advantage of her, as he had already "killed" the idea of marrying her: What if another son should be born? Therefore, Sparrow spent her time happily and peacefully in Max's home. Her status was still that of "surrogate mother."

But who would have imagined that, when the early summer of 1981 was approaching, Death's shadow was already hanging over this modern fashionable glass building. . . .

At dawn of an early summer day, the rising sun was flashing its golden rays on the crystal-like glass mansion when Max Jr. came to his father's bedroom and gently knocked at the door.

Mr. Max led a rigidly patterned life. At six o'clock every morning he would take Max Jr. out and hike slowly along the winding mountain paths, breathing the fresh air of the woods. It was already six twenty, but nobody had seen Mr. Max out of his room. Max Jr. couldn't help feeling slightly worried, so he went to his father's room to see what was the matter.

Ominously, nothing stirred inside the room, despite his unceasing violent pounding on the door. Even when the noise had brought an anxious Sparrow out of her room, the door of Max's room remained tightly locked. Max Jr. pulled Sparrow to the window and peered inside: Max was still lying on the bed!

Had there been an accident? Max Jr. and Sparrow climbed into the room through the window. Not until they reached the bed did they receive their first shock: Max's face was iron-grey, and his lips bloodless. Sparrow felt Max's forehead; it was icy cold. It was plain as day that the multi-millionaire was already in another world.

Mr. Max had no kin except Max Jr., his cloned son. His sudden death, therefore, didn't need to disturb many people. Max Jr. at once sent for Lawyer Wilde and Dr. Darwin, who were the witnesses to Mr. Max's wills. The multi-millionaire was wise enough not to believe any nonsense about eternity, so he had a long time before made the most careful and prophetic plans for this inevitable day. The cloning of Max Jr. was, undoubtedly, only one of his schemes. He had also made two wills and asked Lawyer Wilde and Dr. Darwin for advice. After weighing every suggestion, Max signed the wills and appointed Wilde and Darwin as the executors.

One would deal with the disposal of Max's body. Max wrote: "My body must not be cremated after death. It must be kept under long-term cryogenic preservation. I believe that in several decades there just might be breakthroughs that would enable medical science to restore a cryogenically 'suspended' person. Perhaps I will be one of the lucky people to return to life and enjoy again its happiness.

"I have therefore left a special fund which I believe will be sufficient to keep me in deep freeze for at least a hundred years. Moreover, I have also put another special sum of money, which is to reward the party or parties who might eventually 'rescue' me.

"However, please do not disturb me within the first fifty years after my death, as I am not convinced that the art of 'resurrection' will be perfected within that time. And I certainly do not wish to be used as a guinea pig. Only when the chances for success are absolutely certain can they start doing anything to bring me back to life. Otherwise, I would rather have my body lying undisturbed in deep freeze.

"I also declare now that once I am really brought back to life, I will renounce the right to all my former properties. It is necessary and essential to make this statement, lest my 'offspring' should be haunted by the very idea of my resurrection and even probably do something against me.

"I therefore appoint my son Max Jr., Lawyer Wilde, and Dr. Darwin as the executors of this will."

The other will dealt with the inheritance of Max's fortune. Max wrote: "Max Jr. is the only and legitimate heir to all of my properties. His inheritance is fully legitimated by the common law of blood relationship. Max Jr. is my closest kin. The relation between us, in fact, is even closer than this definition can denote.

"Rorvik, Dr. Darwin, Paul, Mary, and Sparrow are the witnesses to the identity of Max Jr. They have already written the documents testifying to the complete process of the cloning of this child. All the documents have been sealed and properly stored. Only when Max Jr.'s inheritance is gravely challenged can they be made known to the public.

"I repeat that Max Jr. is myself, and that he is a continuation of my life. I am he, and he is I. That he inherits all of my properties is perfectly justified and indisputable. He is the sole heir, both natural and legitimate, to my fortune.

"I therefore appoint Lawyer Wilde to defend for Max Jr. his title to the inheritance."

Lawyer Wilde and Dr. Darwin were both very dependable people. They immediately did what the deceased man had written in his wills. Max's body was at once transported to a modern hospital and preserved in deep freeze.

Max Jr. went through all the legal procedures about inheritance without any difficulty. He rose to the top of his father's vast empire literally overnight. Like Mr. Max, he was self-confident and commanding. His shrewdness awed both Lawyer Wilde and Dr. Darwin who, whenever seeing him, found themselves automatically bending and nodding, as if they had seen the old Max himself.

Extremely ambitious and cunning, Max Jr. confidently formed his plans to double his fortune and to rise to be the number one multi-millionaire in America.

But just as Max Jr. was warming up for greater ventures, a totally unexpected incident arose and got him inextricably into the following whirlpool.

Max Jr. had never dreamed that his inheritance of Max's fortune would be seriously challenged!

No outsiders knew anything about Max's death. Before his last day on earth, Mr. Max repeatedly insisted that no obituary be printed in the newspaper and no funeral be held. For several good reasons he believed that he would not really "die." First, his cloned son—the continuation of his life—would still be alive, which meant that Max himself was still living even after his death. Second, his body was to be preserved in deep freeze, and the chances were that one day he might be brought back to life again. Of course, there was another more subtle reason which he didn't want to state explicitly: the fear that once his death was made known, somebody might conspire to murder or conspire against Max Jr. in order to take over his empire.

The most nosy species on our planet, by common consent, is the journalist. Hardly had Max's body been interred in a cryogenic vault when some newspaper reporters were tipped off about the news. No journalist would ignore such a sensation that would surely make a front-page headline! Hordes of newsmen and camera crews, like flies chasing stinking flesh, swarmed into the hospital and besieged Max Jr. Though Max Jr. and Darwin flatly refused to talk to any newspaper people, some of the resourceful reporters still got some interesting information through other channels. So three days after Max's death, the headline on the front page of every newspaper in the country was printed in extraordinarily large letters:


MULTI-MILLIONAIRE'S BODY KEPT IN DEEP FREEZE!
CLONED HEIR INHERITS ALL PROPERTIES!


As could be imagined, the news swept from coast to coast and catalyzed waves upon waves of gossip, some malicious and some stupid.

The very next day after such publicity, four days after Max's death, a 23-year-old woman flew to the United States and hurried to Marin County, California, bringing a five-year-old boy with her. Though it wasn't very hot in early summer, the woman was already wearing a mini-mini and a low-necked top. A snow-white straw hat topped her head; she wore mirrored sunglasses; and her lips were painted a brilliant red. The boy's dress was rather simple: a checked shirt and a pair of violet trousers. When the woman descended from the plane, she called a taxi and headed straight for the fashionable glass building.

Sparrow scrutinized on the TV screen the woman who was standing before the front gate. A cry of surprise escaped her. AnnaBelle! The woman who was once the other surrogate! Sparrow was lucky enough to get pregnant after the cloning "seed" was sown into her womb and later gave birth to Max Jr. But AnnaBelle was never blessed with such a stroke of luck: She remained barren even after repeated efforts of sowing the "seed" into her womb.

Sparrow thought that perhaps AnnaBelle, after reading the newspaper, had made this long special trip here to express her sorrow for the death of Mr. Max. Precisely because of this notion, she personally went to the front gate to greet them and even bent down to kiss the little boy.

Sparrow led them into the sitting room. Max Jr. was there, but he didn't recognize this stranger. A stunned look suddenly clouded AnnaBelle's face—My God, he looked every bit like Max!

Sitting on the sofa and letting her boy curl comfortably on her knees, AnnaBelle sipped a cool drink and got straight to the point.

All of a sudden her look hardened. The first words she said severely shocked both Sparrow and Max Jr.—"I've come to inherit the fortune left by Mr. Max!"

"What!" Sparrow was stunned speechless.

"What!" From the throat of Max Jr. came forth the roar of an indignant lion.

AnnaBelle didn't care a straw. She lit a cigarette, which was held between her polished nails, and with smoke curving up from her mouth, said affectedly but rather quietly, "You needn't deal with me that way. It is not a weak woman who is now before you."

"Sparrow, you are nothing but, just like me, a surrogate hired by Max. Max Jr., you are but a cloned living being. God knows if you could be regarded as a real man. Well, let me tell you in plain words. Five years ago, when I was a surrogate, though the embryos never made me pregnant, that damned old man Max was infatuated with me and eventually made love to me.

"At the very time, the doctors found you were pregnant. Max, the doctors and the rest of you soon secretly disappeared. Nobody knew your whereabouts.

"I didn't know Max's address and couldn't find you. I had to bear the insult, giving birth to Henry as a bastard. I brought him up in difficulties, treated with disdain by my relatives and friends. I wouldn't throw him into a garbage bin. Anyway, he is my blood and flesh.

"Yesterday I noticed a large picture in the press and recognized it was Mr. Max. I learned from the report that Max was a millionaire. I also learned his home address and something about you and your so-called son. Immediately I borrowed some money to get here.

"I want you to know clearly, only Henry is Max's true son. Max Jr. has no right to inherit Mr. Max's legacy, for it should be taken into consideration whether or not he's even a 'man.'

"I could sue you in court. But I think of the past friendship between you and me, Sparrow, and pity you as a disabled woman. I feel sympathetic for you. Just for these reasons, I've come here to discuss Max's legacy with you, instead of going straight to court. I suggest ninety percent of Max's legacy for me, and ten percent for you, which will be enough for mother and son to live a life of extreme luxury. In this way, there will be no harm to our friendly relationship."

AnnaBelle was talking quite confidently and at length she finished her cigarette and lit another. Her big eyes stared menacingly at Sparrow and Max Jr. But Sparrow was calm and unruffled. She carefully studied Henry.

He looked somewhat like AnnaBelle, but definitely not like Max. After a moment of silence, Sparrow said between her teeth, "Blackmail!"

Originally, AnnaBelle had come with the intention of trying peaceful means before resorting to legal power. But the flat refusal from Sparrow enraged her greatly. She decided to carry the thing through, whatever the consequences. She sued Sparrow.

The judge who had this case was Mr. Louis, a short and fat old man. His bright bald head suggested he had much experience in handling cases. AnnaBelle's charge was so wordy that Judge Louis had to be patient to read it over. Scratching his bald head, he at last caught the point. Merely an exam to decide if Henry was Max's son by blood would settle the case.

So Judge Louis summoned Dr. Gurdon, a legal medical expert. Dr. Gurdon was thin and a head taller than Louis. His deep-lined forehead suggested that he was also a much-experienced person. He had handled several such identification cases, which were usually entangled with the inheritance of a legacy.

Dr. Gurdon started the work right away. He found in Max's medical records that Max's blood was type A. After a chemical experiment, AnnaBelle's blood was found to be type B. Immediately, Dr. Gurdon realized the complexity of the case. If the parents both were type O, their children would be O. If the parents both were type B, their children would have B or O. If the parents had O and B types, their children would have A or B. If the parents had A or B types, their children would have, A, B, AB, or O—four different possible blood types. That meant that when the father had A blood type and the mother B blood type, or vice versa, it would be impossible to identify their children according to their blood. In this situation, the people of A, B, AB, or O blood types all could be blood descendants.

Though the case couldn't be simply solved by a blood test, Dr. Gurdon didn't give up. Instead, he decided to make the examination from various aspects. For example, he could examine the serum factors, earwax and so on. Gurdon had once found damp earwax hereditary. If the parents had damp earwax, their children would also have it. But no detailed record about Max's earwax could be found in his medical dossier. It was fortunate that his body was kept in a cryogenic vault, and Dr. Gurdon hoped to get some clues there. However, when Gurdon suggested a postmortem exam of Max's body to Judge Louis, he started to knit his eyebrows deeply.

Judge Louis knew Max had written clearly in his will: "I shouldn't be disturbed within fifty years after my death." Now, Max's body had been frozen only for five days, how could they disturb him?

Expectedly, when the judge passed the legal medical expert's opinion on to Max Jr. and Sparrow, they opposed it fiercely. Max Jr. definitely turned it down, leaving no room for further discussion. Dr. Gurdon was very angry at this and wanted to withdraw from the case. Flashing with rage and the blue veins prominent on his temples, the legal medical expert shouted to the judge, "I can do nothing except give Max a postmortem exam. Max had written unmistakenly in his will that he couldn't be stirred within fifty years. His reason is: 'I don't so believe that the method to bring people to life from death will be perfected within fifty years. I don't wish my body to be used as a guinea pig!' We would use his body not for bringing life to it, but for a legal medical postmortem exam. In addition, it won't take much time to examine the body. It can be frozen again after the exam."

When AnnaBelle learned that Dr. Gurdon wanted to withdraw from the case, she made a fearful scene. She asserted with great assurance that Henry was Max's son by blood, and of course should be his heir.

AnnaBelle's threats to meet newspaper reporters to publish her charges that Max Jr. was not a real man made Max Jr. very nervous. He found the lawyer Wilde and had a detailed consultation with him. Wilde advised: "Henry's appearances are in no way like Max. I can easily judge him to be a fraudulent son at first sight. She merely intends to blackmail you. A postmortem of Mr. Max's body would thoroughly expose the fraud. What is more, . . ."

Here the lawyer Wilde suppressed his voice and whispered to Max Jr., "the postmortem exam wouldn't matter to you at all. When the body is refrozen after the exam, Mr. Max would never come back to life again! But why should you care? The old man professed that he would give up the ownership of his original legacy when he returned to life. But in reality, he would certainly reclaim everything. By that time, you would. . . ."

Here Wilde didn't continue. He knew very well that the clever Max Jr. wouldn't misunderstand what he implied. But Max Jr. seemed to be very obstinate and held firmly to Max's will, not permitting the legal medical expert to examine Max's body.

The scene AnnaBelle made was as horrible as it was vicious. Her aim was, clearly, to take over the modern glass building and to rob Max's family of all its wealth. Only when Max Jr. realized that a life-and-death confrontation was inevitable did he agree, though very unwillingly, to Dr. Gurdon's demand. Max's legal medical experts came to the hospital. Max's body was frozen in a secret vault with a temperature of one hundred degrees below zero. They removed the body from its secret place and attached it to special cryogenic equipment. Almost instantaneously, the temperature of the body rose as high as that inside the room and the body was restored to its original appearance. It looked as if Max had just died a moment ago.

Originally, Dr. Gurdon wanted to examine Max's body only to help judge if Henry was Mr. Max's son by blood. But unexpectedly, this brought forth new problems.

It was already twelve o'clock at night. The judge was in a sound sleep when the bell rang frantically.

Who would be calling at midnight? Hearing the visitor's voice, Judge Louis, in his pajamas, asked, rubbing his sleepy eyes, "Why are you calling on me at this hour?"

"I never call for nothing," replied Dr. Gurdon. "It is very important."

Dr. Gurdon took a debugging device out of his briefcase. He didn't explain his important news until he was sure that there was no one eavesdropping on them. "I took some of Max's blood for a chemical examination of serum factors. But astonishingly I found the blood had alcohol in it. That meant Max had drunk a small quantity of wine before his death. I went on to a further examination, and to my great surprise, I found an extremely poisonous toxin—AR toxin in it!"

"AR toxin?" Judge Louis was fully awake now. When Gurdon told him this, he was all ears.

"Yes. It is AR toxin," replied Dr. Gurdon. "I have examined Max's death report, which was signed by Dr. Darwin. It says Max died from coronary heart disease. Max didn't have a postmortem exam since his body was supposed to be preserved intact. Now, my finding AR toxin in his blood shows Max didn't die from coronary heart disease. Instead, he was murdered. According to my knowledge, AR toxin dissolves easily in wine. Probably Max died after drinking some wine. Nevertheless, AR toxin doesn't produce an effect immediately, but only two or three hours later."

"Murder?" His chin resting on his hand, Judge Louis was absorbed in thought. After a while, he said, "Max was a multi-millionaire and it isn't unusual that somebody would murder him for money."

"I have been thinking about who the murderer might be. But the case is too complicated to judge."

"Why?"

After a moment's thinking, Dr. Gurdon said, "Max guarded his house like a castle. The tall enclosing walls are installed with electric devices and nobody can possibly break in. And nothing was found missing after his death. Apparently the murderer isn't a burglar.

"The people who used to be around Max were Sparrow, Max Jr., Rorvick, Darwin, Mary, Paul and Wilde. Among those people, Darwin, Mary, and Paul are all scientists who have successfully helped Max in the cloning. Generally, these people are probably not murderers. Certainly, Dr. Darwin is a bit suspicious, because the death report of coronary heart disease was signed by him.

"The lawyer Wilde was one of the executors of Max's will and had a long-standing friendship with him. Possibly, he committed the crime. But he was in San Francisco the day Max died. Therefore, he is excluded from the possibility of committing the crime.

"In this way, only Max Jr. and Sparrow remain as suspects. Only they two were at home that day.

"I don't think Max Jr. could have committed the crime. He is the legal heir already appointed by Max. The murder was unnecessary for him to commit.

"The most suspicious is Sparrow. She was extremely poor, and didn't have a formal marriage with Max. So far as her age is concerned, she is fifty-three years younger than Max and she couldn't have had any affection for him. Additionally, Max Jr. is growing up fast and no longer needs her care. She faced the threat of being driven out of their fine home. Once she murdered Max, Max Jr. would inherit the legacy and she could enjoy everything as Max Jr.'s mother."

Surprisingly, when Judge Louis had heard all this, he shook his bright bald head and said, "My opinion is just the opposite. To my knowledge, Sparrow is a very disciplined and honest woman. Poor as she is, she probably wouldn't stoop to murdering a man for money. Instead, I rather suspect Max Jr. But I can't puzzle out his motive. As you have said, he is already the heir appointed by Max and he needn't murder his father."

What Judge Louis said lacked sufficient evidence and he found it very difficult to convince Dr. Gurdon. But Gurdon knew the judge had much experience in evaluating criminal cases, and his inferences were often exact. So he asked, "You suspect Max Jr., but what evidence do you have?"

"The evidence is obvious—time and again he objected to having the body examined," the judge replied. "If he hadn't anything unnatural on his mind, he needn't have opposed that idea. Evidently, he is quite worried. If the body were examined, probably some traces of the murder would be found. If he isn't the criminal, he should have been in favor of having Max's body examined, because Henry doesn't look like Max. Obviously, he is a fraud. A postmortem could prove that Henry is not Max's son and this would be favorable for him."

What the judge said had much reason in it. After hearing it, Dr. Gurdon sighed, "If Max Jr. is the murderer, it will be more troublesome for me. Max Jr. is Max's copy. The two are not only alike in blood type, but also alike in their fingerprints. Consequently, even if we found the bottle of AR toxin, we still couldn't differentiate the fingerprints left on the bottle."

"That's right. Just like you, this is the first time I've come across such a puzzling case." The judge, scratching his bald head, said, "It seems to me the only thing we can do is. . . ."

The two talked the whole night away before they eventually worked out an effective method to solve the case.

Early in the morning, the sun cast its golden light onto the modern glass building on the hill. Max Jr. had just awakened when Judge Louis and Dr.

Gurdon called. Both guests wore smiling faces; plainly they had brought good news. As soon as the guests were seated in the study, Max Jr. asked, "Have you found out the criminal?"

"No, but we've found a miracle."

The smile faded away from Max Jr.'s face. Apparently he became very nervous. He then asked, "What is it?"

"Well, it's like this, . . ." Dr. Gurdon replied, smiling, "when your father is brought out of deep freeze completely, he should return to life."

"What? Return to life? Impossible, absolutely impossible!" Max Jr. said in one breath.

"Impossible? Why is it absolutely impossible?" The judge asked coldly in retort.

Max Jr. was now panic-stricken at this question and couldn't answer.

"Because you murdered your father with toxin and he could not come back to life. Absolutely couldn't, isn't that right?" Judge Louis told the truth.

Max Jr. was really still only a child despite his size and intelligence, and at these words he started to sweat coldly, out of fright. He began to stutter, "No, I didn't say he couldn't return to life."

Dr. Gurdon took out a mini-recorder from his pocket and pressed one of the buttons. From it came what Max Jr. had just blurted, "What? Returned to life. Impossible! Absolutely impossible."

Max Jr. suddenly felt his legs go weak and he fell down on the sofa. . . .

A very complicated case was easily solved.

As the case concerned a millionaire, Louis decided on a closed hearing instead of a public one for fear of causing trouble. At the hearing, only those immediately concerned were present at the court and Judge Louis presided.

It went very smoothly. Max Jr. acknowledged he had murdered his father.

"You must confess your motive," the judge said in a loud voice.

"I was driven by my natural instincts," Max Jr. said. "No, no, my father drove me to kill him."

"What?" Max Jr.'s words surprised everybody present.

Max Jr. explained. "My father declared that he was an extreme individualist. That is to say, he was a completely selfish man. He racked his brains to make the scientists produce me in his image by the method of cloning. He intended me to inherit his legacy. This is a typical example of his extreme selfishness. I am he and he is I. Therefore, if I inherit the legacy, he can actually still enjoy the ownership of the legacy.

"Besides, he racked his brains to make the scientists preserve his body under ultra-low temperature, so that someday he could return to the world to continue his happy life as a millionaire. It's also another example of his extreme selfishness.

"I'm his copy. We are not only of the same appearance, blood type, personality and manners, but also have the same psychology of extreme selfishness.

"As I'm extremely selfish, I could not bear it when I saw my father growing increasingly younger and more vigorous. I was very jealous. I wished that he would die so that I could inherit his holdings and run them my own way. In other words, a selfish son killed his father who had cloned him."

Max Jr.'s confession astonished everyone in the room. As the murderer made a clean breast of the crime, the hearing soon came to an end.

The court, however, set Max Jr. free because it was judged that Max had committed suicide instead of being murdered. The reason was that Max had written precisely these words in his will: "I repeat that Max Jr. is myself and the continuation of my life. He is just the old Max." With these equations, Max should be viewed as being "killed" by his own image and naturally it should be a suicide. Since it was a suicide, Max Jr. could reasonably be set free and continue to live a millionaire's life of luxury and dissipation.

The reaction from the scientists was also unexpected. Rorvik remarked that Max Jr.'s poisoning of Max decisively proved the unique success of the technique of cloning, for Max's cloned heir, Max Jr., had not only inherited the genetic traits, but also the extreme selfishness from the multimillionaire. This showed sufficiently that the duplicate clone was truly the very image of the original.

Dr. Darwin had studied another problem and decided, "According to my research, though Max's body was again frozen after the postmortem, he had permanently lost the opportunity of returning to life, and he can never return to the world. The body preserved in deep freeze can undergo only one test by raising the temperature. If he can't return to life in the temperature-raising, he will never be able to live again. In this sense, Max has left the world permanently, though he had racked his brains in his lifetime to return to the world again after his death."

*Translated by Pei Minxin*
*and Yang Renmin*

# II
# SPIES
# AND
# TECHNOLOGY

# 4

# The Mysterious Wave

## WANG XIAODA

As a reporter for the Military Science-Technology Press (M.S.T.P.) I went to Base 88 in northern Xinjiang for a news story. The mission: to see how the defensive system known as Wave-45 works; it's unnecessary to keep it a secret now. When I received my orders, I set off that very day. Since my graduation from the Military Academy of Science and Technology, I had been working happily at M.S.T.P. as a science-technology reporter for two years. But this was the first time that I took on such a heavy, single-handed responsibility as covering Base 88 alone. I worked out a plan and outline for my press report that was as detailed as possible. After my arrival at the base, however, very unexpected events occurred.

## AN EMERGENCY AIR-RAID ALARM AND 13−12=0

On my arrival at dusk I found only Ma Gongjian, my old schoolmate from the Academy, waiting for me at the base airport. On our meeting he affectionately punched me on the shoulder and I returned his greeting in kind.

"Pass," said Ma, making a military salute, and then deliberately stretching out his hand just as I was about to ask him something. Off base this behavior struck me dumb, and I handed him the coverage order and service passport in a businesslike manner, silently displeased.

Published in *Sichuan wenxue* (Sichuan Literature), April 1979.

Having had a conscientious look at them, he said smiling, "Routine affairs can't be dispensed with; but there's no need to check your I.D. Get in the car, Zhang the Scholar." He used my old nickname instead of Zhang Changgong. This eased my unhappiness over his seriousness.

While I was sitting next to him in the automatic electric car, zipping along the expressway into the fall wind, he began to chatter away, asking me about our old schoolmates. He had hardly been in touch with those on the outside since coming to this base after graduation. Due to regulations there he couldn't talk about his work beyond the bounds of the base without permission. Therefore, having been a familiar schoolmate in the same field, I only guessed his job was nothing other than the high-energy-radio remote control. In his words, he was very satisfied with it. On our way for less than half an hour, the car made a sharp turn, then descended into a subway tunnel in front of some thick bushes. Then we arrived at No. 1 station at full speed in a little more than twenty minutes. Although we couldn't talk more of Base 88 at that time, I might tell you that it's located over one hundred meters below ground, under a gorge, in precipices along the western frontier covered with thick ice and snow. Top-secret place that it was, you could not see any sentinel or guards above ground because the circumference electronic warning systems were enough to deal with any casual intruders.

At No. 1 station, Ma made a report to the base command, and returned with instructions to settle me at the reception house first, and then for me to begin work the following day. Through my request and Ma's explanation, I was permitted to room with him, as his roommate, Wang, happened to be out on assignment. On the way to the dormitory, I actually forgot we were over one hundred meters below ground. Not only was there fresh air and bright rays, but also flowers, grass, and bushes, with trimmed Chinese ilexes and cannas to divide the traffic from the sidewalk, and mid-avenue gardens at a little distance in which lots of Chinese roses, peonies and dahlias, beautiful and colorful, kept blossoming in varieties under the bright blue sky. Ma told me there was a man-made sky, which turned dark at night. We were able to tell day from night, indoor from outdoor, and see the sunlight, lawns and fresh flowers, too; it was quite another world underground.

The quarters were very spacious and furnished well enough, practical and gracious, beautiful and tasteful. Near the multi-purpose machine on his bookcase, there were specialized books, familiar to me, concerning electron physics remote control, engineering mathematics, circuit and electron components; besides, quite a few sophisticated ones on chemistry and biophysiology. I took out a book of biophysiology which had so many passages thickly dotted and marked that it was clearly not used for lightly skimming. I was puzzled.

"Why do you apply yourself to this?"

"Didn't you come here to cover news of Wave-45?" He turned, taking off his army coat. His words still unfinished, there abruptly came the blinking lines of the red signal lamp on the bedside wall and a bunch of toots from the buzzer.

"Emergency alarm!" he shouted, snatching up his cap and coat on the table, and rushed out. At the door with one hand buttoning his coat and the other waving to me, he said: "Don't move from here, I am going to. . . ." But a critical situation is an order for action. Though I was a reporter, how could I keep out of such an emergency? I hesitated no more, put on my cap and followed him out the door.

People hurried, coming and going, through the passageway, all of them tense but orderly, with clear-cut destinations. The command orders were being issued over the p.a. system: ". . . At the first grade alert. To your posts."

Out of the quarters I kept abreast of him, across the lawn, into a building, down the stairs and around a corner until I was pinned down and embraced round the middle by a pair of machine hands in front of the doorway designated "45-7."

"Ma, Ma Gongjian!" I could only utter a cry, seeing him disappear behind the screen at the front of the room.

"Who are you? What are you up to?" a stern voice came from the screen instead of Ma's answer."

"I'm Zhang Changgong, from M.S.T.P. I have come here as a reporter," I replied, struggling.

"The pass, the base pass, the Wave-45 pass!" Still the stern voice questioned me without any exception as if I were before a judge. How funny! Having just arrived I had had no time to even get a drink of water. How could I get this or that pass ready? I had the coverage order and the service pass delivered to Ma as soon as I got off the plane. However, it would be impossible for me to clearly explain all this to the hateful screen. It would be in vain to struggle against its steel hands. At last I calmed down, but made no reply, standing at ease.

"The pass, the base pass, the Wave-45 pass!" repeated the harsh voice.

"My coverage order and service pass are in Comrade Ma Gongjian's hands, and I haven't had time to get the others." I had no way out but to reply that way. At that moment several soldiers stepped by me without even a glance as they hurried into room 45-7. I was surprised that the cursed screen let them in, and only detained me. Suddenly I thought of my reporting in to the Command at No. 1 station; I loudly exclaimed:

"I came into contact with the Command at No. 1 station half an hour ago. I am a science-technology reporter and am paying a special visit out here to report on the W-45 system. Let me go to the emergency situation."

I also thought of saying some strong words, such as: "You will be responsible for the full consequences." However, facing me was a screen, a mere pair of machine hands with an electronic brain. Severe threatening would not work at all. So I swallowed the words coming to my lips. I didn't expect my words to move this marble-hearted electronic machine. A half minute later he sounded less severe than before.

"On the Command leader's instructions, Zhang Changgong is to be given a provisional pass and join in the battle with Ma Gongjian within the scope of 45-7." Having contacted the Command it set me free and handed me a white silver plate, the 88-45-7 pass. I breathed more easily, and unconsciously made a salute to it. After passing by it, going down another hall, I ran ahead at full speed. At the other end there was a large room in which I saw Ma Gongjian sitting seriously at a big installation with several fluorescent screens, all sorts of meters and signal lights. Wanting to blame him for his leaving me behind, I ran up to him with a little anger. He signed me to take a seat beside him, pointing towards the screen, shaking his hand. This seemed to be a very serious situation with the people all watching the installation and holding their breath, so I had to swallow my grievance.

Outlined against the first screen before Ma were some bright spots approaching the center of a 400 km. scope in the direction of polar coordinate 30 degrees. He told me in a strained whisper that the zero point in the direction of 30 degrees was at a distance of 270 km. from our border; i.e., the bright spots were less than 130 km. from it. When he adjusted the second screen, the magnified spots were able to be seen clearly at a distance of 300 km. only. There were twelve spots.

"Twelve?" he exclaimed at the same time. Why did he make a fuss about this? Seeming to know my doubt, he told me to read a card in the notebook. On the card was a combat order:

By analysis of the satellite information, 13 enemy aircraft from Base SR-17 are taking off to attempt to invade our country. Prepare for action in order to wipe out the intruders and execute plan 4.

Military Commission of Base 88,
19:37 September 20

"How come there are only twelve aircraft?" I cried in surprise, too. $13-12=1$. Nothing could be clearer than that. Where in the world was the other one?

Twelve bright points were pressing on us ten thousand meters high on the third screen, which reflected elevation. It's really rare that such an air fleet would brazenly intrude on our airspace in peacetime. Furthermore, how mysterious a sum was $13-12=0$; a flight squadron with one aircraft missing. Were there any mistakes in the satellite information? While I was sitting there bewildered, there came a second Military Commission combat order accurately repeated by a laser printout.

"There is a Lizard-Type among the thirteen aircraft taking off from the enemy air base SR-17. Start the Wave-45 system at once."

"Lizard Type!" I knew it was a spy plane developed and lavishly boasted about for a long time by one of the superpowers, but it had never come out. It's reported that it's a big powered hedge-hopping scout, and able to fly at zero altitude and make a profiling flight. In other words, it flies so close to hill-slopes, valleys and buildings, keeping a ten-meter space automatically, as to be sheltered under the radar interference of such barriers and hardly discoverable by ordinary radar and electronic monitors. Oh, to turn up and vanish like a flash of lightning. What is more, it's equipped with electron-detectaphone instruments such as laser photographs, anti-missile and anti-interference systems. It's bragged up to the sky: "Go where it likes; do whatever it pleases." Unexpectedly, it did come and display a few wicked tricks, and we could never find traces on the screens.

No sooner did the Command issue the order to start the W-45 system than Ma unfolded the map of the western border on the wall. A faint blue halo indicated the defense belt of Base 88, almost covering the western border above 1,000 km. and deep into the territory for nearly one million square km. On the map there suddenly turned up a flickering yellow speck around the industrial Feng City, more than two hundred km. inside the border, showing a flying object low in the air. No doubt it was the Lizard Type that had disappeared from the screen. Well, we were catching that lizard's tail.

At that moment on the fourth screen, a bright dashing dot was surrounded by a chain of light-rings. While they were tightening their hold steadily, on No. 5 screen there appeared a grotesque airplane with a pair of short and wide wings, a flat fuselage trailed by too long of a tail, and a separate tail-cabin at the end. It was making a devious flight, sneaking around. Abruptly the "lizard" scurried up as if it had taken a beating; immediately numerous bright dots appeared and a number of quite unaccountable curves. The grotesque plane was fading from sight. I could not keep from worrying about it. Did it slip away like this? Ma pressed several buttons with full confidence, and it reappeared clearly on the screen. I didn't know why it was staggering to loop the loop in the sky like a drunkard. He breathed a sigh as if relieving a heavy burden and leaned loosely against the chair-back.

"Why don't we bring it down?" I asked, jerking his hand, anxious to know the lizard's whereabouts.

"Bring it down," he repeated with a smile, giving me a wink. "No need." I did not know the hows and whys. How could we make a show of politeness to an invader? My schoolmate was familiar with my hot temper, and yet in a mysterious way he was not eager to answer my questions but brought me out of room 45-7.

Where should we go? A high speed elevator took us up to an expanse on the ground. To my surprise the lizard on the screen had just then obediently stopped on the field. There were seven or eight soldiers standing around talking and gesticulating. What's the matter? Let Krutch, the flier of the Lizard Type, speak for himself.

## THE CAPTURED LIZARD

I was permitted to make excerpts in detail from Krutch's confession. While reading this copy, I often saw the face of Krutch, blue eyes and a heavy stubbly beard, with a look of perplexity, wavering, upset and full of frustration. Part of his confession is as follows:

"We learned of a new industrial system in Feng City, China, according to satellite reconnaissance. In order to clarify the details, our country specially dispatched batches of high- and low-level scouts, but on crossing the border they all vanished obscurely and unaccountably. Therefore we called the China western border the eastern Bermuda Triangle among our fliers. We decided to use the brand new Lizard Type. It's equipped with electronic reconnaissance instruments, anti-missiles and anti-interference equipment, so we had nearly perfect confidence in its capacities for high speed and minimum altitude performance on flight.

"Of the thirteen aircraft taking off from our base the twelve high-level scouts were just the bait, as it is our habitual practice to distract your attention. I was flying the Lizard Type at zero to steal in. I felt as if I were successful crossing the border and flying above Feng City on schedule. I started to take automatic photos using the electron laser cameras, and yet on checking my bearings I found my position inconsistent with the coordinates indicated by the satellite. Unexpectedly I took some photographs of disguised military sites, for the additional achievement. I was thrilled and even fancied receiving a prize and a vacation.

"I was always afraid of something in your territorial air. Since I'd been rewarded, it would be best to get a move on and return. However, I couldn't return and account for my mission without covering the designated coordinates assigned by my commander. I forced myself to rush forward. I supposed the position should be at the central district of Feng City in line with the chart and my gauges, but in fact I saw a large lake suffused with silver light, surrounded by bald undulating hills. I felt something go wrong and thought the gauges couldn't be trusted. It wouldn't make sense to check my bearing again. That's queer enough! I clearly remembered your The Art of War, by Sun Zi, which says, 'Better make myself scarce.' No matter what my orders and the prize might be, having deployed some interference devices as camouflage, I decided to head home.

"All at once a dozen Lizard Types surrounded me. God bless me! What the deuce was it? We only had three in all that had been completed. The second of them was ready for this mission, but was still at the airport because Evan, its pilot, had gotten drunk and been put in confinement. I believe he purposely avoided being ready for duty. The third was being serviced because a number of specialized instruments had been damaged during a test flight. How could a dozen turn up? They were not ours, of course, but China's. I was done for! And I was struck with great fear and despair. I tried to get rid of their tight ring, dashing here and there, but they dogged me so closely they were like my shadow, madly bustling up close to me. By then I thought I must be crazy. Who would have thought that I could see myself sitting in the cockpit when I looked at the nearest lizard which kept abreast of mine? The pilot, who had the very same figure as me, a heavy beard, glaring eyes and clenched teeth, was rushing at me.

"When it seemed both of us would collide, I raised a cry to God and squeezed my eyes closed. God must have shown his might. When I opened my eyes again, I could hardly believe what I saw: No More Lizard Types but my familiar Base SR-17. With mixed emotions after such a narrow escape, I dived to the runway, and braking, made a wonderful landing. I expected cheers and embraces, for whoever came back form China, even if empty-handed, was a hero, let alone that I had fulfilled an additional task. With bank bills fluttering in my mind's eyes, I began thinking of the typist, Lida, with the little turned-up nose who would no longer look at me disdainfully with her light brown eyes. Slowly I pushed back the cabin-lid and climbed out, waving my right hand pompously.

"If only I could have stayed a little longer in the cockpit! How could I know you were waiting for me. When I got off the plane smugly, what came to my hands were not flowers but cuffs! I needn't say what happened afterwards.

"But I will say something more. I was seized while in an abnormal condition; both the plane and my nerves were shot. Otherwise I should have had a vacation in Rome or Paris, not ended up here."

"Even now Krutch doesn't know he is the 20th prisoner, the 20th to Wave-45," Ma remarked laughingly, looking over the report. And then he gave a brief account of the defense system W-45.

W-45 is a comprehensive high-energy wave system designed by Professor Wang Fan of the Physics Department of Feng City University, with the assistance of the Biophysiology Institute and the Military-Science Technology Academy. The foundation for it is based on Professor Wang's new wave theory. It maintains that each objective substance can be performed by different waves, for all information we can feel is a wave, too; and they are, of course, issued from various real substances. Through further research, a pure information wave can be artificially produced and our sensitive functions—sight, smell, hearing, even touch—can be emitted from real substances. In fact, it is tangible but nonexistent, all emitted by a controllable electron installation.

Uninvited visitors such as the "lizard" and their like will do nothing but peep and bug intelligence in our space, so W-45 lets them see and hear what they want to. In reality, all this is only a few information waves which we just want them to feel. As for the dozen space lizards and Base SR-17, these were a joke on Krutch and his lizard by W-45. It reflected his own wave form, and let him go to hell and fall into the net in a rush. "Heaven wants one ruined, let him go crazy first!" With such a phrase Ma finished his introduction.

It was owing to this emergency alarm that my reporting task was overfulfilled ahead of schedule. The captured lizard provided me with an awfully vivid panorama, which was enough for me to write my special features, and even some stories. By request, however, I was granted another mission by the Command of Base 88, which had contacted the M.S.T.P. As a special envoy I would visit Professor Wang at Feng City to present him with a letter of thanks and a memento—a photo of Krutch and his "Lizard." That's a regular practice at the base. I might learn something more particular from the founding father of W-45. I was certainly overjoyed to be such an "envoy."

## MY MISTAKES AND MOUNT LAOSHAN PRIEST'S WALL

In assigning me this work, the Command once more pointed out that I had to be careful and say nothing of Base 88 to any others except the professor because this trip was also a military secret. As a soldier, I was quite clear about this. Ma still chattered to me about keeping everything secret when we were preparing the materials I would take along. I impatiently remarked:

"Speak of something else. Such words about keeping secrets and heightening vigilance I know already."

One of the base leaders was leaving on business and I got a lift in his special, high-powered car to the airport.

"You, Zhang the Scholar, are always lucky," Ma said, when he saw me off, shaking my hand. He must have greatly admired my errand. But this time my luck turned bad, in fact. How terribly bad from the start!

I got to Feng City early in the morning, boarded the bus to the city-center and transferred to a magnetic car to Feng City University. There were about four or five people waiting for the car at the station, and a tall, lean fellow in spectacles was studying the itinerary on the call-board behind me. When I got on the car, tightening my knapsack straps and habitually pressing on my coat pocket, I felt something hard in it. And then on the chair I unconsciously pulled it out with one more touch. I was startled to find that I had carelessly carried out the provisional card, which must have escaped the check of the electronic sentry because I took the leader's special car. After the emergency alarm that day I had told Ma how I was held up by the machine hands and he explained that it did not trouble them on account of their wearing the alloy sign with the artificial element 117. Then we laughed at Krutch and forgot about the pass. I was accidentally permitted to take it off the base, so I hurried to tuck the small plate, with its silver tint and the sign of Base 88, into my pocket. While I pretended to be calm I looked around; the other passengers looked out the window at the scenery, except for the fellow in glasses who was dozing, holding his forehead sideways behind me. Nobody noticed me and I felt myself very lucky. I would store it at Feng City University until I made a self-criticism for carelessness on my return to base.

At the terminal station of Feng City University, I got off alone and hurried ahead. It's located in a maple grove. In the reception room a young girl read my introduction letter and carefully looked over the code designation, nodding to me with a smile. She struck a row of buttons like playing the piano to make out a card for me.

"With this agenda the professor may receive you," she remarked. "It's a holiday today, however, so you should go straight over to his home." Dignified soldier and reporter that I was, I still was not good at associating with young women and blushed. I made sure of the professor's address at No. 5 Green Maple Village beside the Star Lake. No sooner had I taken the card with a murmur of thanks than I turned around to go along the way she pointed. Then she seemed to say something I did not catch, and a string of ringing laughter accompanied me up to the lake, glistening with golden waves in the sunlight.

I saw a few elegant buildings rising from a sheet of emerald green when I rounded the lake. The large No. 5 on the front one near the lake told me I had arrived. I walked ahead excitedly as if some green maples had been nodding in various postures to greet me. There was a flowered wall around the building that I thought the gate should have been behind, but I was quite bewildered to find it without any gate after walking a full circle. I was struck dumb before this solid wall covered with thick ivy. How could I get in? How could the professor come out? I would not have scrambled in and out with a ladder like Robinson Crusoe. Leaning against a maple tree, I carefully went over the card given me by the girl in the reception room trying to discover something enlightening. But there was only one line on it: "Comrade Zhang Changgong is granted an interview by Prof. Wang Fan at his home in the morning." There was no incantation like open sesame to open a rock door into a cave. I thought she had seemingly said something during my hurried departure; however, I couldn't remember what she'd said but only her large eyes and ringing laughter. I was embarrassed to be seen staring with a vacant look at this impenetrable wall, wondering how to get in.

In my hesitation I caught a glimpse of a shadow up at a window on the second floor and less than two minutes later I heard the noise of a door opening and footsteps approaching. And then I was startled and let out a sudden cry as a child less than ten years old actually walked out through the wall, that solid ivy-leaved wall without a gate or a hole. I could see the child had not climbed over it or gone under it or through somewhere else. It must have been funny to see both my mouth opening wide and my eyes popping out.

"What do you see?" she asked, coming up to me. "You have come to my house for the first time, haven't you?"

"Are you Uncle Zhang?" she continued sagely, giving herself a tap on the back of her head, then reaching out her little hand in a dignified way. "Grandpa is at home. Please come in." I thought I should show a little more dignity before this child. Although I'd not at all recovered from my astonishment, I straightened my cap, calmed myself and looked in the direction she pointed a finger at. I saw nothing but that hateful ivy-covered wall, without a gate or a hole. I recalled thinking of the ancient Mount Laoshan Taoist priest who, as it was said in a Chinese legend, had the magic arts to walk through a wall as she had done just now. If I had to do that, I probably would bust my head open. I still stood there, motionless, with a forced smile.

"That's the wave, my aunt's fun and games. Let's go," said she. Being conscious of my hesitation, she pulled my hand and went through the wall unhesitatingly. I had to force myself to follow her nervously, groping forward. Unexpectedly and without any charms I had no trouble at all going through the wall.

The professor waited for me at the door, and warmly shook my hand, saying, "Comrade Zhang Changgong, I knew you would come, as just now Sister Lin called me up from the reception room. She wanted to play a joke on you because you hurried away without even having heard her out. Since you want to understand what the wave is, it is better to have some perceptual knowledge of it first, so I didn't stop her. I hope you don't mind." I didn't understand all of this immediately, but I guessed the girl in the reception room was Sister Lin and the joke was Mount Laoshan priest's wall. I turned around to look at that hateful wall, but there was nothing there. I took it to be a so-called "cover-up" as they called it in ancient China.

We took seats in the professor's study. Yin Yin, his granddaughter, having shown me in, went bouncing upstairs. Professor Wang looked under sixty with gray hair, a wide forehead, and piercing eyes with a pair of hawksbill glasses emphasizing his scholarly bearing. He was talkative and enthusiastic.

"The troops' senior officers are very polite," he said after reading the letter of thanks and seeing the photos I had brought to him. "I've been longing to visit Base 88 and listen to what they have to say; however, having set up W-45 I joined the design teams for several other projects and have had no time as of yet." He particularly inquired of me how the W-45 system operated. I made a report going into everything on the basis of the materials prepared by Ma. At the mention of Krutch, who was not convinced of his failure, he burst into laughter, and with a heavy southern accent said:

"Those fellows are strong in words but weak in mind. If not convinced, take out some odds and ends! All the vitals of the lizard and its like are merely the second-grade patent of some western European countries. As for bragging, the W-45 is actually the first in the world."

Having learned that I was a science-technology reporter, he gave me a special introduction to the theoretical basis of the W-45 system being as specific as possible. Here he went into the relations between the sense organs of creatures and the information waves, and he told me that in recent developments of all sorts of electronic-information-wave generators, the effects on the primary senses of hearing and sight had been advanced to effects on the senses of taste and touch, such as cold and hot, soft and hard, and smooth and harsh. And the wall I'd seen outside the door was a remote control sight wave, pretty much the same thing as holography but different in the theory. What made me the happiest was that he decided to allow me to visit the experimental station that afternoon to see a number of instruments recently developed.

## MONA LISA'S MYSTERIOUS SMILE

We talked for three full hours. Thus the Dragon-Well tea was freshened several times. Yin Yin came downstairs and said:

"Grandma telephoned from the institute. She can't be back for lunch because she is running experiments and Aunt's on duty, so Grandpa'll have to cook to entertain Uncle Zhang."

"I have to be the cook today. Yin Yin, would you like to be my assistant?"

"Ok, I want to have lobster today," she replied cheerfully and fetched a cassette, laying it before him.

"A simple meal for us," he said to me. "I won't go to more trouble than that. I'm a poor cook and let's have what we have." He pressed some keys on the case and then let her carry it to the kitchen. It turned out to be a pocket calculator to do the cooking based on an entered program. The little girl was very interested in taking care of it.

"Grandpa, you've done something wrong with the program," she soon shouted from the kitchen. "How come the lunch-box's frying the bamboo shoots?" She called this calculator "lunch-box." The professor got up immediately, shrugging to me.

"I've no skill in cooking," he said. "Sure, a wrong program." He shrugged again and hurried into the kitchen.

I was seated alone in the study; outside the window the maple tree was rustling in the fall wind. There lay a pot of narcissus on the windowsill and a vase of wintersweets and nopalxochias on the table near the multi-megabyte computer with three screens. They were actually blooming out of season. In my quiet admiration of this modern gardening, too advanced to be limited by the four seasons, I was suddenly drawn by the painting on the wall. The professor was so proficient at appreciating art that they were all outstanding works by masters at home and abroad, such as Qi Beishi, Xu Beihong, Huang Zhou, Li Keran, Da Vinci, Michelangelo and Miller. As an amateur painter, I was attracted by these masterpieces, handed down for generations, and could not help but carefully study each of them. As far as I could judge, all of them were honest-to-goodness originals! How could that be? Then I came up to the Mona Lisa by Leonardo Da Vinci, eager to find a flaw to refute my own judgement through searching my whole knowledge of art, but evidently it was so poor that I pondered utterly in vain. Instinctively I reached out my hand to touch the clearly drawn, realistic painting, and at once drew it back as sudden as a shock, because there was nothing there. It was the same when I tried again from another direction. As I wiped my eyes and looked at this Mona Lisa with the mysterious smile, which was actually nonexistent, there went floating through my mind a burst of indescribable, contradictory feelings. I looked at her from different angles, standing back, thinking over her smile while this new mystery in my mind kept expanding.

The professor came in, rubbing his hands, and laughed at my astonished look. "It's the same thing as the wall, a miniature sightwave emission." When he guessed I still wasn't quite clear about it, he pulled me to the windowsill and motioned me to smell the light yellow narcissus. I thought this was to help sober me; however, I drew a deep breath and felt drunk with the intoxicating scent, narrowing my eyes. All of a sudden a thick smell of rose fragrance ran into my nose and stunned me with my eyes wide open; the narcissus had suddenly turned into fresh red roses. As I stood there with my mouth hanging open, he laughingly told me that it was a gadget Sister Lin had developed under his guidance, a sight-smell-wave emission. While saying this he led me to lunch. The computer-cook was skilled and the meal well served. Several courses were really colorful, delicious and tasty. There were stewed shad, fried celery, braised prawn in brown sauce, and bamboo shoots with shredded meat in soup. As he helped me to the dishes he explained the wave-theory. I learned how the system emits information waves that are received as sight and smell on the basis of different coding inputted beforehand. I came to a better understanding of the principle of the system W-45.

After lunch I walked over to the study windowsill and forcibly pinched the bright-colored thorny red rose. Sure enough I could see my fingers waving through the roses without any sensations. When I went to sit in the armchair, I braced myself with my hands against the armrests for fear of sitting on a wave. After all, I'd been taken in several times and even suspected my own senses of sight and smell. Fortunately, the professor was not aware of it while making tea, or he would have laughed at me again. He would have laughed all the more if he had discovered that I was even suspicious of whether or not the prawn and shad I'd eaten were the wave as well.

After he handed me a cup of just infused Dragon-Well tea, his local product, he went to have a seat. But Yin Yin, running downstairs, said, "There's another visitor coming here, Grandpa." She pointed at the screen by the door. On it Sister Lin nodded at us with a smile, flashing her large eyes, and then a middle-aged man with spectacles was displayed coming along the path beside Star Lake.

"Who is it?" asked the professor, after carefully watching him for a while.

The visitor with hawksbill spectacles, tall and thin in stature, was in his late thirties and simply but tastefully dressed in a cloth grey coat, blended black trousers, black shoes, and with a very modern briefcase in his hand. A steady impression came to us owing to his sense of calm and deep experience. When coming near the building, he turned to look backward, and then I felt in a flash as if I had seen that figure from behind somewhere before.

He walked to the door, all smiles.

"Who would you ask for?" asked the professor, going out to welcome and look over this unusual guest.

"May I ask if you're Professor Wang Fan?" he returned immediately. "I've just returned from abroad, a colleague of Yang Pin's who left me some papers for your advice." Halting for a while he continued confidentially: "I'm Hong Qin, and work with Yang Pin in the same high energy institute."

"Oh! You're in the institute with Yang Pin," said the professor, hearing his self-introduction, and inviting him in. "Come in, please."

In the study Hong Qin nodded to me modestly, turning an inquiring air to the professor, who then introduced us.

"This is Comrade Hong Qin, a colleague of my student Yang Pin's, working with him abroad now." But I was presented in the following manner: "This is my pupil Zhang, Zhang Lin." I didn't know why. At that moment I perceived that a smile, subtle and profound, seemingly flashed behind Hong Qin's broad-rimmed glasses.

After a few words of greeting, we were all seated. He told the professor that he left so hurriedly that Yang Pin had no time to write until a few days later and asked him to bring the papers here. He took out a bunch of drafts, five or six printed pages concerning the wave research, with two of them singly signed by Yang Pin, and the rest coauthored with Hong Qin. Skimming them over the professor smiled faintly and nodded frequently. When he read the paper "Analysis of Information Waves," however, frowning and tapping the manuscript, he shouted in a much displeased tone:

"Didn't Yang Pin write an article about this problem and send it to me last year? In a special reply I told him that a few experimental conclusions were not all right, therefore he should review them using different data. Why has he directly quoted these conclusions?"

"There are several views of the information-wave analysis circulating abroad," Hong Qin returned with deep consideration. "Dr. Long Hopkins, in charge of our institute, insisted on the original conclusions, or he would deny permission for the paper to be published."

"Publish! Publish!" the professor said furiously. "What we do is scientific research, not speculation or business. If they won't publish, let's do it. Long Hopkins. . . ." He left the last few words unsaid out of courtesy, struggling to restrain his indignation. He served some candy to Hong Qin with a slightly quivering hand to show that he was not cross with him, a first-time visitor. I tried to change the subject to break the embarrassed silence, but Hong Qin didn't mind at all and remained undisturbed. I became conscious of a little elusive smile behind his spectacles. Suddenly I associated it with the Mona Lisa's mysterious smile and almost never figured out all it meant.

Hong Qin took a delicate box from his briefcase, and opened it lightly. There arose an exquisite Eiffel Tower of glistening silver rays with a glittering sapphire at the top. The professor changed his expression to a gentle look immediately. If the excitement of the scientific paper was the tense tenor in his heart, the Eiffel Tower plucked the strings of soft harmony.

"Eiffel Tower! The tower," he whispered and fell into musings of the past. As Hong Qin punched a button and Strauss's "Blue Danube" was struck up in electronic music, he chose this moment to say over the waltz, "This little gift is a token of Yang Pin's regard for you."

"Has he yet remembered I am fond of Strauss and Towers?" said the professor, beating time and smiling.

"How can he forget it! He has often told me how you used to be subtly moved and would linger in front of the Eiffel Tower when you were busy studying in France, and how you used to tell stories to your students about the Pyramid, the Square Tower and the Leaning Tower of Pisa, and took special trips to the Liu He Pagoda, the Da Yan Pagoda, the Bei Pagoda, the Double-Pagoda and the Lei Feng Pagoda when you were taking them to see places and study." The professor was obviously moved and yet exceptionally cheerful and excited, clearing up his anger with the waltz notes and Hong Qin's soft, voluble words. From then on the conversation went smoothly. The professor particularly asked him how they were getting along at the foreign institute. Hong Qin sought his advice, consulting him over quite a few problems. The professor enthusiastically solved some about theoretical research to a suitable extent, but said almost nothing concerning specific research developments at the present time. Sometimes I tried to chip in, but he parried or ignored my remarks. As a result I nearly became a silent audience during the two hours after our meal.

When the electronic clock sounded sweet music, I looked at my quartz watch and could not help worrying about the plan to go sightseeing at the laboratory that afternoon.

"Wait a moment, Zhang," said the professor, conscious of my annoyance with their talk and turning his head to me. Hong Qin surmised that we had something to do and was about to rise to say good-bye. But I rashly showed my good manners by remarking on our planned visit to the labs. Who would have guessed that this could lead to serious trouble.


## I WAS TAKEN HOSTAGE

"Never mind, you go on talking," I blurted out when Hong Qin was trying to say good-bye. "Let's go to the experimental station some other day." As soon as I mentioned it the professor glanced at me, knitting his brows.

"Are you going to the experimental station?" put in Hong Qin at once in a deliberately offhand way. The professor made no reply, but nodded. "Might you allow me to look around, if possible?" he immediately inquired in a very sincere voice. "I have heard abroad that Professor Wang has made a great number of significant, advanced experiments. What a wonderful opportunity to do some sightseeing!" At that moment I was moved by his earnest tone and faithful manner, and cast an appealing look at the professor. He considered a while and agreed. When we began to leave, he took his cap from the coatrack and pressed a green button as well.

The experimental station was an isolated three-story building sheltered by a stretch of pine trees. It revealed itself as a building out of the ordinary by the sets of solar collectors and giant circuit antennas on the roof. Silence reigned and no one was there since it was a holiday. Of course it had an electronic warning system for round-the-clock protection, and we experienced its sophistication as soon as we entered.

In a locker room off the entrance hall we changed our shoes and put on insulated shielding lab coats. No sooner did I walk a few steps down the corridor than a red light began flickering on the wall beside me.

"Are you carrying any pieces of special metal?" asked the professor, walking at the head of our party and turning around. Hong Qin and I were quite upset and looked at each other. As we made no answer, he let us go a few paces further.

"I'm sure it's on you," he said, pointing at me and looking at the signals. When I fumbled through my clothes and touched my coat pocket, I realized, and with terrible embarrassment, drew out the 88-45-7 pass. That startled him, and he gave me a quick look and a glance at Hong Qin.

"What have you done?" he said, and snatched it out of my hand. I flushed, and tried to say something to explain. He waved, put it in a case and tucked it into his pocket; apparently he didn't want to say any more, and led us forward. Hong Qin, next to me, was just adjusting his glasses which seemed his habitual practice.

What we saw at the first several laboratories concerned analysis and research on the wave, in terms of color, spectrum, electromagnetic field, sound waves, and the transmission of various information. The second section contained analysis and research on specialized biophysiological senses, such as hearing, sight, taste, temperature, hardness, bioelectrical current and brain waves. It struck me as very novel that Professor Wang introduced his new wave theory in terms of fundamentals. Trying to follow his explanations caused me much trouble, but made me even more convinced of the awesome performance of the instruments, and I couldn't refrain from praising them in detail.

"You've achieved a better comprehension of the wave," said the professor, praising me once over. All the time Hong Qin, with a smiling face, only listened, took notes, and frequently straightened his broad-rimmed spectacles, quite unlike my being unable to restrain my surprise and putting forward questions one after another.

On the second floor there were several sections designed to develop wave emission. As they belonged to field application, we were much more interested in them. We looked at a pictograph that was shaped like a miniature piano with various buttons as its keys. He told us that button R was for *China Pictorial*, button J—*Jiefangjun Pictorial*, Y—year, M—month, and so on. When I'd popped some buttons, hey! there was a copy of *Feng City Pictorial* before us. I knew it was merely a wave by the touch of my experienced hand. We modulated the angle, pressed button F and Page 1 turned up. There was a photo of the astronauts who journeyed back from Venus with the shuttle "Mount Qomolangma-7" and a big crowd behind them. When I adjusted the pictorial's size to that of two newspaper pages, unexpectedly I discovered Xiao Xu, an M.S.T.P. reporter assigned to the Space Navigation Center, among the crowd. The next few pages showed the Feng City Iron and Steel Combined Corporation and the awards to the labor models who attained a record output and so forth.

In Section 25 of the labs, amid some instruments, stood a table with nothing in the center of its surface. The professor made a few adjustments and there appeared various tropical fish, such as neon lights, black Mary, peacocks, blue immortals and colorful swallows, swimming in a large glass bowl in front of us. Several colorful swallows suddenly pierced through the bowl and came out. Suddenly my casual touch of an instrument made them hover in the air. Immediately the professor's hurried adjustment made them go back into the bowl again. Having recognized them as the wave, I was very interested but not shocked. Unexpectedly, the professor caught me by the hand and put it into the water, I took for granted that I would sense nothing, and yet I fancied that it was soaked in real water and even in hot water. As I drew back my hand, I couldn't help but shake it and took out my handkerchief to wipe it off; but the professor snatched the handkerchief away and made me look at my hand. Oh! Not a drop of water on it. Even the dipped handkerchief was bone dry. It was the sensation of warmth and wetness that the wave gave me. Meanwhile Hong Qin, with his hands behind him, and showing his special smile, looked at all this in silence.

In the following laboratories, the professor performed the wave emission concerning smell and taste. He let us smell all sorts of flavors from rose, peppermint, sandal, osmanthus, and musk to garlic and chives and a taste of sweet, sour, bitter, pungent, salty, peppery, and sweet and sour spareribs, crucian carp braised in sauce, and my chosen dish "beef curry" and Hong Qin's "tiptop liquor-Daqu of Luzhou." All this was merely a taste.

"It's enough to let you have a good taste, but no nourishment," the professor cracked a joke. Finally, we had a taste of multi-flavored beans to finish up. We had eaten too much, but still had an empty stomach as before. After this mental dinner we went up to the third floor.

There he guided us to only two sections. Here Hong Qin was much more interested, appearing quite excited. At section 3-F there was a comprehensive profile apparatus which could produce what we requested on the basis of previously inputted information. The professor conjured some long-haired cats before us. I use the word "conjure" because nothing else could be used here more precisely. Some Persian cats played with each other, tumbling and often mewing softly. Without touching them you'd never believe that they were nothing but the wave, all empty. Had there appeared any ferocious tigers, to be sure, we would have run for our lives. Then there appeared a lake. It was extremely beautiful, with rippling blue waves across a broad expanse reflecting maple trees close by the lakeshore.

"Is it the Star Lake?" I asked the professor, feeling as if it were familiar. With his nodding, my surprise couldn't help changing into admiration. In a moment I remembered Krutch's confession and it became clear why he believed himself to be off his rocker. For some reason Hong Qin kept nodding at the lake.

At section 3-PG, for developing the wave interferometer, the professor put on a demonstration of an electronic sound screen and an echo sounder.

As for the light screen, the reflected wave filter, the silencer and the wave extinquisher, these were only briefly introduced to us.

There was a piano with almost nothing but keys in the corner of the laboratory; I recognized it as the newly developed "Star Sea" holophonic resonator. The professor seated himself at the piano, removed the lid, and while trying the keys, nodded at me. "I will play some stanzas of the symphonic poem of the Yangtze River," he said. I was surprised that he did it so skillfully, expressing all its immense zeal. The melody transported me to the rolling Yangtze River, at one moment a gurgling stream, lithe and graceful like a gentle breeze; the next moment a surging torrent, turbulently rushing down like thunder and lightning. Suddenly not a sound was heard during his rocking about and his fingers bouncing here and there, because the electronic screen rose up. I moved a few steps forward and then it was as if I'd walked through an invisible, thick wall; the piano sounded again, sonorously and forcefully. As he modulated the function-sphere of the apparatus to a half meter, I turned deaf like a post.

The echo sounder was also very interesting. A spoken word could later drift back, with an interval as long as you pleased, clear as an echo in an empty valley with numerous repetitions, like a worn-out record repeating the same tone. Hong Qin delightfully shouted: "I've come." And it sounded repeatedly around us.

Finally, the professor modestly asked for advice from us. Evidently the visit had come to an end. Until then Hong Qin had been almost silent but perhaps he would make up for what he hadn't said and would put forward a bunch of questions to the professor one after another.

The professor led us into his office on the third floor and answered all kinds of problems and questions we raised and showed us a number of design papers. As he was more careful and earnest than I, Hong Qin checked almost all of the data, yet he didn't forget to adjust his spectacles very often.

"I'll go back to my institute abroad in a few days," he said, looking at his watch. "Do you have any words to tell Yang Pin through me?"

"When are you going to set off? I'll buy a few things and ask you to take him some material."

"I'm going to leave for the south tomorrow and go abroad by way of Guangzhou. Perhaps there isn't time for your shopping, but I could get him the materials if you would give them to me today." The time was so brief that the professor had to agree with him. He rose to fetch a few documents from the safe in the wall recess in the corner; in the meantime I began copying some manuals for him. I thought Hong Qin seemed to adjust his spectacles again, and I began finally to pay some attention to this habit of his.

Returning from the safe and sitting at his desk, the professor handed him the materials and began to write a note to Yang Pin. As Hong Qin glanced over them, he frowned and looked at his watch. Abruptly he whirled over to the door, went into the hall, and then coming back in closed the door behind him. All of a sudden he turned round with a sullen look, held a penlike flashlight in his right hand, waved it at us and shouted in an unnatural, stern voice.

"Both of you have finished the play and now it's my turn to direct. Don't protest. Professor Wang Fan, Comrade Zhang Lin, this is a nylon laser gun in my hand. It can kill any living thing at twenty meters in a tenth of a second. However, I won't try its power on you, especially on the internationally famous Professor Wang Fan. Let's have a good consultation."

The professor sat stunned in his chair, looking straight at Hong Qin. I jumped off the chair with the notebook and manual in my hand falling to the floor, and pointed at him.

"Who are you? What do you want?"

"My dear Base 88 officer," he returned with a sneer. "Calm down. I should thank you especially as I couldn't have made up my mind without you. As for what I am, there's no point in telling you. I may be whatever I am. Sit down." The last words were in a sternly imperative tone. Yet I was not afraid of this skinny guy holding a gun in his hand because I could throw him out of the window with one arm so long as he didn't kill me with his first shot. But what if the professor were injured? I had to sit down sullenly. He dragged a chair over in front of the door and sat down.

"Don't play any little tricks," he said, looking at the professor's hand slipping down from the desk. "It's no use. What I have to say is very simple and not a knotty problem for you. Won't you listen?" The professor paled in agitation and then calmed down.

"Speak, please," he replied in a hushed voice. "I'm listening."

"Put it on the table," he continued with satisfaction, jiggling his legs. "I want to get the design papers for Base 88. I won't take them away, but only look at them here. Also I want to see the papers for 3-SB, 3-Z and 3-PG, and I'll go over the blueprints and data as well."

"H'm!" the professor dully uttered and nodded. Though I was very indignant, and had no alternative, I continued trying to figure out how to solve this awkward situation. And I was astonished by his mention of the 3-SB and 3-Z labs, which we hadn't entered, and was even more astonished by the professor's dubious manner.

"The 3-SB Section puts up the self-reflecting wave emission and the 3-Z, the high energy comprehensive wave emission," he said seemingly to Hong Qin and me as well. "Do you want to learn those materials?"

"It's enough for this time and I may come again later. The requirements should be made clear, too. Very generous of us, I must say. First, we must entirely keep this a secret and let those who may do harm to you never learn of this. Second, we are strong enough to pledge your absolute safety. In case you feel in danger, you can flee to some other country with our help. If you want to move and continue your research work, we can provide all the facilities and conditions. Last, the reward is fifty thousand dollars this time. It will be paid in dollars, roubles, marks or Renminbi as you like. If you will open an account in a reliable Swiss bank, we'll do this for you. Mr. Zhang Lin was not under consideration before, but being a facilitator today and a man of merit, I have decided the amount of ten thousand dollars for him by myself. Ha, ha. . . ."

Hearing his shameless words I really wanted to wrench off his bony, pointed head, but the professor was still saying yes, yes and kept nodding speciously. My blood was boiling.

"Let's begin," he said with a wave when seeing us remain silent, staring at the professor with a greedy eye. He rose silently, and went towards the safe. I became muddled with indignation and astonishment. Could he actually give the paper to this scoundrel? Especially if the design materials concerning the W-45 system were revealed, it would have direct, serious consequences for the defense of the western border. I was so disturbed that I stood up wanting to prevent him from doing so.

"Mr. Zhang, none of your tricks!" Hong Qin screamed at me in a sharp voice. "Or I'll kill you and save the ten thousand dollars." The professor looked indifferent, going up to the open safe unhurriedly. Hong Qin was so intoxicated as to burst into laughter, and said, "Professor Wang is really a man to see reason and the situation. . . ." He suddenly stared from the chair without finishing the sentence. Myself, I was surprised and stared happily wide-eyed.

In front of the safe the professor turned around and immediately changed into a dozen Professor Wangs all quite alike. I knew they were phantoms of the wave; however, it was impossible to determine the real one among them. Hong Qin was conscious of himself being fooled and angrily threatened to fire the nylon gun at them, with wrath burning in his eyes. Finally, he put down his hand, because he found himself in a tight corner. If he didn't hit the real one, it would startle the warning system and place him in greater danger. Moveover, at that moment the professor could deal with him at will almost beyond danger. Being the experienced spy that he was, he got close to me at a jump and aimed at my head with the laser gun.

"Dare to make a fool of me!" he roared at the professors, clenching his teeth. "Probably the officer of Base 88 hasn't learned the partition method yet."

In front of him I winked at the professor believing that I could help him get the rascal under control. If we seized him I wouldn't mind if I were shot or even bled to death. But out of concern for my safety, he became one again, standing still before the safe.

## THE SINGER OF "PULLING THE NET" FALLS
## INTO THE NET

Hong Qin became complacent once more, while holding me as hostage. "Professor Wang," he said with derision, "you can always change while I can't. And yet I am at no loss in dealing with your changes. I'm grateful to this fellow," he said and tapped my head with the gun.

His conceit and shamelessness made me lose control of my emotions. With a foot pushing off against the desk I suddenly knocked my chair over backwards and at the same moment I struck down his laser gun while he hastily stepped back. The professor was startled by my abrupt move but came running quickly and stepped on the gun. But Hong Qin was not eager to snatch it up; he drew back to the corner by the door, taking a cube from his pocket and lifting it over his head.

"If you dare to come close, you'll be destroyed along with the experimental station," he cried hoarsely, looking fierce and crazed. No doubt he held a high explosive in his hand. The professor raised a hand to prevent me from jumping on him again. It seemed to me this shameless fellow was also a desperado. If the experimental station were ruined the loss would be no less than the revelation of the secret. What could we do? We both hesitated and the atmosphere became quite frozen.

At length the professor, having no choice, yielded; fetching the blueprints and materials from the safe he laid them on the desk.

"Won't you look at them?" he said with a sigh. "Please make sure of the security of both us and the experimental station." Hong Qin was not so confident and complacent as he had been, still motionless against the corner. The professor lifted his foot from the gun and motioned me to kick it over to show his sincerity. I was still agitated, but considered it unwise to rush headlong without weighing the security of the professor and the station. Furthermore, the professor seemed to have some plan in mind. So I seated myself on the armchair and only then found a scratch on my arm and a big hole torn in my sleeve.

Looking at us, Hong Qin made haste to pick up the gun. He told the professor to show him the blueprints and materials one by one, and he read them from that distance, holding his spectacles with his left hand. At that point I finally understood why he often adjusted them. They were a special-purpose microcamera.

He smoothly completed his task in less than fifteen minutes owing to the professor's coordination with him. It was apparent that this well-trained spy was no amateur when it came to the professor's research. When the professor put aside the last blueprint, Hong Qin said:

"Don't try to stall me with those tentative plans and theory drawings. They don't express the level of your present development, especially the designs for Base 88."

"Only these primary plans are here. As for some assembly drawings for instruments and equipment, they're in the laboratory," the professor said, nodding toward the safe and then shrugging his shoulders.

"Which laboratory?" put in Hong Qin.

"Lab 3-Z," the professor returned at a word.

"Professor, never try to hoodwink me again. If you've any crudities, it's too late for you to repent!" he said word by word, clenching his teeth. Then with a sweep of his head he motioned the professor to lead the way. I was placed in the middle a couple of paces from the professor. We went in single file out of the office. At a corner of the passage leading to 3-Z, the professor suddenly tripped and nearly fell down. I quickly stepped forward to hold out my hand to help him, but Hong Qin viciously warned me away. The moment I reached him, I was shocked to feel nothing at all and instantly realized it was the wave before me. I could hardly hold myself back from laughing with delight. Fortunately, Hong Qin's shriek reminded me that I had better pretend to have discovered nothing, and I obediently kept my distance from the professor.

When the door of lab 3-Z slid open noiselessly, we entered silently. Hong Qin leaned on the self-regulating door, ordered me to stand facing the wall with my hands raised, and told the professor to take out the blueprints and the data. I assumed Hong Qin must be moving his spectacles, hearing the closet open and the papers rustling. Smiling, Hong Qin ordered me to turn around. Flaunting the laser gun before the two of us standing in different corners of the room, he said:

"This task is nearly completed; then we may say good-bye friendly and peacefully. You'll have to put up with a little temporary inconvenience in order to assure the safety between us. It's beneficial to us all. Professor, may I trouble you to tie up the officer so that he is unable to brandish his fists when I go around him. As to you, my elder, I can cope with you." He pointed at a lot of wires near some apparatus.

The professor hesitated for a moment, then obediently fetched a piece of wire to tie me up, and passed even several rings around my neck. Beside us Hong Qin was triumphantly whistling some Japanese ditty called "Pulling the Net." He actually believed that he was the winner, the puller of the fishnet. Meanwhile, however, the gun was still pointed at us. In the course of being tied up I was too puzzled to see how the "wave" professor could do so many specific things. Seeing me rendered immobile and humming his song, he let the professor go to another corner, and went to fetch some wire to treat him the same as me. In order to separate the twisted wires, he put the laser gun and the explosive down for a moment.

Just then there flashed a zigzag lightning from the ceiling. It went straight for Hong Qin and sent him howling like an injured wolf. He raised his right hand to grab the explosive, but was too weak to reach it, dropping his arm halfway and finally curling up and tumbling about on the floor. Suddenly the door opened and Professor Wang and Sister Lin stepped in. She rushed over picking up the laser gun and the explosive, and having an earnest look, said:

"Both of synthetic nonmetallic materials. No wonder the electronic guard worked, but to no avail." Then she took off Hong Qin's spectacles and carefully unwrapped each knot of the wires around me. As they became untangled so did my nerves.

"Luckily the wire is made of superconducting material which can be operated by a high energy electromagnetic field, otherwise the wave professor would have betrayed its true color at that moment," said the professor, wiping the sweat from his forehead.

"He might be numbered the twenty-first," he went on, pointing at Hong Qin curled up on the floor, groaning. I knew he meant the 21st prisoner of W-45. When I turned my head to look at the wave professor, he'd disappeared without a trace.

"What pulsating wave did you use?" he asked Sister Lin.

"Three," she answered, scornfully staring at Hong Qin.

"Two units would have been enough," he said, shaking his head. "We'll have to ask the doctor to help him out."

"I hate the rascal to death," she said bitterly. "At the college gate he pretended to bring things here for Yang Pin and later at home he talked so long with you that I believed you were old acquaintances and didn't pay attention to him. Though you sent out a signal from the lab I only adopted an ordinary precautionary measure. If you hadn't got W-45B to start in the office and let me see the signal at the control room, we'd have been taken in by the beast. It was very clever to lure him into the lab, or the pulse wave couldn't have been used." As she saw me attentively listening to her, she smiled.

"Didn't you get angry when I pulled a joke on you, Mr. Zhang? It really startled me when you swooped down on him in the office. Terribly dangerous if the rascal were to fire. How's your arm?" I became embarrassed at her concern for me, blushed, and didn't know how to reply.

"It's up to you to handle him," the professor said to her, pointing at Hong Qin who was still twitching. "As a technician of the security section, do your duty. And play some tricks with his spectacles." He then motioned for me to leave the lab.

"Dad, Mr. Zhang's arm is injured," she said behind us in a troubled tone. "Please get some bandages and bind it up. The first aid kit is under the bookcase in my room." I blushed again.

I came back to Base 88, and first of all handed in my self-criticism. Unexpectedly, the leader examined his mistakes to me first, and shared the responsibility with me, because he considered that my mistake had exposed a weakness in the warning system. He also ascertained that I was valiant and accomplished my duty very well at Feng City University.

At the dormitory, Ma told me that the Command discovered my taking out the pass through a routine review of the security monitor tapes soon after I had left the base. Supposing that I'd come back before long they didn't try to contact me at once but merely recorded the detail. Later Krutch revealed that when crossing the border he couldn't keep his craft properly balanced. This suggested that someone, hidden in it, had sneaked into our country by means of its low flight capacity, which was in line with the analysis and judgement from the W-45 tracer. The Base Command concentrated its main attention on picking up this spy's trail. No one, however, suspected that Professor Wang was the target. By the time the Base Command had tracked him in Feng City and dispatched a warning to the professor, we'd already knocked him down.

In accordance with the information received from Feng City, Ma told me that the superpowers had taken note of Professor Wang's research work for a long time, collecting his materials wherever possible. For example, Yang Pin's and Hong Qin's papers all came from Dr. Long Hopkins of the foreign institute. In fact, the real Hong Qin worked well with Yang Pin abroad. The fake one was the stowaway, a high-ranking spy, elaborately trained by one of the superpowers. At first his mission was to pry into Professor Wang's research work and its most recent applications. Unexpectedly he discovered my identity from Base 88 on the magnetic cushion car. The provisional pass containing element 177 was picked up by his spectacles and attracted his attention. At the professor's house he learned that the new research work had something to do with Base 88. Originally he intended to obtain intelligence material by relying only on verbal trickery, but in the course of our talks and the lab sightseeing he couldn't obtain any valuable information concerning up-to-date developments, especially those applied to military science and technology, because the professor kept up his vigilance. When he became aware of my having noticed his spectacles, he determined to gain a bumper harvest, with one arrow shooting two birds by uncovering both the professor's research and the secret of Base 88. But what was the result? As Ma put it, "Try to steal a chicken, but end up losing the rice."

My duty to report news was fulfilled awfully well due to various accidents. I had not only a thorough impression and comprehension of Professor Wang's wave theory but secured an intimate relation with the Wangs. When I left Feng City, he saw me to the airport with Sister Lin. I blushed while fumbling with the uniform sleeve which Sister Lin had patched with dense stitches. I didn't know why she, who had been always natural and graceful, was also flushed now. Afterwards I began to correspond with her. The first letter was to thank her for mending my sleeve. I needn't say more because these are personal matters. But Ma learned that I had successively received three letters from Feng City during the week before I left the base and he made a joke of it, saying:

"Thank your lucky stars forever. Even mistakes can often bring you good luck, Zhang the Scholar." I had to crack a smile. It seemed that ringing laughter was drifting over to my ear from the Star Lake shore.

*Translated by Li Lianhan*

# 5
# Death Ray on a Coral Island

## TONG ENZHENG

I am sure that you will not have forgotten the recent mysterious crash over the Pacific of the twin-engined plane, the "Morning Star." According to the news release, the plane had been functioning normally at the time, and had never lost radio contact with airport control at Port X. The early warning radar systems of many countries confirmed that, at that time, there were no other aircraft or any kind of guided missile in the airspace where the accident took place. Nevertheless, the "Morning Star" exploded at a height of 8,000 meters, and the blazing wreck plunged into the Pacific. The newspapers reported that the pilot, an engineer by the name of Chen Tianhong, was missing.

I am Chen Tianhong, the missing pilot. Here, I not only want to tell you about the cause and the circumstances of the accident, but also about what happened afterwards, and my experience will fill you with anger and indignation, and also provide you food for much thought.

I am an overseas Chinese, born abroad. Ever since I was young, the thriving socialist land of my fathers exerted a strong attraction on me. I would avidly read magazines and publications from China, and feel the unceasing call of the land in which my ancestors had lived and died. Each time China achieved a new success, I would feel in my heart an inexpressible joy, an infinite longing.

Published in *Renmin wenxue* (People's Literature), August 1978.

I had tried several times to arrange my return to China to dedicate my youth to her reconstruction, but because my parents were old and ailing, and had no one to care for them, I was dissuaded from doing so. After finishing my university studies in physics, and gaining my degree, I worked in a private laboratory run by my former teacher, Professor Zhao Qian. Professor Zhao, a world renowned nuclear physicist, was also Chinese. Apart from his regular work, he also used his entire income to establish a small, but well-equipped laboratory, in which he carried out research that interested him personally.

Two years later, my parents died, first one and then the other. I felt that it was time for me to return to China, and so I presented Professor Zhao my resignation, explaining to him my reasons. After listening to what I had to say, his wrinkled face was filled with sadness.

"My son, you must go. The leaves of the tallest tree must eventually return to its roots. If I were younger, I would go back too. But," he continued, "I hope you will wait a few months, wait until we have finished assembling our high-tension atomic battery. You can take it back to China. This is the fruit of a lifetime of hard work. I want to give it as my final present, as my contribution, to our country." The old professor's voice became hoarse, and I myself was so moved that I could not say a word.

The small scale high-tension atomic battery was the result of many years' research by Professor Zhao. Its special feature was its ability to release an enormous amount of power in a very short time. Because of this, its future military applications, and its applications in industry, space travel and other fields were inestimable. By the time the research work neared completion, many large business organizations had already offered to buy the rights for incredibly large sums. If Professor Zhao were to have agreed, he could have become a millionaire overnight. It was only then that I realized that during all these years of hard work, forgetting food or sleep, he had been sustained solely by his love for his native land.

I could not refuse such a request. And so, I postponed my departure, and helped Professor Zhao assemble the first prototype of a high-tension atomic battery. In the course of the first tests, all the specifications of the design were met. Our work had finally borne fruit. No words could describe our joy.

I completed the formalities for returning to China very quickly, and booked my plane ticket for Port X. Professor Zhao, in high spirits, prepared a completed set of drawings and technical data, and went personally to the relevant government offices to arrange for the transfer of ownership and the export of the technical material.

On the eve of my departure, Professor Zhao held a small party in my honor, a farewell function to which had been invited the entire personnel of the laboratory (most of whom had been at the university with me). Although there were people of many different nationalities among them, they were all happy that I was able to return home, and drank many toasts to China's continuing prosperity. The friendliness of the scientists towards each other and their good will towards China touched me greatly.

When the party ended, it was already close to midnight. I went back to my bedroom on the first floor. Professor Zhao returned to his study on the ground floor. According to his usual habit, he would work for another couple of hours before going to bed.

I lay in bed for a long time, unable to sleep. My mind was racing, partly because of having drunk too much at dinner, and partly because of thinking of the next day when I would set out on the journey to China, which I had been dreaming about for so many years. Only when the digital clock on the wall signaled two o'clock, did I finally doze off. Suddenly two pistol shots pierced the silence of the night.

The shots were very close, inside the building. I leapt out of bed, threw on my clothes, and raced downstairs. I saw a light coming from the crack under the study door. I ran towards the study, shouting, "Professor Zhao! Professor Zhao!"

There was no answer.

I pushed open the door, and found Professor Zhao lying on the carpet. The light from the table lamp fell on the unnatural pallor of his face.

I ran across, and gently lifted him up. In his chest were two bullet wounds. His jacket was stained red with blood.

"Gangsters. . . . They wanted me to hand over . . . the blueprints." His lips trembled. I bent over him, straining to hear his weak voice. "I burnt the blueprints. . . . My son, you have only . . . take the prototype . . . take it . . . take it back . . . to . . . to . . . China."

His breathing stopped. The French windows were wide open. A breeze ruffled his hair.

In the corner of the room, the door of the safe was open. Without any investigation, I could guess that the precious blueprints and technical data for the high-tension atomic battery which it held had been reduced completely to ashes. For the safe had been designed by Professor Zhao himself. Beneath the keyhole was a hidden button. By pressing it in an emergency, any document in the safe would be set on fire automatically.

What had happened was clear. The gangsters had come specifically to steal the data of the high-tension atomic battery. They had broken into the study, and threatened Professor Zhao at gunpoint to force him to hand over the blueprints. Professor Zhao had, in opening the safe, pressed the button and destroyed them.

This upright scientist had devoted his whole life to this invention, in order to present it to his country. Now he had given his life to protect it.

I gazed at his eyes which had still not closed in death, and could not stop my tears from flowing. My heart was filled with hatred, a hatred such as I had never before experienced in my simple life in the laboratory.

I reported the matter immediately to the police, put off my departure, and waited for the case to be settled before leaving. A week later, in the local police station, a grave police officer, just over middle age, had a talk with me.

"Mr. Chen, we are extremely sorry about Professor Zhao's death." He continued, "Everything points to the work of a thug under the alias of George Zuo, a member of the underground in this city. But behind George Zuo is the head of the secret service of a certain great power ASC."

"ASC?" I could not help asking. According to my knowledge of geography, ASC was situated a long way from the South Pacific. I did not understand what connection there was between our work in the laboratory and that country.

"Yes, ASC!" The policy chief pointed indignantly to the north. "Their fleet frequently carries out naval exercises near our shores. They infiltrate into our city economically and culturally by every possible means. Many well-informed people in our country have been warning us for a long time. Mr. Chen, I'm sure you've often read articles of this kind in the newspapers."

I was silent, knowing what he said was true. I remembered that a columnist had already described the shameless activities of ASC as the "overstretching of its bear's paws." I never thought this bear's paws would finally reach into our tiny laboratory, leaving behind crime and bloodshed.

"What are they after?"

"The high-tension atomic battery. The company which first tried to buy the rights to Professor Zhao's invention was acting secretly for ASC. After Professor Zhao rejected their offer, they resorted to armed robbery. This is their usual pattern. Mr. Chen, their attention is now focused on you."

"What? They dare. . . ."

The police officer interrupted me. "They are capable of anything. In the past year, they have engineered three political assassinations and five kidnappings in this city. We have taken many measures, but are still unable to put an end to this situation. Mr. Chen, you have already completed the formalities for leaving the country. In order to prevent anything unexpected arising from further delay, I would suggest that you leave straight away."

"But Professor Zhao's case has not yet been solved!"

The police officer straightened up, and his face became very serious.

"Mr. Chen, I assure you that, for our country's sake and to avenge Professor Zhao, I will do everything possible to bring the murderer to justice. But it is regrettable that, even if we manage to catch George Zuo, the man really behind it all will continue to hide behind the walls of the embassy, out of the reach of the law."

I considered for a moment, and thought of the task Professor Zhao had entrusted to me as he lay dying. I knew that the police officer's advice was made with the best intentions.

"Thank you," I said finally. "I will leave as soon as possible."

"Mr. Chen, the sooner the better; the more secretly the better," the police officer advised me. "It would be best not to take the regular flight, in case they hijack it. While you are still in this city, we will do everything possible to guarantee your safety. But once you are outside, you're on your own."

We shook hands and parted. While driving home, I noticed two plainclothes detectives trailing me in their car. I knew that the police officer had carried out his promise.

I talked things over with friends, and finally decided to take the high-tension atomic battery with me, and fly directly in the "Morning Star" to Port X. The "Morning Star" was a small plane belonging to Professor Zhao's laboratory, and was used when making contact with scientific organizations outside the city. I was myself a qualified amateur pilot. I had my license and had flown the plane many times before when carrying out assignments given me by Professor Zhao.

Early next morning, my friends saw me off secretly at the airport. On the way, my eyes never left the rearview mirror. I do not know whether it was because I was over-suspicious, or whether it was a coincidence, but behind us, apart from the car of the plainclothes detectives, a light green Ford mysteriously appeared twice.

I took off smoothly in the "Morning Star." As the green fields disappeared from my field of vision, and the vast boundless expanse of the Pacific appeared before me, I cast a last glance at this foreign land which had nurtured me. I silently said farewell to the friends I had left behind, and could not suppress my feeling of sadness at parting from them.

The "Morning Star" was a twin-engined four-seater plane that had excellent performance. At 10 o'clock in the morning, the outline of the XX archipelago flashed past beneath the wings of my plane. The sun was resplendent in the cloudless azure sky. I flew up to 8,000 meters, increasing my speed. I remembered a piece of news reported by the newspapers a few days earlier. The ASC fleet was at present carrying out naval exercises in this area of the sea. But I did not think that they would dare intercept me over international waters. The engines were functioning normally. My mind was thoroughly at rest.

It all happened with extreme suddenness. I heard a noise like a thunder-clap burst through the clear air. Above my left wing appeared a jagged flash of lightning. At such a height, in such clear weather, it was impossible that such lightning could be natural. But this inexplicable phenomenon repeated itself several times. The left engine caught fire. The plane lost altitude rapidly, trailing long tongues of fire behind it.

I did everything possible to regain control and put the plane into a smooth glide. At the same time I looked anxiously for a suitable place to land. But there was nothing but the vast sea all around. I had no choice. The plane crashed onto the sea, bounced back up, landed some ten meters farther on, and then began to sink. During these critical ten or twenty seconds, I managed to pull on my life jacket, and grasping the leather bag in which was sealed the high-tension atomic battery, I jumped out of the cockpit.

The waves surged around me. One wave lifted me up, and then threw me down again. The salty and bitter sea water choked me, leaving me gasping for breath. The currents in the sea quickly swept me away from the scene of the accident. Two helicopters appeared in the airspace above the wreckage of the plane. Several frogmen descended by the ladders hanging down from them, clearly in search of my whereabouts. Judging by the speed with which they arrived, they must have taken off from the naval vessels anchored nearby.

It seemed that even at a height of 8,000 meters, the bear's paws could still stretch out to seize me. The air incident was also the work of ASC's secret service. When they discovered that I had left the city secretly, they had tried to drown me, and remove forever from human knowledge the secret of the high-tension atomic battery. What a despicable motive! What an abominable act! But what had they used to destroy the "Morning Star"? When I thought of this, I clasped the leather bag even more firmly to my chest. While I had a breath of life left, I would not let these pirates succeed in their plot.

My watch had stopped, so I did not know how much time had passed. At dusk, I saw in the distance a helicopter skimming over the surface of the sea. But because I could not distinguish its markings, I dared not signal it. Night approached. I felt my strength ebbing away rapidly. I quickly loosened my belt and tied the leather bag firmly to my waist. In this way, I would not lose it, even if I became unconscious.

I drifted with the current for one day and two nights. At first, I felt an unbearable hunger and thirst, but later felt only weak and debilitated. Only the indomitable will to realize Professor Zhao's dying wish enabled me to struggle to keep myself above the waves.

On the morning of the third day after the incident, I saw the shape of an island. It was so small and so low down in the water that I guessed it to be a coral island. Although the sea was already washing me towards it, I nevertheless summoned up all my strength to swim towards it, afraid of losing this sole opportunity for survival. At last, the shore drew near, and

I swam into a small bay. The sea was as clear as a mirror, and beneath its surface one could glimpse the beautiful white coral hidden below.

Just at that moment, 20 meters away on the surface of the sea, a fin suddenly appeared. I stared at it. It was a shark, 7 to 8 meters long, a fierce man-eating fish known as the "sea-tiger." It was clearly hungry. After circling round me twice, it then turned towards me and prepared to attack. In that moment, I could see clearly its small cruel green eyes and its two rows of sharp white teeth.

I tried to call out for help, but no sound would come from my parched throat. I wanted to flee, but the shark blocked my way to the shore. My whole body froze. There was no way of escape from a terrible death.

It all happened in the space of a few seconds. Just as the shark was about to lunge towards me, a blinding red beam of light flashed from the shore, turning the water suddenly to steam with a crackling noise like lightning. The whole bay was suddenly filled with white vapor. The beam fixed itself on the shark, which, with a piercing scream, leapt out of the water, and immediately sank back again, mysteriously killed, its white belly turned upwards.

I was scalded by the heat of the sea water, struggled to the shore, and crawled out of the sea. The sharp points of the coral reef scratched my hands and feet. I was covered in blood, but felt no pain. Then, from the reef, I heard a voice ask in English, "Who are you?"

I looked all around, but could see no one. I could only answer this hidden voice, saying, "A Chinese, narrowly escaped from death."

"Chinese?" he asked in surprise, and then immediately changed into Chinese.

"Come up quickly!"

I tried to stand up, but my strength was already exhausted. I felt the heavens spin above me. The high-tension atomic battery round my waist felt as if it weighed a ton. I staggered for a moment, and lost consciousness.

When I regained consciousness, I found myself lying in a rather luxurious bedroom, furnished in teak, with a dressing table, wardrobe, armchairs, writing desk and chest of drawers, all neatly and tidily arranged. At the corner of the room was a four-in-one combination console consisting of a TV, radio, tape recorder and record player. The white curtains were flapping in the breeze, and from outside came the sound of the surf beating against the reefs.

I sat up and saw that someone had changed my clothes for me, and carefully bandaged my burns and cuts. On the small table by the bed was a thermostatically controlled ultra-high frequency warming dish containing milk, meat sandwiches and other food. I ate a little, and felt my spirits much restored. I recalled the dangers and hardships I had undergone for the sake of the high-tension atomic battery and quickly got out of bed. Only when I saw the leather bag lying unharmed under the bed did I cease to worry.

I crossed over to a bookcase by the window, and saw on the top two shelves some of the reference books on electronics and nuclear physics with which I was so familiar. But the two lower shelves were full of the incredibly pornographic novels which are so common in the capitalist world, such as *Love on the Isle of Gold, Confessions of a Murderer, The Road to Riches* and so on. The plastic shelves next to the combination console were piled with records and tapes of the Beatles and of Rock and Roll. On the desk was the half-length photograph of a young Chinese. He had thick hair, a square face with a low forehead, thick eyebrows and small eyes, with a slightly sarcastic smile on his lips. This was the owner of the room, surely. But from my very first glance, I found that I took an unaccountable dislike to him.

On the surface, it was the room of a rich playboy. The only thing that did not fit the ambience of the room was a new-type dosimeter hanging on the wall, the kind of equipment normally found in a nuclear physics laboratory. On it the power of any radioactive source can be displayed in figures. I really did not understand why it was there.

The door behind me opened, and someone entered quietly. I turned round, and saw a Chinese of about fifty. His hair was already grey. He had a wide forehead, a high nose, and a pair of deep-set piercing bright eyes. He was not tall, and his movements were smooth but slow. You could tell at a glance that he had long been accustomed to intellectual work.

"Excuse me for not knocking. I didn't know you were better," he said politely. From his soft voice and strong Fujian accent, I knew that it was he who had questioned me the day before, and that it was he who had rescued me.

"Thank you for saving my life," I said. As long as I had not found out what the situation was, I decided not to reveal my identity.

"I'm a passenger. I fell off a ship on my way to Port X. Can you tell me what place this is?"

"Originally, this island had no name. But because I've been working here so long, it's been named after me. It's known as Matthew Island." He clapped his hands twice as he answered. "Come and sit outside. We can talk in more detail. We don't have many guests on this island."

A servant in a white duck jacket entered, slowly and awkwardly. From his wiry black hair and olive complexion, I could see that he was a Malay.

"Would you bring some coffee, please?" Dr. Matthew asked him. The servant bowed, and withdrew silently.

Dr. Matthew explained, "He's called Amang. He's been with me for many years. The unfortunate boy is a mute. There are only the two of us on the island at the moment. Originally, I had an assistant called Joseph Luo. This bedroom is his. He went away on vacation three months ago."

We went out of the room. Outside was a corridor entwined with green wisteria vines and beautiful tropical flowers. At the other end of the corridor were another two rooms. Dr. Matthew told me that the outer one was his study and the inner one his bedroom.

The corridor faced onto the sea. Behind it was another building, white and single-storied. On its roof several different shaped aerials stretched their sensitive antennae in all directions. Behind the building, at the other end of the island, stood a reinforced concrete structure, half built in the sea. From inside stretched several high-tension transmission lines. These were all the buildings on this small island whose circumference was only a few kilometers.

To see such modern equipment on such a bleak, desolate, and remote little island was quite unexpected.

Dr. Matthew seemed to see the puzzlement in my eyes. He explained:

"I'm a physicist. The white building is my laboratory. The one at the back is an automatic tidal-powered generator. It doesn't need anyone to look after it, but makes use of the rise and fall of the tide to generate electricity for my experiments and for my daily needs."

We sat down in the canvas chairs beside the corridor. From here, I could see the beautiful coral island scenery spread out before me. In front of us was a round lagoon enclosed by reefs. Its waters were shallow and clear, its bottom covered with a layer of fine white sand. The lagoon sparkled and glistened as the sun shone on it, reflecting the azure depths of the southern sky like a blue-green mirror. It was surrounded on all sides by a circular reef on which grew a row of coconut trees swaying in the breeze, extraordinarily beautiful, silhouetted against the white clouds. Outside the reef lay the boundless sea. The giant waves of this vast sea surged forward, beating against the reef, covering it with fine drops of spray. The whole coral island was like a gem inlaid in a belt of tiny waves. Everything here was so peaceful, so calm.

However, as I sampled the coffee brought in by Amang, and appreciated the beauty of nature, many doubts and suspicions crowded into my mind.

Who in fact was this gentle and cultivated Dr. Matthew? Why did he live like a hermit in this remote place? What was he doing research on? Who provided him with the necessities of life and the equipment for his research? Who was he working for? And so, in the course of our chat, I asked these questions tactfully but openly.

Dr. Matthew smiled sadly, as if he had many hidden sorrows. He hesitated a moment before he spoke:

"If you will accept one condition, that is, that after you leave this place you will not tell what I have said to a single soul, but keep it a lifelong secret, then I will satisfy your curiosity."

I promised him solemnly.

"I don't know whether you still remember an incident that happened ten years ago. At the time, a Chinese engineer by the name of Hu Mingli became famous for having invented a new kind of laser range-finder in ASC. When the government of ASC wanted to award him a medal and a prize, a dispute broke out between him and the officials over the concrete application of this range-finder, and later he suddenly disappeared. I am. . . ."

"You are Hu Mingli?" I cried out in amazement. Yes. Although I was only a high school student ten years ago, nevertheless, I could still remember that news which had caused such a furor at the time. Hu Mingli, of such illustrious repute, was one of the bright stars in the world of engineering technology. Just as he was to receive the most glorious renown an open dispute broke out between him and government of ASC. Afterwards, he mysteriously vanished. This had aroused every kind of speculation in the newspaper circles of the capitalist world. I never thought that I would unwittingly come across his whereabouts.

"Yes." On Dr. Matthew's face appeared his sad smile. Only a man who had in his spiritual life suffered great stress and gone through many crises, a man who had lived in a complicated inner world, could have given such a bitter smile. "I am that unfortunate man."

And so, in a voice light, but nevertheless of restrained fervor, he told me the story of the first half of his life.

Dr. Matthew was originally born into a Chinese family which had taken up residence in Japan. When he was in primary school, he had a teacher who had been disabled as a result of fighting in the Second World War. The entire family of this teacher had died in the atomic bomb attack on Hiroshima, and he himself had only narrowly escaped death on the battle-field. Although he was luckily still alive, he had survived with only one arm. Because of this, he hated war, and continually instilled in his pupils' minds the horror and cruelty of war. This kind of education made a deep impression on the mind of the young Dr. Matthew.

After graduation from high school, Dr. Matthew moved to ASC to study crystallophysics, and showed great ability in his research on lasers. After graduation, he was immediately invited to join a research organization and quickly established his reputation. In fact, before inventing the laser range-finder, he already had many other inventions to his credit.

At that time, Dr. Matthew was in the prime of life, but the words of his primary school teacher were deeply engraved on his mind, so that his hatred of war was as strong as ever. He took no interest in politics, and had never thought about the direct consequences of his work. He considered that in his lofty scientific enterprise, he was working solely in the interest of promoting the happiness of mankind, and that was all. His comfortable life and his work away from all social activities caused him to pay little attention to the changes in the outside world.

After the successful testing of the laser range-finder, the government of ASC, in order to stimulate him to work harder, prepared to honor him publicly with a prize. Only at this time did his superior give him some memoranda published by the Ministry of Defense, among which was a piece which spoke of how the laser range-finder, after some slight modification, could be used to control the release of bombs from a plane or as the aiming device in a tank. Some other documents spoke of his earlier inventions. They had all been used in military applications, and had been highly effective.

So that was it! He had been honored and employed only because his work was useful in the service of war!

If a bomb had exploded before Hu Mingli's eyes, he could not have been more shocked. Everything went dark before him, and for a moment he could not utter a word. When he recovered his senses, he flared up angrily and protested vehemently. He said that he had been cheated. He demanded that the government of ASC offer him an apology, and destroy all the military equipment that had been made on the basis of his inventions. He immediately went to the capital, from one department to another, from one officer to another, excitedly expounding the principles which his primary school teacher had taught him so many years before. But, at first, although some people listened to him tolerantly, eventually, no one would listen to what he had to say, and all kinds of pretexts were used to drive him away. The last time he went to the Ministry of Defense, he discovered that instead of the officials with whom he had made the appointment, the doctors from the mental hospital were waiting for him. He felt a new and deep humiliation. From that moment on, he abandoned all ideas of trying to reason with such people.

But what was he to do next? Some newspapers had already published stories about him, describing him as having become an abnormal psychotic who was mentally ill, satirizing and ridiculing him to every extreme. He was exceedingly angry, and personally met with several groups of reporters in order to explain the real situation to them. But his words were deliberately distorted so that people who read the reports were strengthened in their belief of the previous articles. Although Hu Mingli was a laser expert, he was a kindergarten child in dealing with the world. He regarded public opinions in capitalist society with too much naivety, and this persecution and attack produced in him a kind of hatred for the world and its ways. He not only did not desire to live in ASC any longer, but also did not want to live in any other kind of society either. He dreamt of finding a utopia where he could forget this hideous world ruled by utilitarianism.

Just as he was hesitating in the midst of his conflicting feelings, unable to decide what to do, a friend of his named Bryan came especially from Europe to ask after him, showing concern for him in every possible way, so that Hu Mingli felt completely comforted. Bryan had been at a university with him and was at present assistant manager of the Lovell Electronics Group, a diversified and multinational corporation.

Bryan sympathized completely with Hu Mingli over his predicament, and highly praised Hu Mingli's lofty ideals. He castigated the corruption of society in ASC, condemning the leaders as a group of warmongers. He said that he himself was also a pacifist working consistently for peace. That was why he was serving the Lovell Electronics Group. This company was a purely private organization, with no connections whatsoever with any government. The aim of the management was not profit, but to be of benefit to humanity and to eliminate war. Finally, he proposed that Hu Mingli should accept the invitation of Lovell Electronics to contribute to their lofty goal of saving mankind.

Hu Mingli was completely taken in by the net woven by Bryan's sweet words, and so he poured out to Bryan his own weariness of the world. Who would have thought that, here again, Bryan would sympathize with him.

"Respect others' feelings, protect others' ideals—this is the very purpose of the Lovell Electronics Group," he said. "You have only to agree to work for us, and we will find for you a place far from human society, and set up a laboratory there, so that you can devote your life to the sacred cause of science and never again be worried by the ways of the world."

Hu Mingli agreed to his proposal. And so, under Bryan's clever arrangements, he disappeared from ASC. Six months later, the Lovell Electronics Group really did buy an unnamed island in the Pacific, and on it built a power generating plant and set up a well-equipped laboratory. Hu Mingli changed his name to Matthew, and came to the island in secret. At first, only he and Amang lived there; but afterwards, he trained Joseph Luo, the son of an old friend, as an assistant.

For ten years, Bryan kept his word. Apart from the seaplane which regularly transported the necessities of life to him, no one else came to disturb the quiet. Dr. Matthew selected his own research topics, and the Lovell Group made no specific demands of him.

After Dr. Matthew had finished speaking, I said nothing for a moment, but thought back with misgiving. For the name of the Lovell Group was rather familiar. It had appeared in a newspaper report recently. Finally, I remembered what the news items was. It had cited a great deal of evidence to show that the Lovell Company was being secretly manipulated by ASC, and was a transnational company receiving large funds from this power.

Since this was my first meeting with Dr. Matthew, I could not speak to him too directly about the problem, and so I hinted at it in a round-about way.

"Dr. Matthew, have you never investigated the political background of the Lovell Company? I seem to remember newspapers reporting recently that it has some slight connection with ASC."

Dr. Matthew answered angrily, "I never read newspapers. If the newspapers say that, then they are rumor-mongering. I believe what Bryan has told me."

I couldn't pursue the matter, and so changed the subject.

"Doesn't the Lovell Company want anything in return for the investment of such a large sum in you?"

"Of course!" Dr. Matthew replied. "During this period, I have made a few minor inventions, and they are all for peaceful purposes. The company gets the rights; from the business point of view, they find it worthwhile."

I was silent, thinking how to express my thoughts. Having lived in a capitalist society since I was young, I could understand the torture and the pain suffered by this upright spirit. He had been cheated by this unjust society, persecuted as an odd-man out. He could not find the right road. Like a monk in ancient times, he imagined he could escape from the reality of life by staying on this dimly discernible Pacific island. But was it possible to escape from the reality of life?

"Dr. Matthew, war is only a social phenomenon. What produces it is the system of exploitation of man by man," I said as gently as possible. "Because of this, we should make a concrete analysis of wars. There are just wars and unjust wars. Moreover, to completely eliminate war requires that we use the means of revolutionary war, and first of all change the inequalities in society. To hate war without analyzing it is not the way to solve the problem."

"Look how complicated you make it!" Dr. Matthew stared at me innocently. "I don't understand these things, and I don't hope to. All I hope for is to use what remains of my life to do some little things for the benefit of mankind."

Looking at his simple face, I was filled with complex feelings, which I myself could not distinguish clearly. Was it pity? Was it sympathy? Was it anxiety? From Dr. Matthew's simple narrative, I instinctively felt that things could not be as simple as he thought they were. Bryan could not be as honest as he had described. There was something wrong somewhere, perhaps even a plot. Unfortunately, I could not make Dr. Matthew believe me. Scientists like him always judged society by the laws of science. He believed in facts, not in words.

Nevertheless, it was my duty to awaken him. And so I said, "As you are a scientist, I don't think I need to draw your attention to how extremely difficult it is to decide beforehand whether a scientific law or scientific instrument is to be used for the purposes of peace or of war. How can you guarantee that your inventions, after being sold to the Lovell Company, will not be used, directly or indirectly, in the service of war?"

"Bryan has reassured me on this point that the products of the Lovell Company are used solely for the benefit of the people. Even if some other countries have signed contracts with them, this is for weapons to defend peace."

Dr. Matthew spoke in a relaxed manner. What was a "weapon to defend peace?" This was simply playing with words. I could not help asking.

"But aren't they weapons?"

"Hum, yes," Dr. Matthew replied reluctantly.

"Using weapons to defend peace? Doesn't this conflict with your stand against all weapons?"

Dr. Matthew frowned for a moment in thought, and finally shook his head.

"I can't argue against you. A reporter once said that I had no ability in this field. It seems that he was right."

"Dr. Matthew, please excuse my frankness. . . ."

Dr. Matthew waved his hand. "Please don't apologize. The language of science is always frank."

I tried to change the subject.

"Dr. Matthew, the weapon you used to kill the shark the other day, is it a new kind of laser?"

My words seemed to sting him to the quick.

"Weapon? I don't have any weapons on this island." He stood up. "You'd better rest quietly for a few days! Bryan and Joseph Luo will be back shortly. You can go back on their plane."

When he left me, I noticed that his back was slightly bent, and his footsteps heavy.

In this way began my monotonous life on this desolate island. Dr. Matthew was very busy, locking himself up in his laboratory all day. According to him, his research was entering its final stage. I could see that my last talk with him had made a deep impression. Because of this, even if we met by chance, he did not wish to raise any political issues with me. And Amang, apart from looking after us, in the evening would sit on the rocks, playing some ancient sad melody on his pipe. The sound of the pipe made me think of the silvery beaches under the moon, the palm trees swaying in the soft breeze, and the white sails gliding on the crystalline sea. I knew that this was a lonely spirit pouring out his homesickness for his country. It seemed that under his cold exterior lay a warm heart.

In Dr. Matthew's study was an extremely well-stocked medicine cabinet. My wounds had been very light, and after two or three days' treatment, had basically healed. When I went to the study to change my bandages, I was amazed once again that the Lovell Company should provide Dr. Matthew with such excellent equipment. Apart from a rich collection of books, there was also a large electronic storage and retrieval system such as only the largest scientific research centers possess. The technical material appearing in newspapers, magazines and books published daily in every country of the world was transmitted by wireless in facsimile reproduction from the research centers of the world, and could be received automatically by this machine, and stored in the memory system of its computer. The user needed only to press a button for the explanation, formula or diagram he required to be accurately displayed on the lighted screen. In this way, Dr. Matthew, although living on a barren island, was still able to maintain close contact with science and technology circles throughout the world, and feel the throbbing pulse of scientific development at any time he wished. No wonder his work could continue to develop anew.

In a concealed bay behind the island, Dr. Matthew kept a small motor boat. When I had nothing to do, I would take the boat to go fishing. On the coral reef, I came across sharks several times. This would remind me of the frightening event two days earlier. From my general knowledge, I deduced that the shark had been killed by a laser. But what kind of laser could produce a strong beam of light of such efficacy?

One afternoon, after getting up from a nap, I heard a knock outside. When I opened the door, it was Dr. Matthew. He was still wearing his white coat, and a pair of green sunglasses were pushed up over his forehead. His face showed tiredness and joy. Without his saying a word, I knew that his research had reached a final satisfying conclusion. He was now feeling the euphoria from his final victory, and was so happy that he needed someone to share his joy with.

After we had made ourselves comfortable, we began to chat. Dr. Matthew did not speak of his present work, but recalled some episodes in his laboratory life. His memory was very good, and his description lively, and I found them full of interest. It seemed that he wanted to chat as a way of relaxing mentally.

Amang served afternoon tea. On the tray that day was a birthday cake, decorated with cream, on top of which were ten candles. In addition, there was a bottle of wine.

"Is it your birthday today?" I asked.

"No," Dr. Matthew smiled, stood up and shook Amang's hand. "Amang is very good at showing consideration for others. Every time I succeed in inventing something new, Amang bakes me a cake. Today's is the tenth invention since I've been here on this island."

He poured three glasses of wine, gave me one and offered one respectfully to Amang. "My dear Amang, the two of us depend on each other for survival. In all my inventions, there is a part of your labor. Today, I want to express my gratitude to you in front of our visitor."

We drank the wine. Amang did not say a word. His respect and affection for Dr. Matthew could be seen in his richly expressive eyes. He crossed his arms over his chest, bowed deeply and withdrew. We continued to chat. When Dr. Matthew told me about an accident in which a radioactive element had escaped from the laboratory, I pointed to the dosimeter on the wall, and jokingly asked, "This preventive measure is the result of the lesson you learned?"

Dr. Matthew laughed. "There is no such meter in my room. But Joseph Luo is a bit nervous. Wait . . . Wait. . . ."

He suddenly stopped speaking, and went quickly over to the dosimeter. I followed him to have a look, and discovered that the radiation level in the room was slightly above normal. This was something I had overlooked, but it had not escaped Dr. Matthew's keen observation.

"You haven't brought anything radioactive with you, have you?" he asked suspiciously.

I remembered the high-tension atomic battery.

By then I had some understanding of Dr. Matthew and so took the battery out for him to look at, telling him that it was the invention of my professor, who had entrusted it to me to take to Port X.

Dr. Matthew examined the battery carefully, and asked about its construction. He spoke very highly of Professor Zhao's invention. Then he sighed. "If this battery could be combined with my laser excavator, then mining, tunneling and underground engineering would enter a new age. What an enormous benefit that would be for mankind."

"What laser excavator?"

Dr. Matthew looked at me in dismay. He realized that he had said too much, but he was not a man accustomed to lying. He considered for a moment, and then continued firmly. "It's my latest invention. If you're interested, I can show it to you."

I knew that the riddle which had been turning in my mind these last few days was about to be solved. Of course I was interested.

Dr. Matthew, in high spirits, led me to the laboratory. The most conspicuous object in this laboratory, apart from the usual oscillators, oscillographs and computers, was a large semicircular control console in the center of the room. A milky-white fluorescent screen took up a huge area in the center of the console. Below it were row upon row of meters, indicator lights and buttons. On the ceiling connected to the control panel hung down something that looked like a periscope. One end of the equipment clearly extended out through the roof.

On the stainless steel bench beside the control desk was a laser machine.

Dr. Matthew led me to the side of the machine, opened the case and began to explain it to me.

In general, this laser still belonged to the category of solid-state continuous laser machines. But the material which it used was not glass or crystal, but a new kind of plastic. Dr. Matthew had made a completely new and original improvement to the resonator, so that the energy output was several times greater than that of an ordinary laser. Apart from this, Dr. Matthew has also successfully solved the problem of focusing the high energy light and had increased its distance of transmission several times over.

"I designed this machine for excavation work. That's why I've called it an excavator," Dr. Matthew continued. "Any hard metal or rock will be immediately vaporized by this kind of laser. In future, tunneling through underground layers of rock will be even easier than cutting through butter with a knife. But this kind of machine can only transform energy, transmit energy and focus the energy. It cannot create energy. Because of this, in application, it needs a high-tension energy source, which means clumsy peripheral equipment. Now that we have your high-tension atomic battery, the problem is solved."

"Did you use it to kill the shark?"

"Yes."

"Were you on the beach then?"

Dr. Matthew turned on a switch at the control desk.

"I was sitting here."

The big fluorescent screen began to light up. I seemed to have been suddenly transported to the edge of the coral reef, with the sea lapping at my feet. Rocks jutted behind me and in front of me, to my left and to my right. I involuntarily moved aside for safety, to prevent the tide from wetting my clothes. But I immediately realized that I was still in the laboratory. It was only that the scene of the seashore that appeared before my eyes seemed completely real.

I understood. "A laser holographic television?"

Dr. Matthew smiled. "This is another of my inventions. That day, I was just experimenting, when I saw you floating in the sea. Then I saw the danger you were in. Because the situation was so urgent, I had to use the laser to kill the shark."

"How did you aim the laser so far away?"

Dr. Matthew pointed to the instrument that looked like a periscope. "By means of this light refraction system. I can aim the light beam accurately at any point on the surface of the sea around the island."

"How could you speak to each other?"

"That's even simpler. I have installed a transmitting and receiving system on the island."

I stared at this new and original laser machine, and couldn't help thinking of an ancient legend. Two thousand years ago, when the Roman navy closed in on the Greek city of Syracuse, the Greek scientist Archimedes tried to use brass plates to form many hexagonal mirrors in order to focus the rays of the sun to destroy the enemy ships. Who would have thought that the heat ray machine which Archimedes had dreamt of should now exist in reality before my eyes?

"Archimedes' dream!" I couldn't help exclaiming.

"No. It is not Archimedes' dream." Dr. Matthew was doubtlessly familiar with the story. "His dream was to kill people with heat rays. But what I have created is an instrument for the benefit of mankind."

I said, "Dr. Matthew, I would not ask you to turn your laser machine into a military weapon, but I cannot agree with your attitude towards military weapons. For example, don't you agree that your saving me from the jaws of the shark was an act of humanity?"

"Of . . . of course," Dr. Matthew stammered.

"If you had not used your laser beam as a weapon, would you have been able to save me?"

Dr. Matthew did not reply.

"So you see, the question is not whether a weapon is evil or not, but in whose hands the weapon lies, and the use to which the weapon is put. Don't you agree?"

Dr. Matthew shook his head. "No matter what you say, a man is not a shark. I can kill a shark, but I cannot kill a man. There are more than enough weapons in the world already for killing, without my invention."

I said, pained, "Dr. Matthew, one day you will understand, but there is a very great contradiction between your good intentions and reality."

"Perhaps you're right. But I'm old already. It's too late for me to change the principles I have lived by." Dr. Matthew said, a little sadly. "But in the last ten years, I believe that I have done a little to improve man's ability to live in peace. I have improved the laser operating scalpel, invented a laser welding machine, and I have done some research in producing an atmospheric electric discharge."

"An atmospheric electric discharge!" Something suddenly clicked in my mind.

"It's a by-product from my research on long-distance wireless transmission. I invented a powerful kind of microwave oscillator. It can produce an extremely narrow beam of wireless waves and produce an electric discharge on a far distant target. Actually, I haven't yet discovered a practical application for it as yet, but the Lovell Company is very interested in it."

"Good Heavens!" I exclaimed in astonishment. "Then the 'Morning Star' was shot down by artificial lightning."

"What 'Morning Star'?" Dr. Matthew stared at me. "You're not . . ."

Only then did I tell him my true background. I told him of what had happened to Professor Zhao, and what he had entrusted me to do. I told him of the police officer's conjecture, and of the incident of the "Morning Star." Dr. Matthew questioned me in great details about the height I was flying at, the weather conditions and the form of the lightning flash.

"Only the ships of ASC were in the vicinity at the time. After the loss of the 'Morning Star' they sent out helicopters in search of me. When I think of what has been said about the connections between ASC and the Lovell Company, I think that there must be whole volumes to be written," I added finally.

"No, that's not possible!" Dr. Matthew staggered a few steps, and fell dejectedly into a chair. I saw his face suddenly go white, and he clutched his chest in pain. I couldn't help crying out in alarm.

"What's the matter?"

"My heart. It's nothing. I've had it for years." Dr. Matthew said in a low voice. "There's some special medicine in the medicine chest. Would you call Amang to give me an injection?"

If I had known the state of his health beforehand, I would not have spoken to him so bluntly. I was full of remorse.

But when Amang gave him the injection, and took him to his bedroom to rest, still another important question came into my mind. "Dr. Matthew, does Bryan know that the laser excavator has already been completed?"

"He only knows that I'm working on it, not that the prototype is finished."

"And Joseph Luo?"

Dr. Matthew thought for a moment. "He doesn't know either. The final assembly has been done by myself these last two months."

"In that case, before the true nature of things has been cleared up, is it possible for you not to let them see this machine?"

"Of course," Dr. Matthew answered briskly. "Tomorrow, we'll move it into my bedroom. But, the machine is very heavy. Amang and I are not strong enough. You will have to help us."

In the days that followed, Dr. Matthew was very kind to me, and frequently asked me about new developments in China. In our conversations, I found it astonishing how cut off he was from the outside world. In fact, he had at hand every kind of advanced communications equipment, but because of abetting by others and his own prejudices, he did not receive any news apart from technical material. It was as if he had built an invisible wall around himself, completely separating life on Matthew Island from life in the rest of the world. Only then did I understand Bryan's attention to secrecy. He played on Dr. Matthew's pessimistic hatred of the world and was willing to pay any price to help him achieve his ideal. His aim was to mold Dr. Matthew into a purely scientific tool in order to serve his ulterior motives.

One day at dusk, I was taking the air in the corridor with Dr. Matthew, admiring the brillant sunset on the Pacific. Just as we were talking, the outline of a naval vessel appeared in the far distance. It was heading directly for the island. When it dropped anchor about two km. from the shore, I recognized it as a P-missile carrier belonging to the ASC navy, which had been carrying out naval exercises nearby.

Dr. Matthew raised his telescope. He could see clearly the ASC flag. He frowned. "A warship! What's a warship doing here?"

A thought flashed into my mind. "Dr. Matthew, can it be Bryan and Joseph Luo returning?"

Dr. Matthew shook his head. "It can't be. Why should they come in a foreign warship?"

I persisted. "In any case, you mustn't on any account tell anyone my true identity."

"Of course."

We saw a helicopter leave the warship. There was no doubt that someone was coming to visit the small island. I knew that my words had had their effect on Dr. Matthew. He must have been pondering over many questions, too; for he suddenly turned towards me and asked me to take the high-tension atomic battery into his bedroom, and not to come out again until he called. However, I could still see what was going on through the window.

The helicopter landed by the side of the lagoon. The door of the cockpit opened. The first to descend was a young man in a floral shirt, who I recognized from the photo on the bedside table. There was no doubt that he was Joseph Luo. The second was a tall, thin European, rather Slavic in his bearing, with gold-rimmed spectacles, smiling urbanely. What was surprising was that from the helicopter also descended a naval officer together with six naval ratings. What was it all about?

The group came slowly over. The setting sun cast long shadows before them. A tense atmosphere covered this quiet, pleasant island.

Dr. Matthew welcomed Bryan into the study. The six ratings stood at the door, expressionless.

I tiptoed to the side of the door leading to the study, and through the crack observed what was going on.

"Let me make the introductions," Bryan said, indicating the naval officer. "This is our famous Dr. Matthew. This is Captain Shapunov." Shapunov was tall and of stalwart build, looking like a polar bear in his well-ironed starched white naval uniform. Although his face was covered in smiles, he could not hide a domineering manner. He shook Dr. Matthew's hand with excessive politeness, and then said in perfect English, "I am so honored to meet you."

"Please sit down, everyone," Dr. Matthew answered coldly.

"We haven't seen each other for a year, old boy. I've been thinking a great deal of you," Bryan said in a very affectionate manner. "You don't look too well. You're not working too hard, are you?"

"Dr. Matthew, you really ought to rest," Joseph Luo interrupted. "Mr. Bryan and I have had a first-rate holiday. The nightclubs on the Ginza in Tokyo, beach parties in Honolulu, Hawaii, the casinos in Monte Carlo—that's real life for you!"

"Holidays are for the young," Dr. Matthew replied. "How is it that you've come by warship?"

Bryan laughed. "It's completely by chance! Captain Shapunov's ship carries equipment from our company. He invited us to inspect it, and so we took the opportunity to come over and visit."

"Equipment? Is it an atmospheric electric discharge machine?" Dr. Matthew still appeared calm, but his voice showed his suppressed excitement. I began to worry.

There was a moment's silence. Joseph Luo shifted uncomfortably in his chair.

"What is an atmospheric electric discharge machine?" Bryan pretended not to understand.

"Like the one that shot down the 'Morning Star.' "

Dr. Matthew had said earlier that the language of science was direct. He could not dissemble, and so now once again he spoke aloud the guesses he had already made. But this action, completely unprepared, had an unexpected result. Dr. Matthew's words doubtlessly attacked Bryan at his most vital point. He did not know how much Dr. Matthew actually knew, and did not know the source of his information. And so he said nothing for some ten seconds, unable to think of an appropriate answer.

Captain Shapunov realized that there was no use prevaricating. He cleared his throat, and answered for Bryan. "Dr. Matthew, we have a contract with the Lovell Company. We have asked them to make us all kinds of . . . equipment. Among them are perhaps some that are your inventions."

Dr. Matthew still stared at Bryan. "Then the promises you gave me . . . ."

Bryan suddenly found his voice. "The equipment is for defense. They are not military weapons. There is no conflict between that and our ideals."

Dr. Matthew did not continue his questions, but said in a tired voice. "Let's talk about the 'Morning Star.' I'm only interested in technical problems."

"That's right. You really are a great scientist," Captain Shapunov said, beaming. "Ten days ago, a drug trafficker, after being condemned by our courts, attempted to escape by hijacking a plane. Our navy happened to be doing exercises in this region, and so we used the Pluto flame thrower on him."

"What Pluto flame thrower?" Dr. Matthew asked.

Bryan explained. "It's a piece of defense equipment, based on the principles of your lightning discharger. Only, on the basis of this test, we have found that this wea . . . this piece of equipment has no future. It's too difficult to aim accurately, and goes wrong easily. Its power is not sufficiently great, and so we want to offer Captain Shapunov the plans of some other piece of defense equipment. That's why we've come to see you, old boy."

"What do you want me to do?" Dr. Matthew seemed to ask casually. It was already getting dark. He lit the lamp, and turned the lampshade slightly so that his own face was hidden in the shadows.

"I know that your high-power laser machine is finished. The company is preparing to put it into production. We have already constructed a laboratory for you deep in the mountains of one of the countries of Europe, and we want you to direct it. . . ."

Dr. Matthew said nothing. I knew that remorse was gnawing at his heart. Only now did he see Bryan's true features clearly. He realized that he had been tricked and deceived these ten years. He had committed a gross blunder. His lifelong belief in honesty, friendship and confidence crumpled in an instant like a castle built on sand.

But Bryan had underestimated Dr. Matthew's ability to distinguish right from wrong. For ten years, he had played with Dr. Matthew, and now, intoxicated by his victory, mistook Dr. Matthew's silence for agreement, and so was even more pleased with himself. "I'm so happy that we have reached a new understanding. Mr. Luo has already expressed his willingness to cooperate with you further, and has agreed to let us have your designs."

When he heard Bryan's words, Dr. Matthew glared angrily at Joseph Luo. He leapt up and, shaking with anger, cried out hoarsely, gritting his teeth:

"You bunch of pirates! You have filled the world with your fine words and your evil deeds. You can trick one person like me, but you cannot deceive millions and millions of others. It's taken me until today to see through your jackal's faces. It is already too late, but as long as I have a breath of life left in me, you cannot hope to take my laser equipment from me." Joseph Luo ran up to put his arms around him. "Dr. Matthew, you mustn't be angry. Science is a commodity. We have no responsibility for how the customers use what they buy."

Dr. Matthew pushed him away angrily. "You're despicable! You've dishonored science. How much did they pay you for your soul?"

Joseph Luo lowered his eyes, and stood aside shamefaced, not daring to look into Dr. Matthew's angry eyes.

Bryan and Shapunov exchanged glances. Shapunov took out a whistle and blew it. The six naval ratings immediately appeared at the door.

Bryan said mildly and even sweetly, "You mustn't misunderstand, old boy. This is for the sake of your sacred work, and also for the great cause of peace. We are worried about preserving the secrecy of this island, and so have decided to blow everything up tonight. You'd better pack a few things and leave with us."

Dr. Matthew's eyes swept over the dark faces of the ratings. He knew that they would use force to seize him. He became even angrier, his chest heaved up and down, and he cried out at the top of his lungs, "How can you be so vicious. . . ."

He wanted to say more, but his weak heart could not sustain him. He staggered back, glared at them all angrily, his eyes filled with remorse and with hatred, so that even someone as cunning as Bryan, as arrogant as Shapunov was afraid. There was a moment of dead silence. Dr. Matthew flung out his arms and fell heavily to the ground.

Shapunov was the first to recover. He bent down and quickly examined Dr. Matthew. Then he took out a white handkerchief and wiped his hands, saying indifferently, "He's had it."

Watching this tragedy, I felt my blood boiling, and I was overwhelmed with grief. I seized the doorknob, and was about to rush out to revenge him at all costs, but Shapunov's words stopped me cold.

"It really is a pity that we didn't get the high-tension atomic battery," he said to Bryan. "Otherwise, we could have put the death ray machine into production immediately."

Now at last, I knew the beginning and the end of the whole affair. The murder of Professor Zhao and Dr. Matthew's tragedy were both part of a plot by this great power ASC: to build a death ray machine. Even though they would be able to master the design of the laser equipment with Joseph Luo's help, nevertheless, they did not know that Dr. Matthew had already completed a prototype, and still less that the high-tension atomic battery was in this very room. If I ran out now and sacrificed my life, that would be a small matter. But if I let them get two inventions, then the result would be disastrous. And so I clenched my teeth, fighting to control myself and remained where I was without taking any action.

I guess that in my excitement I must have made a sound. Bryan, who was closest to the bedroom, suddenly became vigilant, looked in my direction and started to come over. I was so tense that I began to sweat, and my heart beat furiously. I looked around desperately, searching for a weapon with which to defend myself, but there was not even a wooden stick in the room. How I wished that there was a bomb near at hand, so that I and this valuable machinery could perish together with these beasts.

Bryan's hand was already on the doorknob. We were separated by only the thickness of a plank. I bent down slightly, the muscles in my body taut, determined to fight him to the death. Just at this critical moment, a cry of anguish made Bryan turn round.

It was Amang. He had just brought in a tray of glasses and a bottle of wine. As soon as he saw his master on the ground, there came from the depth of his throat a heart-rending cry such as can come only from a mute person. Mindless of his own life, he threw himself at Bryan, and knocked him over with one blow. Only then did the naval ratings react, rushing over to seize Amang, forcing his arms behind his back.

Joseph Luo helped Bryan up. One side of his face was swollen, and blood flowed from the corner of his lips. It looked as if it was the first time in his life that he had been in a fight.

"Where are the blueprints?" he asked roughly.

"In . . . in the laboratory safe," Joseph Luo answered fearfully.

Then, one of the naval ratings hurried over to report. A signal had been received from the ship. There was a change in plan. They must leave the island immediately. On hearing this, Shapunov at once said to Joseph Luo, "Get them quickly!" Then he, pointing at Amang, issued the order, "Get rid of him. Prepare the explosives for demolition, and set them to go off in an hour."

Joseph Luo pointed to Dr. Matthew lying on the ground. "What . . . what about him?"

Shapunov laughed sardonically. "We're using nuclear explosives. It will remove Matthew Island forever from the map. The flames of the atomic blast will provide him with solemn funeral rites, and the ocean will be his last resting place."

The naval ratings dragged Amang out. A moment later, from outside the door, a rifle shot sounded in my ears, announcing the death of this loyal servant.

When he heard the shot, Joseph Luo shuddered. Then, as if struck by a whip, he ran out, head down.

Bryan wiped his face with his handkerchief, sat down in a chair and spat fiercely onto the ground. "What lousy luck!"

Shapunov came up to him, slapped him on the shoulder, smiling contentedly. "I say, Ivan (that was probably his real name), you've done a beautiful job. You have the boldness of vision of a politician, and the shrewdness of a capitalist. Look what rich fruit the seeds you sowed ten years ago have finally borne. We have only to construct the death ray machine now and we can shoot down at will the enemy's satellites, missiles and planes, sink their ships, and destroy their tanks. Then we will not only become masters of the world, but masters of the universe. We will prove by actual deeds that we are worthy successors to our mighty ancestors. Let's bestir ourselves. Let's examine the laboratory thoroughly, and leave nothing behind."

Bryan stood up, and followed Shapunov out.

I couldn't wait any longer. I ran out at once, carried Dr. Matthew into the bedroom and lay him on the bed. I discovered that he was still breathing, that his heart was still beating faintly, and so took the special medicine from the medicine cabinet and gave him an injection. Then, with mixed feelings of grief and anger, I concentrated my attention entirely on saving the patient, completely forgetting the imminent danger that was facing me.

I heard Shapunov and his men leave the laboratory. I knew that they had taken the blueprints. Then, the lights on the island went out. I knew that they had already destroyed the power station. Then the helicopter took off, leaving this island to its doom.

The bright rays of the moon streamed through the window. Quiet reigned all around. Somewhere on this little island, the timing device was ticking away, moving closer, minute by minute, second by second, to the final explosion. In the bay, a small boat was floating on the water. It could help me to escape. But I could not leave this helpless sick man alone. To move him now would be tantamount to hastening his death. I could only sit quietly at his bedside and wait for the last moment to come. There was no fear in my heart, only a profound regret at not having seen my ancestral land, at not having accomplished professor Zhao's dying wish.

Suddenly Dr. Matthew uttered a groan and slowly opened his eyes. He looked up at me and grasped me firmly by the hand. His tears flowed, and for a moment he could not say a word.

"Have they gone?" he asked with effort, after a long moment.

I nodded.

"The blueprints . . . ."

I nodded sadly.

"The ship—has it gone?"

"Not yet."

Dr. Matthew's eyes suddenly opened wide. In a superhuman effort he struggled to sit up, and pointing to the laser machine in the corner, cried, "Quickly . . . quickly. Move it to the window!"

"Dr. Matthew," I said anxiously. "You mustn't get excited. Your health . . ."

"This is not a question of one individual's life," Dr. Matthew said, struggling for breath. "If they get away with the blueprints, it will be the death of millions."

I could not disobey him. Three days before, Dr. Matthew, Amang and I had exerted all our strength before we could dismantle the machine, and move it in three parts into the bedroom. But now, in this moment of life and death, I managed single-handedly to push it to the window.

I helped Dr. Matthew to the side of the machine. He deftly connected the high-tension atomic battery and adjusted the strength of the laser to its highest intensity. Under the powerful electric current, the red beam from the laser machine became blinding, cutting through the silent night sky like a sharp avenging sword.

On the surface of the sea in the distance, the warship was preparing to lift anchor. Its outline began to disappear in the fog over the sea, but the deadly ray was already pursuing it from behind. There was no way in which it could escape its fate.

The laser beam in its first sweep cut down a row of coconut trees on the reef. They fell with a resounding crash. In its second sweep, Dr. Matthew's hand trembled a little. The laser beam struck the surface of the sea, cutting a track through it. Great clouds of steam rose up, obscuring the moon. At last, Dr. Matthew aimed the beam at the warship. I saw a flash, followed by a resounding explosion, and the warship sank in flames and smoke.

Dr. Matthew let go of the knob, and fell sideways. I hurried to help him. But this act of revenge had exhausted his last ounce of strength. His breathing became weaker and weaker, and his pulse could scarcely be felt. Under the moonlight, his face was as white as a sheet of paper. His lips trembled. He wanted to tell me urgently all that was seething in his mind, to tell it to all those who would come after him.

"I was wrong!" he said slowly. "If I had not killed those 'sharks,' the world would have known no justice, no peace. . . ."

He wanted to say more, but death was already close. I saw his head fall suddenly onto his chest. I had witnessed the death of two scientists in the space of a fortnight.

My eyes filled with tears. I laid him out on the bed and covered his body with a white sheet. Then I remembered that I had perhaps still ten to twenty minutes in which to escape, and so taking the high-tension atomic battery, I ran towards the bay. The laser machine was too heavy, and so I had no way of taking it with me.

The motorboat was still anchored by the shore. I jumped into it, loosened the mooring rope, started the motor and headed with full speed for the open sea. The motorboat roared away, leaving a trail of foam behind it.

Just as I was four to five kilometers from the coral island, an earth-shaking explosion resounded behind me. The force of the waves almost lifted my small boat right out of the water. It needed all my strength to keep it steady. Then I turned to look and saw a white column of water rising from the sea, topped by a thick mushroom-shaped cloud of black smoke. A moment later, the cloud dispersed and water fell, coming down like rain. When the bubbling of the sea finally ceased, only the moon was left reflected in the vast surface of the sea. The tragic Matthew Island had disappeared forever from the earth.

Seething with hatred and yet full of confidence, I sped the small boat towards the land of my fathers, ready to face a new life of struggle.

*Translated by S.F.W.*

# III
# IN AND OUT
# OF
## SPACE

# 6

# The Mirror Image of the Earth

## ZHENG WENGUANG

The planet appeared yellow in the distance, as if it were a lemon drifting in a space of dark purple velvet. So the spacemen aboard *The Explorer* thought there was nothing but barren desert, until their craft drew near enough for them to discern a layer of dense, yellow atmosphere studded with green clouds, like so many islands floating about in the atmospheric ocean.

The spacemen surveyed the deadly silent planet with great care. They discovered that the chief component of the atmosphere was oxygen, which meant people could breathe there, and could drink water in the streams. However, though luxuriant plants grew profusely on the planet, there were neither birds nor animals, let alone any higher form of civilization. But when they climbed up the cloud-capped mountains, they could vaguely discern the upturned eaves and turrets of palatial buildings. Yet there was not the slightest sign of living beings. The visitors named the planet Uiqid, and then returned to Earth, with the suggestion that the next team of astronauts include a cosmic archaeologist.

Thus, three and a half years later, Cui Yining landed again on the lemon-like planet aboard a new spaceship, *The Hundred Flowers*. "Hey Cui, do you know why it's called Uiqid?" asked the young biophysicist Linwu Sheng, captain of *The Hundred Flowers*. The astronauts were standing in a

Published in *Shanghai wenxue* (Shanghai Literature), October 1980.

springy grass field, while their two women colleagues lingered by the ramp
of the ship, fascinated by the enchanting spectacle of this strange planet.

Cui Yining turned, and shook his head. "By reversing the letters, the
word Uiqid reads Diqiu!¹ The meaning is quite clear: The Mirror Image
of the Earth," said the captain.

Cui Yining curiously surveyed the landscape on all sides of the spaceship. They had landed on a desolate, vast grassland. The color of the grasses
was a bit varied, but mostly of a pink-red hue that made the land look
ablaze. Ripples shimmered in the distance—could it be a lake? The water
was not blue but bright yellow, like Shaoxing Wine. Further away lay a
range of green mountains. At one side of the spacecraft there was a sparse
wood with tall trees like poplars, only the trunks were brown and the
leaves red as a rose, looking more beautiful than the red leaves in the
Fragrant Hills.

"I don't see anything similar to our Earth," muttered Cui Yining.

"Really?" Linwu Sheng said mischievously, "Then ask your lady to have
a look. Hey, Du Yinlin!"

Du Yinlin was slim and agile, with delicate features. She was a geologist
as well as a photographer (every astronaut had to be trained in two disci-
plines). Standing by her husband, she studied the strange landscape with
excitement. All of a sudden she grasped Cui's hand, mumbling "Complementary . . . color. . . ."

Linwu Sheng gave a hearty laugh, and cast a knowing glance at Gu
Mingwei, his fiancée. She was both a chemist and a physician. At the
moment she was so entranced by the colorful view that her pretty eyes
didn't even blink.

Linwu Sheng took the camera off Du Yinlin's shoulder and snapped a
quick shot of the surroundings. In a few seconds, a color negative dropped
from the cassette. Linwu picked up the photo. The instant he saw it he
cried, "It's just like a picture taken at the Ming tombs or the Western
Hills. . . ."

Because of the optical characteristics of complementary colors, the picture taken with a negative was very similar to that taken with ordinary
color slides on Earth. The astronauts were excited at this discovery.

"It *is* the mirror image of the Earth. . . . Exactly. . . ." Cui said, in
short breaths.

"We'll find the Uiqidians yet. Must be living beings like you and me,
only blue all over. . . ." Linwu Sheng said loudly, with an impish wink.
Then he quickly climbed into the cabin of the spaceship. Soon he emerged
at the controls of a hovercraft.

"Do you really think there are blue people?" asked Gu Mingwei, who
had kept silent all the while. She was young and beautiful, with large eyes
like fathomless lakes—lakes on the Earth, to be sure.

"I think so . . . I would believe anything!" answered Linwu cheerfully.

Then stretching out a hand, he said, "Come on, envoys from the Earth, aren't we like Alice in Outer Space?" They climbed into the hovercraft one by one. Du Yinlin was thinking to herself: Yes, exactly. We *are* like Alice entering the mirror world, but it's a real world, not the wonderland in the dream of the little English girl. . . .

The hovercraft traveled at the speed of 180 km. per hour. It took them four and a half hours to move up the gently sloping mountain. The time, of course, was shown by their wristwatches in Earth time. During this period, the sun shining over Uiqid had not moved in the least. It seemed the day was quite long here.

They stopped twice on the way to have a rest, a snack, take a few pictures, and collect specimens of rocks and plants. They had not come across any animate forms of life, not even a tiny insect. The first astronauts had probably been correct in guessing there were no other animate beings on Uiqid. But then, who built those upturned eaves and turrets?

Referring to a map computer-generated by the original surveyors, they spent two hours trying to find the magnificent palaces, but their efforts were in vain. The map was accurate: mountains, lakes, woods, and various directional bearings—every indication was perfectly correct, yet . . .

"Maybe it's only their imagination," Cui Yining muttered, "just like the mirages we see on Earth."

Linwu Sheng shook his head slightly. As a biophysicist, he was sure that on a planet whose natural conditions were much the same as those on the Earth, the development of life should be more or less the same, too. Somewhere in Uiqid, there must be animals, even human beings—undoubtedly their color, features, and lifestyle would be different, but living beings nonetheless, with the faculties of reason and emotion, capable of creating a civilization.

The only explanation was that in the past three and a half years, a catastrophe must have befallen Uiqid.

But there was not the least trace of crumbled walls and toppled houses. Was it really a sort of mirage? Impossible. Even a mirage is not a total illusion; it is a reflection of actual scenes—distorted, of course.

The hovercraft progressed up the slope with bursts of steam. They were trying to reach the summit. On their map, it was called Mount Amgnalomoq, the reversed name of Mount Qomolangma, though not so steep and towering. Moreover, it was not covered with white snow but looked black, and awesomely majestic.

A huge crater gaped wide in front of them.

"Perhaps the place has been destroyed by a volcanic eruption?" said Gu Mingwei in her sweet silvery voice. Since their landing on Uiqid, she had looked unusually rosy and bright. Whenever Linwu glanced at her his heart would beat faster.

Du Yinlin, the geologist, shook her head. It was merely a lapse of three and a half years. What kind of volcanic eruption could it be that left no sign of destruction at all? She looked doubtfully at her husband, Cui Yining, who was examining the crater with the expert eyes of a cosmic archaeologist. After a while he said resolutely, "I must get in there, but it's a twisted path. The hovercraft won't do. We have to go on foot; Linwu, just the two of us, O.K.?"

"Let's all go down," said Du Yinlin, earnestly. Immediately she took down from the hovercraft a coil of thin but durable rope made of fiberglass-reinforced plastic. Each person carried a mini-jet engine on his back to help with the upward climb later on. Grasping the rope, they went down into the gaping crater, one after another. They had a short rest, drank a little water, and presently reached the bottom. Linwu Sheng looked at his watch. It had taken them only an hour and ten minutes.

"Look here—light!" Cui Yining said, excitement in his hushed voice.

Indeed, an uncanny light was reflected from the rocky lava; a peculiar optical phenomenon. A faint purple light lit up the bottom of the volcano, presenting a miraculous scene, like a fairy tale wonderland. Du Yinlin clutched her husband's hand, while Gu Mingwei clung to Linwu, who stood stock still, hearing only his heart beating like an African battle drum.

"Here's a passage," Cui whispered to Linwu. "Shall we go on?"

They moved along the narrow corridor one by one, and in a few minutes came to an immense cave. A hazy light glimmered from the arched ceiling. The walls were quite smooth, as if they had been finished. There were even several doors on one side.

The four astronauts stood before a door. Perhaps they would soon meet the intelligent beings on Uiqid? They stood there with bated breath, exchanging wondering looks. The door was not made of wood, but of a kind of black opaque plexiglass. Rows upon rows of protruding big nails were embedded in the door in the style of the gates of ancient Chinese architecture, but these were smaller and arranged in a closer pattern.

Linwu touched one of the door nails. Good Heavens! He was so astounded his jaw dropped and he stared, mouth agape. The change was sudden. The cave disappeared, and instead there emerged the boundless, wild, surging billows of a blue sea; then a succession of gigantic ships in full sail came into view. As the rolling waves swept towards them, Gu Mingwei gave a cry. Instantly Linwu steadied her. He was the first to realize what was going on.

"Don't move. It's just a holographic movie," he said in a low but firm voice.

He was right. The scene was exceedingly lifelike, but it was soundless. They could see some sailors moving to and fro on the ship, dressed like warriors of the Ming Dynasty, but they couldn't hear the roaring sea, nor any noise from the ship. They heard nothing but their own heartbeats.

Then a crowd appeared on the deck of an enormous ship. The image drew nearer and nearer. A hefty man with a clean-shaven pale face stood on the deck, just ten paces away from the astronauts. He was speaking, but they could only see his mouth opening slightly without hearing any words. In a moment, there loomed on the sea the back of a blue whale, its huge tail pounding the waves, beating up columns of water like splashing fountains. Soon the whale swam out of view.

"It's . . ." Cui stammered to his wife, "it's the scene of Zheng Ho sailing to the Western Ocean."

Everyone understood at once. Certainly it was a movie shot of historical scenes on the Earth: the sea, the ship, the whale, the characters. . . . That man, no doubt the celebrated eunuch Zheng Ho. The scene was truly vivid. However, the astronauts were so spellbound that they didn't even stop to wonder: How could a holographic movie of fifteenth-century events on the Earth be shown on a strange planet?

The ship vanished, so did the sea. It was the same hollow cave all around, lit up by the uncanny hazy light. The astronauts seemed to have awakened from an eerie daydream, but none wanted to speak.

"Shall I press another door nail?" Linwu finally asked, glancing at his three companions. Now they were sure that what they had called "door nails" were really buttons for showing holographic films.

No one replied. Linwu Sheng stretched out a trembling hand and touched another button. He was so taken aback that he jumped aside.

A horrible scene of war and slaughter unfolded before them. It was not on a battlefield, but in a courtyard. Ancient armor-clad warriors, armed to the teeth, were raising glittering swords at frightened women in imperial dress. Blood flowed like a gushing fountain. Suddenly, a fire broke out and rolling flames spread swiftly, enveloping the entire space in no time. They didn't hear anyone crying or shouting, nor did they feel the scorching heat but still their hearts quivered. Look at those dim contours, amidst the towering tongues of fire—aren't they mansions, pavilions, and terraces with carved beams and painted pillars?

"The burning . . . of O Fang . . . Palace . . ." Cui stammered.[2] God knows if it really was, but the armor, the royal dress, and the weapons were definitely fashioned in the Qin Dynasty style.

This time Linwu didn't ask for any advice but pressed yet another button right away. Now no one doubted any more. The new scene displayed dozens of young people with red armbands, standing there in regular columns and waving booklets with red covers in the same direction towards a remote figure. Then a second group of teenagers flung themselves upon the first. Immediately a tangled fight broke out. Leather whips were lashed about, daggers and swords glistened in the air, bricks were thrown at random. Blood oozed from the forehead of a young boy; his face was twitching, and he was staring at the astronauts with lusterless eyes.

Cui Yining gasped, swayed in a swoon and fell down.

"Yining!" shrieked Du Yinyin. Linwu and Gu Mingwei hurriedly helped Cui to his feet and heard him mumble "Oh, my poor brother. . . ."

It was incredible that they should see, on this strange planet, the picture of that foolish, brutal conflict in the twentieth century with the image of his brother who had died of his wounds. Now, all of them were aware of the fact that these holographic films had not been shot in a studio, but were truthful records of history, made on the spot.

But who could have been the cameraman? And who had carried the films to Uiqid through a distance of so many light years and kept them in a cave? After all, when O Fang Palace was burned down and Zheng Ho set sail to the Western Ocean, the motion picture had not even been invented on the Earth, much less the holographic movie.

All this perplexed and puzzled the astronauts beyond words. They were scientists, so none of them believed in divine power or miracles, but without divine power and miracles, how did all these spectacles come about? How could they be explained? They looked at one another, dumbfounded.

Cui Yining came to in half an hour and said to his companions, "Someone must have kept here a number of holographic movies of historical scenes. How were they produced? I think we could get the key to the answer right here. Let's press more buttons, one by one. What do you say?"

"I don't want to see cruel scenes of slaughter any more," replied Gu Mingwei, her voice still quivering.

"There won't be pictures of war and fighting all the time," Linwu consoled her. "Maybe we'll see some interesting scenes like the Dance in Rainbow-hued Feather Dress performed by female dancers to the court of the Emperor Tang Ming Huang, or a royal banquet, or a grand wedding ceremony, and the like—joyful pictures anyway. . . . You could pass over anything you don't like to see, just as though you were watching TV."

Scenes in the holographic movie followed each other in quick succession. There were few battle scenes, but neither were there any pictures of joyful celebration as predicted by Linwu. Most of the views showed the ordinary, poverty-stricken, and humdrum life in the countryside of old times: close-ups of a boat struggling in whirlpools; a fierce wrestle between man and animal; fishermen trembling like leaves in a storm. Cui Yining was absorbed in watching the shifting scenes. To an archaeologist, what could be more valuable than pictures depicting the life of ancient people? Others thought that all those dresses, utensils, tools, and buildings were quite ordinary. Only he was able to make out whether they had prevailed in Early or Late Tang Dynasty, in the Southern or Northern Dynasty; whether they had been made by the Han race of people or the minority nationalities. It seemed that the unknown cameraman had deliberately shot varied scenes of life in different periods and different areas.

One of the pictures showed people praying for rain: Naked men acting as Devils of Drought danced wildly under a scorching sun. Looking at the gaunt, pale-faced, skeleton-like people worn out with thirst and exhaustion, Gu Mingwei turned a little and murmured to Du Yinlin, "We're simply like strange animals locked up in a cage on exhibition."

"It looks like the cosmic beings have been observing and studying us over thousands of years," replied Yinlin. "But all the views are about China. Why? There are lots of other countries on the Earth. Are the cosmic beings blind to them?"

"Oh," Linwu interrupted in his cheerful tone, "obviously because the drama on the Chinese stage is the most attractive—in the eyes of cosmic beings. . . ."

Cui was a little taken aback. The archaeologist had never pondered these questions: Should sensible beings outside the Earth want to study our history, what would they do? Probably those movie shots had not been carefully chosen, just as visitors to the zoo don't invariably choose to watch the caged animals that look most powerful, beautiful and energetic.

In studying our own history, can we be as unbiased, level-headed and impartial as the cosmic beings? Is it true that we've tried to embellish and modify history at will, consciously or unconsciously? On the other hand, when we see historical scenes shot by others, we feel very awkward, as though we were viewing our own naked bodies pitted all over with ugly scars.

All of a sudden Linwu cried, "Look, a UFO!"

So it was! A scintillating green object raced across the blue sky over the globe, like a couple of dishes stuck together. Most likely the historical scenes had been shot by this strange object. If living beings in outer space wanted to investigate the Earth, this was the best way, the most skillful and direct means.

This planet Uiqid seemed to have developed civilization at a high level thousands of years ago, and the Uiqidians had been observing everything that happened on the distant Earth. Then, the Earth sent its delegates to this planet. . . .

Suddenly Cui Yining grasped Linwu's hand.

"Now I know!" His voice betrayed excitement. "They had recognized that our spacemen were Chinese, so they have prepared the films shot about China produced over thousands of years to welcome us with. . . ."

Linwu nodded in agreement. Then he pressed a button: Atop the hill in Uiqid, near the crater through which they had come a short while ago, stood an extraordinarily gorgeous palace. A few people came out . . . ah, blue men! Behold, they were turning round, high-browed, unfathomably large eyes, enigmatic smiles, glossy blue skin—facing the astronauts. The strange people waved their hands, muttered something, and climbed into a spaceship near the palace. In the twinkling of an eye, the spaceship took off, the launchpad broke down, and the palace fell to pieces, leaving a heap of ashes. . . .

The scene faded out. In the silent cave, still enveloped in the faint purple light, there was not the slightest sound, except the hard breathing of the astronauts.

After a long lapse, Linwu Sheng said, somewhat sadly, "They've gone away . . . to other planets; they don't want to meet us. . . ."

"But why?" asked Gu Mingwei almost inaudibly.

"Perhaps . . . they know us better than we do ourselves," said Cui Yining gently.

"But," Du Yinlin was impatient, "living beings on different planets should have friendly exchanges, shouldn't they?"

Cui shook his head emphatically: "They don't live in the same stage of civilization as we do. While we were burning books and burying scholars alive, they had already mastered the technique of laser holographic photography and the means of long-distance space travel. They have developed thousands of years earlier than we have. So, to them, we're simply barbarians. Now, why should they be friendly and believe the savages? They would naturally think we might attack them any moment with machine guns and tanks, or with old weapons like flintlocks, spears, big swords, and bricks. . . ."

"How about ourselves," Linwu chuckled. "Do we believe in ourselves?"

"But," Du Yinlin cut in, "if their civilization is more advanced than ours by thousands of years, why should they be afraid of tanks and machine guns?"

"Oh," her husband murmured straight away, "historically speaking, all advanced civilizations did not necessarily triumph. Genghis Khan was a perfect case in point. His nomadic tribes wiped out all the flourishing civilizations in Asia and Europe, but. . . ."

"Well, I see," Linwu said with a sudden realization, "why there are no animals on this planet. Because the Uiqidians have packed them off. They are the modern Noah."

"Are we, people from the Earth, so terrible?" Gu Mingwei said sorrowfully.

"Sure, but people on the Earth aren't all the same. We all know that some are just like . . . fierce flood and savage beast . . ." said Cui Yining, stressing every word of the simile.

On the various planets the astronauts visited later on, they did not find the Uiqidians who had emigrated from their native planet. It did not necessarily mean that they had evaporated, or "exploded" like a supernova. They had just gone to some unknown place inaccessible to humans.

No matter how hard human beings try to probe the universe, they cannot uncover all of its wonders, as they are so multicolored, inexhaustible, and mysterious. Is this not true?

*Translated by Sun Liang*

## NOTES

1. Diqiu—the Chinese word for the Earth, in pinyin.

2. The spectacular palace built by the decree of the first Emperor of the Qin dynasty [221–207 B.C.]. It was located in the northwest suburb of present-day Xian, in Shanxi Province. Towards the end of the Qin dynasty, the palace was burned to ashes by insurgent troops.

# 7

# Corrosion

## YE YONGLIE

A snow-white helicopter, with a big red cross painted on each side, hovered over the vast desert in northwestern China, only four or five hundred feet above the ground. Inside the chopper, everyone looked grave and a bit anxious. In contrast to the white coats and caps they wore, their faces appeared gloomy. They were all silent, listening to the monotonous moaning of the engine. The hatch window, shaped like the eye of a golden fish, protruded from the front of the chopper. A girl craned her neck, absorbed in looking out the window at the immense land below.

The desert, boundless sea of sand, appeared in a variety of strange forms: some looked like tree-rings; some took the shape of a huge flat piece of paper made of sand. The hot summer sun, a fiery ball above the fiery desert, baked the sand with its blinding rays. On this sea of sand nothing could be seen except one tiny black spot, moving steadily. That was the shadow of the chopper.

At the beginning of the flight, they could strain to see the green spots here and there, though they were no larger than the sesames sprinkled on a Chinese pancake when seen at such a height. But gradually even those few tiny dots faded out of sight like the outgoing morning stars at the approach of dawn. At last, they could see nothing but an immense yellow below—light yellow, golden yellow, ashy yellow, brown yellow, soil yellow, and milky yellow.

Published in *Renmin wenxue* (People's Literature), November 1981.

The girl's big, black, diamond-like eyes kept on staring out the window. She had a beautiful figure. Her cheeks were rosy and her nose small and straight. She bit her lips slightly and appeared very self-confident. Now, with her eyebrows knitted, she seemed to be searching for something.

"It's there! It's there!" All of a sudden the girl burst out in ecstasy, as if she had discovered a new continent. At the same instant, the people sitting on the left side of the helicopter also cried out in unison.

Down on the left a waving mass, painted red and white, was lying conspicuously on the light brown sand. Beside it was a cone-shaped dark brown object, slanting skywards.

The chopper churned toward them. Again the girl cried out, "The parachute! That's the 'Silver Star'!" They descended. Yes, the huge mass in red and white lying on the sand was the parachute. The cone-shaped object was the control capsule of the spaceship "Silver Star."

China's spaceship "Silver Star," after its long voyage in outer space, had finally landed on the desert. The spaceship was manned by one astronaut. But on its voyage home, the astronaut lost radio contact with the control center on earth. No cause had been discovered, which only suggested the great possibility of an accident.

The chopper landed over a hundred meters away from the "Silver Star." The rotor kept revolving like a huge electric fan and blew the brown sand across the ground. At once the atmosphere was filled with a brown mass; the sky suddenly looked menacing.

The air conditioning inside the hatch was turned on. But as soon as the door was opened, a wave of scathing air greeted them. Wearing dark sunglasses, they limped through the soft sand. Every step left behind a shallow pit, but kicked off a screen of dust and sand.

Striding foremost in the team was Han Pin, the head of the "Space Emergency Rescue Team." He stopped before the capsule and skillfully opened the tightly sealed door. By this time, the girl and several other team members, gasping and sweating, had all rushed over. They peeped inside; a strong sickening smell, like that of rotten garlic, greeted their totally unprepared nostrils and almost made them vomit. The astronaut was there, leaning motionless against a corner. His helmet and seat were broken. Obviously, he had died a long time ago.

Han Pin crawled into the capsule, but he nearly screamed as soon as he put his feet in: the floor was like the soft sand; one step would produce a deep hole and send off a wind of dust!

Everything inside was in a terrible mess. Han Pin randomly picked up the cushion on the astronaut's seat. At his touch, unexpectedly, it disintegrated into pieces and slipped through his fingers as if it were a newly curdled piece of beancurd snatched up by mistake. He moved toward the dead astronaut. Barely had his gloved hand contacted his space suit when he found his fingertips had made big holes in it. The space suit was made with over ten layers of synthetic fibers, but now it was like a piece of thin paper!

"Corrosion! It must be the most terrible corrosion!" The team leader's judgment was quick and instinctive. He started withdrawing toward the exit, but stepped right on the girl's toes. She had crawled in too, and in spite of the unbearable smell, was collecting into a sample bottle bits and pieces of the broken equipment scattered across the floor.

The radio immediately brought the shocking news, from the heart of the desert, to the headquarters of the Chinese Space Center. "Interior of 'Silver Star' found most horribly corroded. Cause unknown. Astronaut dead." This short message exploded, like a powerful bomb, at General Control in the center.

Most horribly corroded? Nothing of the kind had happened since people's first conquest of space in 1957! China's spaceships had often visited stars both near and far away, but never had this kind of thing happened to them!

General Control immediately held an emergency meeting.

Again the radio waves relayed new developments in the desert: "General Control, from the sample I collected from the 'Silver Star,' I've discovered an ultra-corrosive bacteria hitherto unknown from outer space. Its color is bright yellow, and its shape X type. Everyone in our team has been contaminated. The patient's symptom is feeling cold and shivering; one has already died. The team leader has lost consciousness. The other members cannot be expected to last long. Please don't organize any rescue. We want to make it clear that we would rather die in the desert than live to see the spread of this ultra-corrosive bacteria as a result of our rescue. Please pass the above information to our teacher, Professor Du Wei of the Department of Biology at Bin Hai University. Over. Li Li."

Five minutes later, Li Li sent an additional message.

"General Control, it has been discovered in the capsule that only the engine, certain instruments, and the hull and frame of the ship, which are all made of titanium, remain uncorroded. The team leader is dead. We will be gone soon. Over. Li Li."

While all this was going on, Professor Du Wei, shaded by a grapevine, was drinking Long Jing green tea and playing *Weiqi* (a game played with black and white pieces on a board of 361 crosses). Professor Du was short and thin, his gray hair was cut short. This most prominent authority on biology was once Li Li's teacher, but his appearance gave one an impression that he was an old watchmaker!

It was a Sunday. The summer afternoon was so stifling that Du Wei found it impossible to get any work done, so he retreated to his cool backyard and played *Weiqi* instead.

His opponent was a youth about thirty. His figure was like a bean sprout, tall and thin. His face was white, and his cheeks hollow. His eyeballs were like the black pieces they were playing, big and sparkling. A mere glance at the young man and one would say, "He must be extremely intelligent." Dressed in his pants and shirt, he slowly waved the foldable fan in his hand. He was Wang Chong, nicknamed "Small White Face." He was one of Professor Du Wei's best students.

They had already "fought" two rounds, Du Wei winning the first and Wang Chong the second. This was the last and decisive round. "Ta!" Professor Du Wei put a black piece on the "Star Position" in the upper-right corner. "Ta!" Wang Chong placed a white piece on the "Star Position" in the upper-left corner, as a direct countermeasure. The "battle" grew more intense. After some time, Wang Chong was sweeping over the field when he suddenly noticed his professor's dismal look. He at once deliberately made a "strategic error" in his advance and rapidly lost part of his field. The game ended in a draw.

Just then they heard footsteps approaching. Du Wei's wife showed in a young man. The man was of medium stature, about thirty years old. He had a big square face, thick eyebrows and big eyes. His lips were rather full. He was wearing a shirt and shorts, his muscles looking strong and well-developed. He was Fan Shuan, another of Professor Du Wei's assistants. As he would smile before speaking and would unwittingly show his white teeth, which looked like the white pieces the other two were playing, people had nicknamed him "Blacks' toothpaste."

"Professor Du, the department has just received an urgent telegram for you." Fan Shuan handed Du Wei the telegram.

When Wang Chong saw the beads of sweat oozing from Fan Shuan's forehead, he at once offered him his fan.

"Too careless!" Du Wei finally let out a long sigh. He well remembered that at the beginning of space travel, his professor and other authorities on geology warned that some kind of terrible microorganism may exist on other planets in space. Therefore, the astronauts must go through a most thorough disinfection by a chemical composed of iodine-oxygen-hydrogen-sodium. But later, after so many successful space voyages, people had never encountered the feared "terrible microorganism." The worry was thought to be completely unnecessary. The process of disinfection was abolished and the disinfectant equipment on the spaceships removed. Many people even laughed at Du Wei for worrying too much! Though Du Wei's professor had been dead a long time, his prediction was finally proven by the events today. The luckiest thing of the whole tragedy, however, was that the spaceship "Silver Star" landed in a desert, which meant that it would be extremely difficult for the ultra-corrosive microorganism—or bacteria—from outer space to reproduce and spread. Just imagine if the spaceship had landed in the sea; that tiny monster from outerspace might have literally eaten up the earth and reduced everything to dust.

Du Wei handed over Li Li's telegram to the two young assistants.

When Fan Shuan read it, the face of this young man, who would usually smile before speaking, suddenly became stiff and expressionless, as if his muscles had become petrified. His heart seemed to be filled with lead, unbearably heavy.

When Wang Chong read the telegram, the young man's face instantly grew pale and his eyes lost their sparkle. Fan Shuan and he had both taught Li Li. This charming and intelligent girl had made him feel something strange and exciting. After Li Li had graduated, they kept a correspondence which was growing more frequent and intimate. . . . Now, this telegram out of the blue hit him in the head like a violent blow. He found himself shivering and trembling. He seemed to witness his love fall down in the desert and the ferocious wind roll along the brown sand, enshrouding the girl's body and burying her deep in the. . . .

"What do you think?" asked Du Wei, looking at the two grief-stricken assistants. But both of them remained silent and only watched the old professor with questioning eyes, as if to say, "We're waiting for your decision, Professor."

A moment of silence. Then Du Wei stood up and, in his slow but serious tone, expressed his plans:

"This is a matter of life and death for the entire human species. I'm flying to the Space Center right away and then leaving for the desert.

"I think we must set up a special lab for research on this outer space microorganism. But the lab must be built in the desert lest the ultra-corrosive bacteria spread by some chance. I'm going to the desert to build the lab and do the research. But I'm now old and feeble. I hope one of you will go and work with me. But please understand that this will mean a three or five years' isolation in the desert. Who's going and who's staying; I'm now waiting for you to decide."

As soon as Du Wei finished, he watched Wang Chong expectantly, for in Du Wei's mind Wang Chong was a rung above Fan Shuan as far as intelligence and ability were concerned. In the face of such important research, naturally enough, Du Wei would hope to take with him the most competent and helpful assistant.

"I'm going!" Fan Shuan was quick, and his words were quicker.

"Then I'll let you decide, Professor!" Wang Chong answered, after a pause. "Going is work; staying is also work. I don't mind if I go or stay."

"All right. I'll decide after my talk with President Yang of our university," said Du Wei.

\*     \*     \*     \*     \*

Five years had passed.

During this period of time, Du Wei and Fan Shuan had led a completely isolated life. In this sea of sand, they had greeted and seen off five springs and autumns.

Five years ago when Du Wei and Fan Shuan flew in a chopper hovering low over the landing site of the "Silver Star," they saw with their own eyes many people, dressed in white uniforms, curled up—dead—on the brown sand, some of them already half-buried in the sand. Du Wei and Fan Shuan found their eyes blurred. Tears streamed down Du Wei's cheeks along the deep wrinkles leading down from his eye sockets, while Fan Shuan, who always remained calm and tough, suddenly found tears welling up and overflowing his eyes.

The chopper continued flying forward and Du Wei chose the heart of the desert for the site of the lab. For a few days helicopters continually landed and took off from the chosen site. The Space Center sent over a group of young men and soon the lab was completed. The round-shaped lab was built half above ground and half under ground, resembling a "pillbox."

Inside the lab, everything was bright and shiny: the walls, ceilings, floors, and all kinds of equipment; almost all of them were made of titanium.

Titanium was a kind of metal that possessed the qualities accorded to a hero: It was bright, light, but extremely hard. The most powerful chemical corrosive liquid could reduce silver and even gold to nothingness, but would be powerless when dealing with titanium. When the metal was discovered in the 18th century, it was called "titanium," derived from the name of the heroes in Greek mythology. In ancient Greece, the "Titan's Spirit" was a synonym for courage and determination. By the information given by Li Li before her death, Du Wei chose this "heroic metal" to help conquer the monster from outerspace.

After the silvery "pillbox" was set up, Du Wei ordered the engineers and workers to leave, in several batches, by chopper. At last only he, Fan Shuan, and a minihelicopter remained behind.

Everything had by now been carefully prepared. Du Wei and Fan Shuan put on special protective suits, which looked like space suits, but with their surfaces plated with titanium. The helmet was also titanium-plated. When seen from outside, it seemed to be a mirror; but when looking from inside, the wearer could see everything. Du Wei and Fan Shuan looked at each other and immediately burst into a hearty laugh: Both of them were radiating silvery light from head to toe. Du Wei remarked that they were the medieval armored knights, while Fan Shuan joked, in plainest words, that they looked like two naked thermos bottles!

Fan Shuan liked sports and could drive a car, a motorbike, a speedboat, and even fly a helicopter. When he settled into the pilot's seat, he suddenly turned around and told Du Wei that he had left his water bottle behind. Could he go back to the lab and bring it?

Fan Shuan had never sent his teacher on an errand before. Du Wei thus believed that he had really forgotten to bring the bottle. So he descended from the chopper and walked toward the lab. Just then he heard the sudden roaring noise of the engine. He looked around; the rotor of the chopper was revolving at high speed and blowing sand high into the air. In seconds the chopper was airborne and left Du Wei alone in the vast desert. Watching it disappearing into the distance, Du Wei once more found big and crystal-like tears rolling down his eyes. He knew clearly the enormous danger in collecting the sample at the landing site. But Fan Shuan almost forced him—his teacher—to stay behind and went alone, in the "Titan's Spirit," to the place that was even more dangerous than a burning fire or a pot of boiling oil!

And Du Wei's mind was tormented with fear and anxiety until Fan Shuan returned, safe and sound, two hours later. He hurried toward the chopper. But unexpectedly, when Fan Shuan climbed out of the chopper, he simply shouted at his teacher, like a furious lion, "Move away!"

Completely wrapped in his silvery protective suit, Fan Shuan gripped a glittering sample bottle and rushed directly to the disinfection room. He immediately locked the door from inside when he got in. Automatically, beams of disinfectant liquid rushed out in all directions and washed him clean from head to toe.

Only after this most thorough disinfection did Fan Shuan take off the armor-like protective suit and walk out of the room.

"I've collected the sample of the ultra-corrosive bacteria," he told Du Wei. But he didn't smile and his eyebrows almost drew together. It was after some time that he released a long sad sigh, "Nobody survived!"

He related the heart-rending sight he had seen. After he had collected the sample, or the "seed," of ultra-corrosive bacteria from the capsule of the "Silver Star" and shut it in the sample bottle made of titanium, he went to see the Emergency Rescue Team. They had all been so corroded that their faces were hardly distinguishable.

"If the disinfection was not thorough enough, we would soon meet the same tragic end." Du Wei said calmly and slowly, his eyes glittering. "Doing scientific research is as risky as fighting a war. Sometimes the fruit can only be picked at the price of human lives. Please record what you have seen on the landing site. If we should run into the same bad luck, perhaps the notes would leave something to our successors."

From that day on they had made a very detailed record of their work each day. They were fully prepared to say, at any time, a final farewell to this world.

Fan Shuan also took on the radio communication with the Space Center. Whenever they needed something, they would radio the Center to send choppers to drop it. Since the completion of the lab, Du Wei had forbidden any aircraft to land there, or anyone to visit them. The danger of the spread of the ultra-corrosive bacteria could thus be eliminated. Of course, neither of them was going to leave this place.

Life in the desert was like the desert itself: dull and dry. Except wind, there was no rain, no snow, no dew, nor frost. Occasionally they would see the clouds gathering and drops of rain hanging in the sky. But they were evaporated and dispersed by wind even before they reached the ground.

Water here was more precious than gold. Their only supply came in by air. Du Wei and Fan Shuan used most of the water for experiments; as for their daily needs, they would have split each drop into pieces to make it plentiful if they had been able to! Before going to bed each night, they would take a walk, barefooted, in the desert, "washing" their feet with sand, the substitute for water.

Time flew by rapidly. Day by day, week by week, Du Wei and Fan Shuan closely studied the "monster" which they had securely confined to the containers made of titanium. They had studied its shapes and formations, its living habits and biological history, and its reproduction. After the first year's work, they had had some plausible answers to these questions.

Another question that followed was more complicated but fascinating. It had cost most of their energy and time. Why did the ultra-corrosive bacteria possess such extraordinary power? Could they make use of it in the interests of mankind?

Industry was invariably rewarded with a big harvest; sweat and sleepless nights would lead to ultimate successes. After a few more years' research, Du Wei and Fan Shuan finally discovered that the ultra-corrosive power of the bacteria lay in a kind of corrosive fluid the bacteria secreted. Though the bacteria would contaminate and destroy human lives, the corrosive fluid it secreted would only corrode objects, but would not harm, even slightly, human beings. The case was analogous to that of penicillin: The element the bacteria secreted would be made into medicine to cure and save people. Finally, Du Wei and Fan Shuan, after a series of difficult and energy-consuming experiments, succeeded in extracting from the bacteria the pure corrosive fluid—a kind of light yellow oil-like fluid. Even when it had been diluted by water at the proportion of one drop to several million, it would turn hard rock into dust when a few drops of the mixture were poured over the surface of the rocks. When splashed on a safe, the steel would instantly become a heap of rust. When poured into a glass bottle, the bottle would be reduced to nothing in a fraction of a second! Even silver and gold had to succumb to this monster; they immediately lost their brightness merely at the touch of the mixture.

In the evenings Du Wei and Fan Shuan sat in their "pillbox" watching the numberless stars decorate the sky. Then they would imagine what would happen if they succeeded. In the future people would only need to use a little corrosive fluid to demolish a concrete skyscraper. If people encountered mountains when building highways or railways, they would use the fluid to "raze" them to the ground. The disposal of million of tons of urban garbage would no longer be a tiresome burden; they would be turned into soil and used to level the swamps. When man wanted to dig up the valuable minerals buried deep under the ground, shafts and tunnels would not be necessary as they could readily resort to the fluid to remove the rock shell and exploit an open cut. . . .

The imagined beautiful future made Du Wei and Fan Shuan quite forget their physical discomfort caused by the aridity; forget the dullness and loneliness in the desert; forget the overhanging danger that was likely to take their lives at any moment. . . . They became more confident and worked even harder.

Wang Chong spent these five years quite comfortably at Bin Hai University.

But a small incident not long ago made him feel quite unhappy.

That was an unusual day. He took off his Chinese jacket and put on an ironed Western suit. He was now slightly fat. His face was white and round and, after shaving off his beard with an electric razor, looked handsome and pleasant. An important delegation of scientists was coming to visit the university that day, and President Yang asked him to receive them.

When greeting the foreign scientists, President Yang introduced Wang Chong to them. "This is Mr. Wang Chong, associate professor and acting chairman of the Department of Biology."

All of a sudden, Wang Chong's face clouded, though only for a second. But he resumed his smiles at once and shook hands with the guests one by one. For a whole day and deep down in his heart, however, he felt very unhappy.

The words "acting" and "associate" really hurt his pride.

In the past five years, Wang Chong had been quite successful. He had published many theses and was promoted from lecturer to associate professor. He was also now the acting chairman of the Department of Biology, but only *acting* since the real chairman, Professor Du Wei, was still alive.

However, people always addressed him as "Chairman Wang," instead of "Acting Chairman Wang," and "Professor Wang," instead of "Associate Professor Wang." Whether this resulted from custom or an inclination to shorter and simpler titles it was hard to determine. Though President Yang's introduction was perfectly correct, Wang Chong, who was used to being called "Chairman Wang" and "Professor Wang," felt as if someone had just rubbed salt into an old wound.

Then he suddenly remembered Professor Du Wei, his memory of whom had been gradually fading away—

When Du Wei and Fan Shuan went to the desert five years before, they kept a very frequent correspondence with Wang Chong. Du Wei would cable the Space Center every two or three days to relay his messages to Wang Chong. There were sometimes requests for new equipment, or sometimes questions about some data, or sometimes questions about the situation in the department. At that time Wang Chong always did everything possible to meet Du Wei's needs, as he felt a kind of guilt for not going to the desert with Du Wei.

As time passed and when word came that Du Wei and Fan Shuan had made little progress in the bleak desert, their communication became less frequent. After Wang Chong was promoted to acting chairman of the department, he was so busy with his work that he could seldom afford the time to help them or even ask about their work. But Du Wei continually sent in requests, through the Space Center, for all kinds of information and data. As he was too busy, Wang Chong would shift these chores to his assistant.

Things went on like this for a long time, but whenever on holiday or festival, Wang Chong would, no matter how busy he was, visit Professor Du Wei's wife to show his concern and a student's respect for his teacher.

On the Mid-Autumn Festival this year, Wang Chong, holding a box of mooncakes in one hand, again went to see Mrs. Du. Among all of Professor Du's best students, the one Mrs. Du liked most was Wang Chong. He was urbane, intelligent, and considerate.

Wang Chong put down the mooncakes and asked Mrs. Du, very concernedly, if she was all right and whether the Pay Office was sending over Professor Du's salary every month. But he was greatly surprised when Mrs. Du told him that Professor Du had sent her a short cable a few days before, saying that they had made tremendous progress in their research.

Though Mrs. Du could give no details of that "tremendous progress," Wang Chong instinctively felt that this was an extraordinary message.

On his way home, he constantly looked up at the full moon. It was so bright, so pure, like a silver ball, but the image that appeared in the center was not "Chang E"—the Moon goddess in Chinese mythology, but Professor Du Wei. Wang Chong kept on asking himself, "Will they really make an earth-shaking discovery?"

He was already at the door of his own home when he suddenly turned back and went to his assistant's home. Wang Chong carefully examined Du Wei's messages relayed to the department through the Space Center. Now he was convinced that Du Wei and Fan Shuan were approaching a really important breakthrough!

He paced the room pensively, his hands locked behind his back—his habitual gesture when he was lost in deep thought. But his mood was both confused and complex. All those years he had been feeling fortunate that he didn't get "buried" in the desert. If he had followed Du Wei at that time, he would never have been the acting chairman and associate professor, as he was now. There would never have been any promise of a bright future for him. But now he suddenly came to realize that, after several years' hard work, a launching pad had been erected in the heart of the desert and was going to catapult a "star" that was sure to shake the whole world! Wang Chong had at his fingertips the current situation of the international scientific community, and was certain that his judgment was right. He was also aware of what it would mean if the monster from outer space were captured and conquered in the desert.

As to what would happen if the "star" in the desert was successfully launched, Wang Chong made the following predictions. It would mean very little to Du Wei, as he was already the No. 1 authority in China in the field of biology, though the new success, of course, would do much to increase his international prestige. As a Chinese saying goes, "A good teacher will never fail to bring up the best students." The rise of his teacher Du Wei's fame would have a beneficial side effect on Wang Chong. But he was most afraid of Fan Shuan. They used to "ride neck to neck" in class; they graduated from the same class at the same university; they were assigned to work at this university at the same time; they completed their graduate studies under Professor Du Wei at the same time; they became assistants and later lecturers also at the same time. Wang Chong was very clear that he was a rung above Fan Shuan as far as their special field and ability were concerned. During the past five years, Wang Chong's numerous publications had brought him the title "associate professor." If the situation lasted, a full professorship was a sure thing for him in a few years. But Fan Shuan had published nothing during this period and was still a lecturer. Most people knew that it wasn't very difficult to rise from an assistant to the position of a lecturer. But it was no easy thing to get promoted from a lecturer to an associate professor—there were many people who had achieved little in their fields and were still lecturers when they retired! However, if Fan Shuan made an earth-shaking discovery, it would astound the international field of biologists. By the time Fan Shuan returned triumphantly from the desert, he would be very possibly promoted to a full professor, which was in itself unusual and significant. He would even have full credit to a membership in the renowned "Academy of Science!"

Jealousy was the hostile reaction by a common mind against uncommon talent. Wang Chong's heartbeats quickened at once, his face felt hot, and his eyes grew green.

Early next morning, Wang Chong sent a cable to Du Wei, "Happy to learn of your progress. Glad to help if you need me."

But he didn't expect that the answer would come so quickly. On that very afternoon the Space Center relayed to him a message from the desert: Professor Du Wei would welcome Wang Chong to join the research to conquer the ultra-corrosive bacteria! Professor Du Wei believed that after the molecular formation of the corrosive fluid was discovered, the next step would be to synthesize it by chemical and artificial means. But this complex and big project could not be carried out in the desert because of the poor conditions there. He hoped Wang Chong would organize a special team which would include faculty members of the Department of Chemistry, in order to work on this project of unusual importance. Since the ultra-corrosive fluid was a lifeless matter and would not reproduce and contaminate as the ultra-corrosive bacteria did, it would be safe to start this research at Bin Hai University.

Wang Chong's face beamed, all his worries thrown away. He replied, "O.K.!"

In order to facilitate direct communication with Professor Du Wei, the university set up a special radio station. From then on, messages didn't have to go through the relay system of the Space Center.

A mysterious looking special lab soon appeared in the enormous building of the Department of Biology. Its ceilings, floors, walls, doors, windows, furniture, and equipment were all made of the shining metal, titanium.

Wang Chong proved to be a real talent. Under his leadership, the synthesis of ultra-corrosive fluid made a promising start after only a year's work.

Just then a group of foreign biologists came to visit the department. Again dressed in his well-ironed Western suit, Wang Chong showed the visitors around the building and talked to them in his fluent English. When they passed by one lab, its glittering doors and window, shut tightly, at once aroused their attention.

Although Du Wei had repeatedly warned Wang Chong, "Don't open the cover of the pot until it's the ripe time," now when he found himself focused on by so many imploring eyes, the temptation to show off was simply irresistible. His words automatically flowed out and briefed the visitors on this extraordinary research under way.

The visitors were completely taken by surprise. They at once beseiged Wang Chong and earnestly begged him to let them see the lab. At last, Wang Chong had to refuse their request under the pretext of "preventing contamination."

Fifteen days later, the chairman of the International Association of Biology, Dr. Johnson, sent a telegram inviting Chinese biologists to speak at a convention on the first "monster" from outer space that humans had ever captured—the ultra-corrosive bacteria. The journal *International Microbiology* also cabled the university, offering to publish the Chinese biologists' paper on this topic.

A word said was like a bucket of water poured out—it could never be retrieved. Since the international biological circle was so enthusiastic and concerned about the project, it was fully justified to send people to speak. But who should go? The only candidate was Wang Chong! Neither Du Wei nor Fan Shuan could leave the desert. What would happen if they, or their transportation, should be contaminated with the ultra-corrosive bacteria. It was impossible to imagine.

Therefore, Wang Chong again seized the chance that he had craved for, without any difficulty or pains. It was soon decided that Wang Chong would go to speak at the convention. His white face again beamed.

He immediately set to work on the greatest part of the whole scheme—writing the research paper. It was precisely at this point that the smiles lingering on his face disappeared. As the work was done by Du Wei and Fan Shuan, at a price of so many years' sweat and blood, Wang Chong knew very little of its specific details. Even though Wang Chong was quick and smart, "a first rate cook cannot make a meal out of nothing." He had only done the work concerning the chemical synthesis and he could write only that part.

What could he do? The only thing to do was ask Du Wei and Fan Shuan to write the paper.

After he cabled them for the paper, he began to pace the room, with his hands habitually locked behind his back. Would they "hold back something?" Would they not write down the key data? Especially Fan Shuan, who "rode neck to neck" with him? Perhaps he would hold back something. According to Wang Chong's experience, holding back some important data was quite a frequent phenomenon in scientific circles. If you didn't hold back something, how could you win when the crucial moment came? If they held back something—

He kept on pacing to and fro, now worrying about another question: How should the paper be signed? The signature on the paper was an important thing that indicated to whom the honor should belong. This was as divine a thing as the signature on a patent certificate. Wang Chong thought the authors of the paper were, of course, three people—Du Wei, Fan Shuan, and himself. The order of the signatures would most likely be Du Wei, Fan Shuan, and Wang Chong. By the recognized convention, it was natural to put Du Wei, the renowned authority, first. The key issue was where would Fan Shuan's name stand. If Fan Shuan's signature was arranged before his, then—

Du Wei once remarked that Wang Chong was "exceptionally bright but too smart." Here and now Wang Chong was still pacing the room, his mind tortured by his over-smartness. And he never expected that the torture would last for more than a week. Du Wei and Fan Shuan had not replied—whether they were really going to keep back something or whether they were busy drafting the paper, it was hard to tell. This "long" period of silence made Wang Chong impatient, unhappy, nervous, and even caused him to suffer insomnia.

After more than a week, a long, long cable was at last received from the desert. Obviously, it was the paper.

Wang Chong could hardly wait to read it. Below the title were the signatures of the authors. Though Wang Chong was "exceptionally bright," this time he could not believe what he saw, for he had never anticipated that the first name was not Du Wei, nor Fan Shuan, nor Wang Chong, but Li Li!

As if in a dream, he saw a girl's beautiful figure appear before his eyes; her face was rosy, and her nose small and straight. Her lips were slightly pouted, her big eyes a pair of black diamonds. . . . She was so familiar to Wang Chong! He once gave his heart to her. But after six years, he had forgotten. . . .

Wang Chong's eyes opened wide. He never imagined that Du Wei and Fan Shuan still remembered her and put her name first in the line. His eyes fell upon the deciphered cable. After Li Li were the names of the other three authors; the order was Du Wei, Wang Chong, Fan Shuan.

This again surprised Wang Chong. He had feverishly hoped that his name would be put before Fan Shuan's, but he could not believe that the cable from the desert would arrange the names this way!

He read the long paper word by word. Himself an expert, he could tell, at the first glance, that the paper was logical, well-organized, carefully detailed, and had real substance. There was no sign of "holding back something." This made Wang Chong very happy. The paper highly praised Li Li's role in the research and called her "The discoverer of the ultra-corrosive bacteria." She was also the first one to define clearly the shapes and formations of the bacteria. She was the first to find that the metal titanium was immune to corrosion by the bacteria. These discoveries of hers paved the way for the later research. The paper recommended that the bacterium be named "Li's Bacterium," in memory of this young female scientist who gave up her life for this research.

However, why Wang Chong's name was written before Fan Shuan he could not understand. He read the paper three times at one sitting. By its style and diction, Fan Shuan was evidently its author. As the writer of the paper, Wang Chong reasoned, Fan Shuan might fear that, if he put his own name before Wang Chong's, he would have trouble when he gave the paper to Professor Du Wei for approval. So he had to stand in the second place. Though it was done quite unwillingly, he had no choice. . . .

Except for inserting his part on the chemical synthesis of the fluid, written at Professor Du Wei's suggestion, Wang Chong left the other parts completely unchanged. He translated it into English and had it sent to typing.

When the typed English translation was brought in, Wang Chong's eyes stayed on the signatures for a long time, saying to himself: "Li Li is dead. It doesn't matter that she stands first in the paper. It's natural to put Du Wei in the second place. I'm the third because on the draft it was arranged this way!" He felt elated and comforted himself.

His wishes were completely fulfilled.

His sharp black leather shoes shining, Wang Chong stepped on the soft red carpet and strode toward the podium. Tide after tide of ovations were ringing in his ears. The light flooded the dais. Numberless cameras, television and film crews all focused on him.

Though Wang Chong had been abroad, his short experience and low status made him no more than an ordinary representative at conventions. But he was totally changed today. He was now the "celebrity" in the press. His image appeared in newspapers, on television and film screens.

"Wang—Hero Who Has Conquered Monster from Space," "Wang—Titan Who Doesn't Fear Corrosion," "Wang—Founder of Space Biology," "Wang—Opening a New Epoch in Biology. . . ." These headlines, printed in big letters, filled the front page of every newspaper to introduce to the readers the distinguished Mr. Wang Chong, who was overwhelmed with self-content and elation whenever looking at them. He had never enjoyed such great honor. But whenever the thought of the desert flashed through his mind, whenever he realized what little idea he had about the down-to-earth research out there, his light heart would suddenly grow heavy. He was preoccupied with an unspeakable feeling of emptiness. Honor and vanity were woven into a complexly patterned net of emotion. His mind was in a ferment. For so many years Wang Chong had been yearning, or rather dreaming, to rise to international fame one day. But he had never thought that, when that day really came, he would feel so inexplicably pained.

Invitations to banquets flew at him like snowflakes. Wang Chong could hardly manage it. A private banquet was given by Dr. Johnson, the chairman of the International Association of Biology. After several toasts to Wang Chong, he said jokingly, "Mr. Wang, have you ever thought that your extraordinary discovery and success may win this year's Nobel Prize?"

"Oh?" Wang Chong was surprised. He had not given a thought about it.

"You are really fortunate," Dr. Johnson smiled, his blue eyes half-closed. "The Nobel Foundation stipulates that, if the work is done with the collaborated efforts of many people, only three of them will be chosen as winners. To win this prize is an uncomparable honor, and trouble always arises because only three people can be the winners. But luckily, your work was done by Mr. Du, Mr. Fan and you—just three people. So there won't be any problem about who shall be the winners. Mr. Wang, let me wish, though rather too early, that you will win the Nobel Prize!"

The speaker was not serious, but the listener was. The chairman's casual remark was at once imprinted in Wang Chong's mind. Wang Chong knew that the annual Nobel Prize was decided in extreme secrecy by the Swedish Academy of Science. Even the winners themselves didn't have any ideas about it until the results were announced, nor would the international science community learn anything about the selection beforehand.

Dr. Johnson's words were, of course, dinner table jokes. But they alarmed Wang Chong into remembering the paper he hadn't turned in. It was signed by four authors! Throughout his speeches, Wang Chong had mentioned that the discovery of the ultra-corrosive bacteria had cost Li Li her life, but, when talking about the research, Wang Chong only mentioned Du Wei and Fan Shuan. Naturally, Dr. Johnson took it that the paper was written by three people.

Though the clock had struck twelve, Wang Chong was still slowly pacing in his hotel room, his head hung low, his eyebrows in a tight knot. On the desk lay the typed paper, and the correction fluid he had just bought.

"Three or four. Four or three, one more. . . ." These two figures were leaping up and down in Wang Chong's mind. The associate professor found himself hopeless before this simplest of arithmetic problems. The convention would terminate tomorrow and the paper would have to be turned in. Wang Chong felt lucky that Dr. Johnson brought that up today.

He stopped and sat at his desk. On the paper the names of the four authors were clearly typed out:

Li Li        Du Wei        Wang Chong        Fan Shuan

He took the bottle containing the correction fluid in one hand; the lid had a small brush underneath. If the brush was to dip on anyone's name, that name would disappear from the paper in an instant.

But whose name should go?

Du Wei? No, it wouldn't be possible; neither was it necessary. Wang Chong himself? Of course not! Fan Shuan. Yes, that was exactly what he secretly hoped. But wait a minute. Oh, no! He couldn't go! If Fan Shuan's name were not there, everyone would see that he had gone too far. That would give him endless trouble. Fan Shuan had already been treated unfairly as his name was arranged after Wang Chong's!

He racked his brains and concluded that the only name he could erase was Li Li's. Looking at the name, Wang Chong suddenly visualized her charming and pleasant image; the memories of those sweet and happy meetings came alive. If only she hadn't met that disaster. . . .

The unforgettable past made Wang Chong hesitate. If he erased Li Li's name, he would be permanently tormented by a guilty conscience.

But finally he managed to list the reasons for erasing Li Li's name. First, Li Li didn't participate in the research, so why should she be one of the authors? Second, she was highly spoken of in the paper and her name was recommended for the title of the ultra-corrosive bacteria. That was the honor she deserved.

Wang Chong took up the small brush, his hand slightly trembling. But when the brush was approaching "Li Li," the slight trembling became violent shaking. He stopped again. Should he tell the truth, and let the

Swedish Academy of Science make the choice? The reasons to get Li Li's name off the paper were clearly out there. Others would see them . . . , but if. . . . He bit his lips hard and tried his best to calm down. At last he decisively pressed down the brush, the fluid "covered" Li Li's name quickly and thoroughly, as if it had never been there.

Again, the tragic scene of Li Li falling down in the desert flashed across his eyes. Though he wasn't there to see it, the imagined scene made his heart writhe in unspeakable pain.

He confusedly grabbed a newspaper and hastily covered the paper on which only three names remained now. But unexpectedly, the big striking headline on the front page of that newspaper read: "Wang—Hero Who Has Conquered Monster from Space!" Again, his heart was filled with guilt.

Not long after he had returned to China, Wang Chong received three copies of *International Microbiology*, sent by its editor. Their paper was printed on the front page; three names: "Du Wei, Wang Chong, Fan Shuan," printed in bold letters under the title. His immediate reaction was unusual. Rather than show off, as he customarily did, he quickly locked them into his desk, as though he had committed some sin. Of course, he didn't have the courage to send them to Du Wei and Fan Shuan.

Du Wei and Fan Shuan continuously sent in news about new progress. They were making a kind of corrosion-proof fluid so that, when the ultra-corrosive fluid was used, they could cover and protect with the fluid the part that didn't need to be corroded. This would be an important weapon in the conquest of the "monster" from outer space. Du Wei and Fan Shuan greeted their sixth winter in the desert.

The snowflakes danced with the howling north wind. At eight sharp in the morning, Wang Chong stepped into his heated and spotlessly clean Chairman's Office. As usual, he made a cup of Long Jing green tea, and turned the desk calendar to a new page—November 10.

The phone rang. The operator's voice sounded very clearly from the receiver. "Department of Biology of Bin Hai University? This is the satellite-transmitted international call from Stockholm in Sweden. Can you get Du Wei, Wang Chong or Fan Shuan to answer the call?" This sudden international call almost made Wang Chong's heart jump out of his chest.

Stockholm? The Nobel Prize? The idea lanced through Wang Chong's quick mind. He at once realized it was an important call, and simultaneously pressed the "Record" button on the phone to tape the message.

He listened to the call almost without breathing, and was afraid he was dreaming. He replayed the tape and listened to the recording once more. Now he was sure it was not a dream.

The call notified him that professor Du Wei, Associate Professor Wang

Chong, and Lecturer Fan Shuan had been awarded this year's Nobel Prize for Medicine and Physiology for their outstanding contributions to the research of the Li's Bacterium from outer space. The ceremony would be held on December 20th, in commemoration of the date of Mr. Alfred Nobel's death.

Again Wang Chong's eye fell on his desk calendar. Then he realized today was November 10th; in a little more than one month it would be December 20th. It was a marvel! Dr. Johnson's dinner table joke had now turned out to be an accurate prediction!

Trying his utmost to suppress the excitement that was nearly exploding inside him, Wang Chong copied the recorded call, took the tape, and ran all the way to the office of President Yang. Du Wei and Fan Shuan can wait, he thought, but President Yang must be told first. Perhaps he would have to explain to Du Wei why he had erased Li Li's name from the paper. But Du Wei might not feel displeased about it because, if Li Li's name had not been removed, the fourth author in the line, Fan Shuan, would not have been one of the winners of the Nobel Prize. This argument not only held water, but showed that all this was done in favor of Fan Shuan. Let me explain to Professor Du Wei with this reason. . . .

He pushed open the door of the President's Office, forgetting to knock first. He at once saw Mrs. Du was there talking with President Yang. President Yang stood up and said to Wang Chong, "You came just in time. I've asked my secretary to ring you!"

Wang Chong sat down beside Mrs. Du. Only then did he notice the unusual atmosphere in the room. Mrs. Du's eyes were full of tears! What had happened? Wang Chong felt as if he had again fallen into a dream world, and found himself totally incapable of dealing with the sudden change.

When President Yang saw Wang Chong sit expressionless and fixed on his seat, he said, "You don't know? Please listen to this recording of a long distance call."

At his press of the button, a slow and heavy voice came out of the loudspeaker.

"President Yang? We're the Space Center. We have very unfortunate news. Today is November 10th. On the 10th, 20th, and 30th of each month, we always airdrop supplies for Du Wei and Fan Shuan at the scheduled time, three times a month. At five o'clock this morning, when we tried to get in touch with them by radio, they didn't reply, which has never happened before in the past six years.

"The jet transport plane took off on schedule and got to the destination, the heart of the desert, at ten to eight. But no one came out to receive the supplies, and this has never happened in the past six years, either.

"Because the jet plane couldn't land in the desert, it had to drop the supplies as usual and, at the same time, sent us an emergency call by radio.

We presume that Comrades Du Wei and Fan Shuan might have had an accident.

"We're going to dispatch immediately a rescue team. The General Control thinks that the team must include a biologist to direct the operation. We're looking forward to your reply."

This sudden and totally unexpected news exploded inside Wang Chong like a bomb, and cooled his over-heated head.

He looked up and saw President Yang watching him with expectant eyes. Wang Chong understood what it meant—he hoped that Wang Chong would go to the scene. Obviously, Wang Chong was the only person who was fit for the mission. He was Professor Du Wei's best student, Fan Shuan's colleague, and also an expert on the ultra-corrosive bacteria.

When disaster befell Li Li six years ago, Du Wei decided to take one of his assistants along. At that time it was one out of two. But now they simply had no choice.

Facing the president and his teacher's wife, Wang Chong bit his lip hard and finally found his tongue. "I leave it for you to decide."

"Then you go there at once!" President Yang's order was firm and forceful.

Wang Chong stood up. Mrs. Du gripped his hand and implored in a trembling voice, "Wang Chong, please be careful! Just look down from the plane. Don't go down!"

Wang Chong was about to leave the office when he suddenly turned back, took out from his pocket the recorded international call from Stockholm and handed it to the president.

A snow-white helicopter with a big red cross painted on each side was flying over the vast desert in northwestern China, maintaining a height of four or five hundred feet above the ground.

Inside the hatch, everyone was dressed in white uniforms and caps, their faces grave. It was dead silent except for the monotonous moaning of the engine.

The half-globed hatch window protruded out like a golden fish's eye. Wang Chong was sitting exactly on the same seat that Li Li had sat on six years before. He carefully observed the earth below. Desert, the boundless desert. Wang Chong had never seen with his own eyes this lifeless, monotonous, bleak, and lonely sea of sand.

It was not until the afternoon that the chopper arrived at its destination. The silvery "pillbox" stood out alone among the brown sand. In the bright afternoon sun, it looked very conspicuous.

The helicopter's engine filled the air with its deafening noise while it circled over the "pillbox," but there was not even a stir on the ground. They watched the "pillbox," but nobody came out to greet them.

They did not dare land on the desert without knowing what was going on down there. If the bacteria had contaminated this place, the rescue team would end up in the same tragedy as six years ago.

The commander of the General Control decided to throw down the rope-ladder first and send one man down to find out what was happening.

The only man suitable for this task was, naturally, Wang Chong. Having no other choice, Wang Chong put on, rather reluctantly, the titanium-plated protective suit and climbed down the rope-ladder rung by rung. He and the commander had agreed that, if everything was normal when he entered the lab, he would fire a green signal. The chopper would then take him back at once. If he needed the help of other team members, he would fire a yellow signal. Only under extremely dangerous circumstances could he fire the red signal, which would mean that he himself was contaminated, and could not return. The chopper would leave him there and fly back.

Wang Chong's feet touched the desert for the first time in his life. Only then did he feel how soft the desert was and how difficult it was to walk on it. He scrambled to the shining lab. Every step left behind a clear footprint.

Wang Chong went into the lab. Three minutes passed; five minutes passed; ten minutes passed; fifteen minutes passed. But nothing happened down below. The chopper stayed in the air, all the members of the team watching the "pillbox" worriedly.

The commander was more anxious than anyone else. He put on one of the protective suits and prepared to go down himself. The other members all put on suits and volunteered to go down first.

Twenty minutes passed. Still nothing happened. The commander began climbing down the rope-ladder. One second before his feet touched the sand, "bang!" a fire ball suddenly flashed out of the window of the "pillbox," immediately a bright red signal was hung in the clear blue sky. The commander had to climb back to the hatch.

The chopper flew home. A ferocious wind began to blow on the desert. What had happened to Wang Chong? People guessed, and worried.

That evening, President Yang received Wang Chong's long cable from the desert.

President Yang:

I have found out the truth. When I came into the lab, I saw someone sitting at the experiment desk, his head sunk low as if he were asleep on the desk. I hurried over and shook him violently to wake him up. Then I discovered that his body was stiff and he had been dead a long time!

But who was he? I couldn't tell. His long and disheveled hair was mingled with white and gray. His face was the color of bronze and heavily bearded. If it hadn't been for the conspicuous scar on the left of his forehead, I would never have believed that this was Comrade Fan Shuan! In my memory he was as strong as a horse and had an athletic build. But now he was simply all bones!

I am certain that his death was not caused by the contamination of the ultra-corrosive bacteria, because there was no trace of the corrosion on his body. From his posture, I could tell that he was still working just before his death. He died of overworking! But what surprised me was that there was no sign of Professor Du Wei in the small "pillbox."

I found a thick notebook on Fan Shuan's desk. The work they had done each day after their arrival at the desert was clearly recorded in the book.

I learned from this book that Professor Du Wei, whose health had become worse with old age, suddenly died of heatstroke on an unusually hot summer day last year. I then realized that when the paper was sent by radio from the desert, Professor Du Wei had already passed away!

"Please forgive me," Fan Shuan wrote on the notebook, "for not reporting to you the death of Professor Du Wei. The reason is that I'm afraid you would send other comrades to work here if I let you know. The conditions here are so bad that one can only come in without any hope of leaving. I think I will be able to cope with all the work here, so I decided not to inform you of Professor Du Wei's death."

Honestly, when I descended from the helicopter, I planned to get back as soon as I had a glance at the place. Therefore, I had already loaded the pistol with the green signal. All I needed to do was pull the trigger. But after I entered the "pillbox," I was so moved by the selfless sacrifice of Professor Du Wei and Comrade Fan Shuan that I decided to remain to carry on their unfinished task. I reloaded the pistol with the red signal.

When the helicopter had gone, I busied myself with the burial of Fan Shuan for a whole afternoon. Again from the notebook I learned that Professor Du Wei was buried beside the lab. I found the tomb, before which stood a shining tombstone made of titanium. On this was inscribed:

"My dear Professor Du Wei's tomb. Built by Fan Shuan, with great respect."

I buried Fan Shuan beside Professor Du Wei's tomb and also erected a tombstone made of titanium: "My dear friend and colleague Comrade Fan Shuan's tomb. Built by Wang Chong, with great respect."

Under a small light I read carefully the record of their experiments. As I went on, I couldn't help feeling very guilty. Though I'm physically strong and healthy, my soul has already been corroded by a kind of invisible ultra-bacteria, which cannot be seen even by an electron microscope! I've long been contaminated, but I didn't feel it. Though Li Li, Du Wei, and Fan Shuan have all passed away, their souls remain uncontaminated and pure. Their scientific ethics are the noblest. They are the people made of special material—the metal titanium. They are really the "Titans," the true heroes.

I'm determined to work here for a very long period, in order to make the corrosion-proof fluid. This will be used not only to deal with the ultra-corrosive bacteria but will have other benefits as well.

Don't send over any assistants. I'm strong and healthy, and can do the work on my own.

Lastly, Wang Chong asked President Yang to call at once the Swedish Academy of Science to request the following correction:

"The authors of the paper should be Li Li, Du Wei, Fan Shuan, and Wang Chong. Because only three can be the winners, they should be the first three authors of the paper. They are Li Li, Du Wei, Fan Shuan." This cable was sent by Wang Chong from the desert on the night of November 10th.

*Translated by Pei Minxin*

# 8
# Boundless Love

## JIANG YUNSHENG

**1.**

Far, far away, that light-blue star. He saw it again. It hung in the vast space, like a dream, like a riddle, exerting an eternal attraction to a person who had returned home from afar. In his childhood, he had watched television shows about the first moon landing and listened to the astronauts who were talking about the spectacular view of Earth as seen from the Moon. He was greatly amazed. Later, he went on a moon trip with his parents and enjoyed the sight of Earth from the Moon. What an enormous revelation! When he put his feet on the footprints Americans had left on the Moon two hundred years before, he uttered a long cry at the tiny, round and beautiful Earth. It was probably that very moon trip that decided his life career—space transportation. It was his daily routine now to shuttle from star to star in the universe. Each time on his return trip, however, he would watch Earth from afar with deep love and let her light-blue light reflect his glistening drops of tears. . . .

Shema was pretty, indeed. She could be counted as a beauty according to Earth standards, and even according to Oriental standards. He could never have expected that there would be such beautiful women on W-Plant, a space colony. Apart from a few natives and Earth immigrants, the majority of the population came from planets outside the solar system. Where did Shema come from? Could she be . . .

Published in *Kexue wenyi* (Scientific Literature and Art), November 1987.

When Shema, in bikini, suddenly appeared in front of him, he thought that if her golden skin should turn white, she would be exactly like a Caucasian on Earth.

"That organ behind her G-string might also be exactly like that of an Earthwoman?" he guessed. However, when Shema was going to take off her G-string, he stopped her. At that time there were only two of them at the hotel.

"How can I make love anywhere like a stray dog?" he queried.

Yes, Shema wanted to play love with him, but he refused. It was not because he regarded it as sinful. He just did not want to; or, in other words, he was not in that mood. It was true that Shema was very pretty, and very sensual. He really appreciated her curves, her grace and vigor. She looked like a living statue—and the color of her skin was like pure gold! But beauty was one thing, and sex another. There was no equal sign between the two. Yes, she once said with sincerity about her view of sexual life, "It must be a kind of materialization of emotional communication. . . ." He saw his wife in his mind's eye. Mai was a delicate and charming woman. Except with her, he had never had that kind of materialization of emotional communication. Why? Well, he himself had never given a thought about it. It seemed needless to give a damn thought about such a thing—wasn't lovemaking without affection like mating between dogs?

He uttered a sigh, and that lovely girl Shema disappeared, together with her fragrant whisper and fall-like beautiful long hair. . . .

When the spaceship entered the atmospheric layer, the hull shivered slightly. At this distance, the light-blue Earth was surrounded by white clouds like a pretty girl carelessly wearing a scarf. How wonderful, Mother Earth! Once again I am returning to your side. How wonderful, my delicate and lovely wife! Once again I am returning to your embrace!

All of a sudden, he saw Shema's face emerging from a distant place. Gazing at him grudgingly, her eyes seemed to convey so much.

"Well, Shema! Shema . . . ," he muttered in a low voice.

## 2.

He did not know why his director wanted to have a talk with him at the bureau office. Spaceship *Zhonghua* had returned to the station safe and sound, and all the papers and cargo had been transferred and checked, and space quarantine completed. An ominous cloud shadowed his mind. . . .

He entered the office building of the National Space Navigation Bureau. He had thought to first give his wife a call, but the assistant director kept on urging him to see the director. Everyone he came across in the corridors of the building, whether acquaintances or not, raised his or her head and looked at him. All eyes seemed to hide something behind them. He became worried.

The assistant director opened the door for him and the director left his desk to greet him as he stepped into the office. "A good trip, Wang Kang!" The director shook hands with him tightly. He discovered that there were some other people in the office. He took a careful look and found they were all doctors. One of them was a psychiatrist, tall, plump and of fair and clear skin. Whenever their eyes met his, they would change directions immediately. They would lower their heads and stare at their toes. The tall psychiatrist smiled at him, but that smile was a forced one. He felt that his hand, still in the director's grasp, was becoming colder and colder.

Everyone sat down, and the office was dead quiet as if it were empty. Then, the director coughed lightly, fished out a denicotined cigarette, and struck a match.

A whiff of smoke spread out.

"What has happened, Director?" He heard a quivering voice speaking. Strange. Is that my voice? he asked himself.

"I must tell you some bad news, Wang Kang. Your wife died in a traffic accident. . . ."

He jumped up from the sofa, and then collapsed and blacked out. . . .

*I'm going first, Kang.* Where are you going? *To meet you!* Am I not home now? *I'm going first.* No, you won't go first, Mai. *Why?* You're too timid to go to hell alone. *You're disgusting.* Am I? Why did you marry me, then? *You ran after me so hot!* How about you? *You're disgusting, Kang!* Tell me the truth, Mai. Do you love me? *If not, would I be willing to marry you? I hated that pale-faced guy.* Who? *You know very well who.* Do you mean my cousin? *Damn it! Ignorant of eugenics in the 22nd century! I still hate him!*

*Do you really love me so affectionately, Kang?* Yes. *What if I should die?* I won't allow you to say so! *Are you so terribly superstitious?* No, I'm not, but why talk about such terrible things! *But terrible things do happen. For instance, traffic accidents.* They won't get you. *Why?* Because I can't live without you! *What if without me?* I don't know.

*I can work out a way for you.* What is it. *Produce one of my image.* You mean a clone—a clone without a navel? *What's the use of a navel? It would be exactly my duplicate. Wouldn't it be nice?* I need a Mai with a navel. *Why fuss about a navel? That's nothing but a sign indicating that a life is conceived in the womb and delivered from it.* I just want a baby delivered from the womb, and from your womb. *Shame on you!* By no means. You're my wife; otherwise you wouldn't make love to me. *Without love, I wonder if. . . .*

Do you feel happy? *Yes, how about you?* I like it.

*Lovemaking is in fact a kind of materialization of emotional communication, isn't it?*

Why, Shema's here. *I am seeing you off, Wang; and I'll come again though you don't like me.* I like you Shema! *I mean you don't love me.* I love you, Shema. *You know you are loving me as a piece of art.* Isn't that kind of love also very precious? *I envy your wife, Wang.* She would also envy you—

you're so beautiful! *How do Earthpeople wish others a happy marriage?* Live to ripe old age in conjugal bliss. *Then I wish you to live to ripe old age in conjugal bliss.* Thank you, Shema. . . .

Oh, no, that couldn't be true. How could you really go first, Mai? Mai, my Mai!

Mai was gone, gone forever. According to her last wish, her ashes were carried into space by rocket and scattered. The burial ceremony was very impressive. As the angry rocket was darting skyward with trailing fire, over one thousand people of the Bureau staff set off black balloons from their hands. They darkened the already cloudy sky, and it seemed that the sky was so impressed that it began to rain. . . .

After the ceremony, the bureau director offered him a ride in his sedan.

"Brace up, Wang Kang!"

With tears in his eyes, he looked through the windowpane of the sedan and saw the mourners walking in the rain. He switched down the windowpane and, stretching himself halfway through the window, waved his hands to express his thanks to them all.

"Another thing I must tell you," the director said while lighting up. "Following your wife's other behest, we have duplicated her with one of her cells. . . ."

A clone?!" He half stood up.

"Yes. The clone looks exactly like your wife. . . ."

No, not exactly alike. It has no navel, but Mai had one. I need Mai with a navel. *Why fuss about a navel? That's nothing but a sign indicating that a life is conceived in the womb and delivered from it.* I just want a baby delivered from a womb, and from your womb. *Shame on you.* By no means. You're my wife. . . .

"That's your wife's wish, and you actually do need one to look after you. . . ." The director's words seemed to come from a far, far away place. "But I regret to say that the duplication technique at present can not include memory restoration. Otherwise, we could have almost claimed the revival of your Mai."

The rain was getting heavier and heavier. The car was racing in the rain. All around was a vast expanse of whiteness. He felt that his mind was also a vast white expanse.

**3.**

Slightly, slightly he heard some subdued weeping, repressed as if there were lots of hidden bitterness at heart. He opened his eyes and turned his head. She (it?) covered her face with the pillow, her shoulders shivering now and then. He felt sorry. So, he extended his hand, held her lightly, and patted her white and plump arm.

She was motionless, still weeping in grief.

Some time later, they went on a trip. He was badly in need of emotional readjustments: His lovely wife had died of a sudden death and left an eternal vacuum in his heart; the 22nd-century science took only half a year cloning a duplicate with her cell. The face, body, and voice were all alike; and the same smile, and habitual movements of hands and feet. Everything was as alike as two peas. She was exactly the image of Mai. He recalled to his mind how Mai teased him and felt even more sad. The clone had no navel, unable to reproduce, without memory of the past. All these reminded him from time to time of that vacuum in his heart. The clone was after all not his Mai with whom he had enjoyed good company since childhood.

It was still a pleasant trip, though he would not say so frankly. It was in fact his second honeymoon. And they had chosen a quaint region of rivers and lakes in the south. In May, orioles were singing, grass growing, flowers blooming and trees thriving. In the south, the 20th-century tile-roofed village houses were well-preserved. Surrounded by the blossoming rape plant, they were classical holiday inns, indeed. Clothing, eating, housing and transportation, all the basic necessities of life followed the patterns of two hundred and fifty years before; even the robots were dressed like farmers. Some knelt down in the water, weeding the paddy field, and some carried double manure buckets on their shoulder poles to the field. . . .

On the first day, they took lodging in a small inn with clay walls. They just wanted to experience at night the simple life of old days in the same way that they had enjoyed that day. That could be as interesting as space travel to the moon or other stars. It was at this ancient village inn that they made love for the first time—the materialization of emotional communication. Then, he held her lightly, combed her disheveled hair with his fingers and kissed her on her slightly hot lips from time to time. Filled with gratitude to science for its grace, he muttered, "Mai, Mai. . . ." And she returned his affectionate attentiveness with sweet kisses, her black eyes glistening with happiness.

Later, they went climbing, angling, and then swimming in a hot spring at the foot of a little hill near the entrance of the village. There were no other people around. Naked, they jumped into the hot spring pool and chased each other for fun, totally forgetting the world all around.

During their rest, he cast a glance at her bare belly just at the moment she lifted her head and looked at him. She was sensitive of his attention and abashed. He immediately turned round and held her waist. "You're a good swimmer, indeed! Just like a mermaid." But she did not respond to his compliment. Lightly she pushed off his arm, got up without a word and went to dress herself, up behind the trees. Stupefied, he sat motionlessly, thinking of another mermaid, a mermaid with a navel. . . .

One day, they went boating in Green Ripple Lake outside the village.

There were lots of lotus which stood straight up like many opened-up green umbrellas. Myriads of water drops like pearls rolled to and fro on the lotus leaves in the wind. The slim lotus stems all held high pink or light purple flower buds. The sun glittered numberless gold and silver beams on the surface of the lake, and off stretched a vast expanse of enshrouding mist. With a pleasant cry, she jumped up from the grass, clapping her hands. He seemed suddenly struck by an inspiration and rushed to untie the cable from the willow. They both got aboard the boat and pulled on the oars. The small boat passed through the lotus slowly and sailed towards the center of the lake, leisurely and carefree.

"What a beautiful sight! Really beyond my expectation," she said with a slight smile at him. Without a word, he produced a handkerchief to wipe the sweat from her forehead. Their eyes met and brightened. They put down their oars and embraced, releasing the boat to drift at its will.

That day could have been the sweetest and happiest day during his second honeymoon, but a minor episode spoiled it all. That happened at dusk when they, dog-tired but perfectly content, were paddling back to the pier. When they got near the shore, a pair of water birds were startled. Flapping their wings, they took flight from the patches of lotus. She cried out in happy astonishment, "Look, water birds." While pulling on the oars, he recited with facility a poem written in the Sung Dynasty.

> Sunset at the pavilion by the brook, I remember,
> So intoxicating I lost my way back.
> With heart content, I returned late by boat,
> And went astray into the recesses of lotus pond.
> Pulled long, and pulled long,
> But only startled herons on the shore!"

"What are you reciting?" she asked.

"Li Qingzhao's 'As if in a Dream: A Song.' Isn't it your favo—?" Waking up to reality, he stopped halfway. She, in front of him now, was not Mai! Mai had been Li Qingzhao's disciple, but she had perhaps just heard of this name "Li Qingzhao" for the first time. He regretted having made such an indiscreet remark, and felt distressed at her ignorance and stupefaction. "Oh, my Mai, Mai!" He lifted his head and saw the sunset glow reddening the whole western sky. He seemed to see Mai emerging from the red clouds, and in the innermost recesses of his heart he cherished boundless love for Mai. . . .

That night they did not exchange a word. Both felt rather embarrassed.

**4.**

On W-Planet, a big, tall policeman from the Ministry of Punishments unlocked No. 7 Cell with urbanity and gestured him to walk out of it.

Dull and numb, he strode a few steps forward and then heard the door behind him lock lightly by itself. He could still hear the footsteps as the policeman was walking farther and farther away from him, but he remained there motionless, trying to put his thoughts in order. . . .

Yes, as memories could not be duplicated, we often had moments of embarrassment. She knew that I cherished a deep love for Mai because we had been childhood sweethearts. And I knew that she felt inferior and pained because she was unable to reproduce or to share the weal and woe with me from the past.

It was that psychiatrist who relieved us of the distress. He suggested that we both should work for the National Space Navigation Bureau. That was a great idea, indeed! She first joined the ground crew, and later piloted a small spaceship with me to the Moon, Venus, Jupiter. . . . We collaborated quite well. While working and living together with her, I got rid of all psychological hostility towards her and finally assured her that I, unlike my ancestors, did not take reproduction as the sole justified reason for sex. We then lived in conjugal happiness. We were husband and wife, colleagues and bosom friends. Like Mai, she began to appreciate Chinese classics in literature and loved reading poems by Li Yu and Li Qingzhao.

Maybe we should not have accepted this mission to W-Planet. We were transporting some seedlings of Chinese plum and mottled bamboo to W-Planet via Spaceship *Zhonghua* when something unexpected occurred during the final part of our voyage. Our spaceship came across a meteor shower which damaged our air storage. Even the emergency oxygen tank was hit and began leaking. The alarm meter jumped to the highest point. For a moment we both were dumbfounded. Then we quickly calculated all our losses and soon came to realize that all the remaining air, food and water could only sustain one person to reach our destination. We dispatched S.O.S. messages into space but finally admitted that they were useless because there were no spaceships in the vicinity that could help us. Our spaceship was just like a solitary boat in a vast sea. Hoping against hope, we tried to repair the deep-freeze cases, but in vain.

Then, we had a fight between us. While I was stupefied by the hopeless situation, she, my love, suddenly produced her proton gun which was to be used only for self-defense in space. She pointed her gun at her own head and ordered me to sit still, otherwise she would commit suicide that instant. I sat motionless and listened to her, but in mind I was trying desperately to work out a way to grab her gun. I could not live without her now. I could not lose a second Mai! I knew clearly that only one of us could reach W-Planet alive, but I would prefer myself to make the sacrifice. I was unable to suffer from repeated deaths of my love any more!

Standing near the cockpit, she looked entirely different from her usual self. She sternly ordered me to take control of the spaceship and strive by all means to reach W-Planet alive. She said that I must carry these seedlings of Chinese plum and mottled bamboo there safe and sound and let the Earth culture develop in space. I tried to persuade her, and even begged her to put down her gun. I suggested that we should work out other ways to solve the problem. But she simply took off her helmet to show her determination to sacrifice her life. The scene of those last minutes has been unforgettable all my life: She pointed her gun at her temple and admonished me with tears to live on. She said that she was passionately in love with me and that she was grateful to me for the short but sweet conjugal life we had lived together. She asked that after my return to Earth I should scatter her ashes in the space so that she could merge with Mai and ever accompany me in my space career. . . .

But I seemed to discover a chance. When she was wiping off her tears with one hand, I threw myself on her. That was beyond her anticipation. She fell down. I desperately snatched the gun from her hand and smashed her fingers. I thought I could save her life once I grabbed the gun. Who would have thought that she would swallow a pill of hydrogen fluoride while falling down! When I saw the empty bottle on the deck, her face had already turned terribly pale and her eyes rolled upward. Her last words were: "I love you, Wang Kang."

That afternoon, the police bureau examined all the video records from Spaceship *Zhonghua* and finally became convinced that he, a citizen of the People's Republic of China from Earth, was absolutely innocent. Hence he was released from detention.

As the spaceship was getting ready to set off, a golden shadow suddenly ran toward the launching pad from a far away distance.

Oh, it was Shema!

. . . 4, 3, 2, 1, 0!

Set sail!

"Farewell, Shema!" he waved his hand to that distant shadow, muttering to himself in his mind that this was his last trip to W-Planet. At that very moment, he could not help but cherish some passions of love for it while watching the desolate sight outside through the port of the spaceship.

Far, far away, that light-blue star. He saw it again. It hung in the vast space, like a dream, like a riddle. Several days later, he scattered her ashes into the limitless space. Oh, Mai! Mai. . . . Why, did he really see Shema again? No, it was the golden face of the Sun emerging in the far away recesses of the tiny, round and beautiful Earth.

*Translated by Wu Dingbo*

# Chronological Bibliography of Chinese Science Fiction

## 1904

Huangjiang Diasou. *Yueqiu zhimindi xiaoshuo* (Tales of Moon Colonization). Shanghai: *Xiuxiang xiaoshuo* (Portrait Fiction).

## 1905

Donghai Juewo [Xu Nianci]. *Xin falu* (New Absurdity). Shanghai: *Xiaoshuo lin* (Fiction Forest Press).

Zhi Ming. "Shengsheng dai" (Lively Tales about Life). Shanghai: *Xiuxiang xiaoshuo*, no. 55.

## 1906

Bihe Guanzhu. "Wanjin shijie" (The World of Gold). Shanghai: *Yueyue xiaoshuo* (Fiction Monthly). Commercial Press.

Chun Fan. *Weilai shijie* (Future World). Shanghai: *Yueyue xiaoshuo.*

Li Baojia. "Bingshan xuemei" (Snowy Plum on Icy Mountain). Shanghai: *Yueyue xiaoshuo.*

Wu Woyao. *Xin Shitouji* (A New Story of *Dream of Red Mansions*). Shanghai: Gailiang Fiction Press.

Xiaoran Yusheng. *Wutuobang youji* (Journey to Utopia). Shanghai: *Yueyue xiaoshuo.*

Zhang Mianzhan and Chen Wuwo. "Xin Zaishengyuan" (New Romance of Rebirth). Shanghai: *Yueyue xiaoshuo*, no. 1: 5.

Zhou Guisheng. "Fei fang Muxing" (Forward Jupiter). Shanghai: *Yueyue xiaoshuo*, no. 1: 5.

**1908**

Bao Tianxiao. "Kongzhong zhanzheng weilai ji" (Future War in the Air). Shang-
    hai: *Yueyue xiaoshuo*, no. 2: 10.
———. "Shijie muri ji" (Doomsday). Shanghai: *Yueyue xiaoshuo*, no. 2: 10.
Bihe Guanzhu. "Xin jiyuan" (A New Era). Shanghai: *Xiaoshuo lin*.
Wu Woyao. "Guangxu wannian" (The Ten Thousandth Year of the Guangxu
    Reign). Shanghai: *Yueyue xiaoshuo*, no. 2: 10.
Xiaoran Yusheng. "Xin Jinghuayuan" (A New Story of *Flowers in the Mirror*).
    Shanghai: *Yueyue xiaoshuo*, no. 2: 10.

**1909**

Xu Zhiyan. "Dian shijie" (Electric World). Shanghai: *Xiaoshuo shibao*, no. 1.

**1922**

[unknown]. *Ertong youji* (Children's Travels). Shanghai: Commercial Press.

**1923**

Jing Feng. *Shinian hou de Zhongguo* (China Ten Years From Now). Shanghai:
    *Xiaoshuo shijie* (Fiction World), no. 1:1.

**1933**

Lao She [Shu Sheyu]. *Maocheng ji (Cat Country)*. Shanghai: Modern Book Co.
    (English edition: Translated by William A. Lyell. Columbus: Ohio State
    University Press, 1970).

**1940**

Gu Junzheng. *Heping de meng* (Dream of Peace). Shanghai: Cultural Life Press.

**1941**

Xu Dishan. "Tieyu de sai" (Ironfish Gills). In *Selections of Xu Dishan's Works*.
    Beijing: People's Literature Press, 1958.

**1950**

Zhang Ran. *Mengyou Taiyangxi* (Roaming around the Solar System in a Dream).
    Tianjin: Zhishi Bookstore.

**1954**

Zheng Wenguang. *Dierge yueliang* (The Second Moon). Beijing: *Zhongguo qingnian
    bao* (Chinese Youth Daily), November 23, 25, 27 and 30.

## 1955

Zheng Wenguang. *Taiyang tanxian ji* (Search the Sun). Shanghai: Juvenile Press.

## 1956

Chi Shuchang and Wang Wen. *Sanhao youyong xuanshou de mimi* (Swimming Contestant No. 3's Secret). Beijing: Chinese Juvenile Press.

Cui Xingjian. *Xiaolulu youli Taiyangxi* (Little Lulu Travels Through the Solar System). Taiyuan: Shanxi People's Press.

Guo Yishi. *Sunwukong danao yuanzi shijie* (Monkey King Sun Wukong Turns the World of the Atom Upside Down). Beijing: Chinese Juvenile Press.

Yu Zhi. *Dao renzao yueliang qu* (Trip to the Man-Made Moon). Beijing: Chinese Juvenile Press.

## 1957

Chi Shuchang. *1979 nian de hai lu kong* (Sea, Land and Sky in 1979). Shanghai: Juvenile Press.

Xu Qingshan. *Dao Huoxing shang qu* (Trip to Mars). Hangzhou: Zhejiang People's Press.

Yang Zijiang. *Huoxing tanxian ji* (Venture to Mars). Shanghai: *Zhongxuesheng* (High School Students), no. 9.

## 1958

Guo Yishi. *Kexue shijie luxing ji* (Travel to the World of Science). Shanghai: Juvenile Press.

————. *Zai kexue shijie li* (In the World of Science). Shanghai: Juvenile Press.

Xu Qingshan. *Shiqian shijie luxing ji* (A Trip to the Prehistoric World). Nanjing: Jiangsu People's Press. Reprinted in 1979.

Yan Yuanwen. *Jiari de qiyu* (Happy Encounters on Holiday). Shanghai: Juvenile Press.

Yu Zhi. *Shizong de gege* (The Missing Elder Brother). Beijing: Chinese Juvenile Press.

Zhao Shizhou. *Huo Sunwukong* (Monkey King Sun Wukong Lives). Beijing: Chinese Juvenile Press.

## 1960

Tong Enzheng. *Guxia miwu* (Dense Fog over the Old Gorge). Shanghai: Juvenile Press. Revised edition, 1978.

## 1962

Lu Ke. *Qimiao de dao* (The Wondrous Scalpel). Shanghai: *Ertong shidai* (Childhood), no. 7.

Tong Enzheng, et al. *Wuwannian yiqian de keren* (Guests Fifty Thousand Years Ago). Shanghai: Juvenile Press.

Xiao Jianheng, et al. *Buke de qiyu* (Pup Buke's Adventures). Beijing: Chinese Juvenile Press. Revised edition, 1979.

## 1963

Chi Shuchang. *Dajing muchang* (The Whales' Pastureland). Beijing: Chinese Juvenile Press.

Ji Hong. *Shenmi de xiaotanke* (Wondrous Minitanks). Nanjing: Jiangsu People's Press.

Tong Enzheng, et al. *Shiqu de jiyi* (Loss of Memory). Shanghai: Juvenile Press.

Wang Guozhong. *Heilonghao shizong* (The Ship *Heilong* Is Missing). Shanghai: Juvenile Press.

## 1965

Xiao Jianheng. *Qiyi de jiqigou* (A Strange Robot Dog). Nanjing: Jiangsu People's Press. Revised edition, 1979.

## 1976

Ye Yonglie. "Shiyou danbai" (Strange Cakes). Shanghai: *Shaonian kexue* (Juvenile Science), no. 5.

## 1978

Ji Hong and Miu Shi [Ji Wei]. *Haidi konglong* (Dinosaurs on the Seabed). Nanjing: Jiangsu People's Press.

Song Yichang. *V de bianzhi* (The Devaluation of V). Hong Kong: *Wenhuibao* (newspaper).

Tong Enzheng, et al. *Wuwannian yiqian de keren* (Guests Fifty Thousand Years Ago). Beijing: People's Liturature Press. [A different book from the same titled one of 1962.]

Ye Yonglie. *Xiaolingtong manyou weilei* (Little Know-It-All Travels to the Future). Shanghai: Juvenile Press.

## 1979

Cheng Zhongyi. *Jinniuhao shijian* (The Incident of the Ship *Gold Ox*). Fuzhou: Fujian People's Press.

Deng Yanlu. *21 shiji tielu manyou ji* (Roaming Around the 21st Century's Railroad). Changsha: Hunan People's Press.

Guo Zhi. *Xiaopingpong bian le* (Little "Pingpong" Fan Changes). Beijing: Chinese Juvenile Press.

Liu Houyi. *Banbo ren de gushi* (A Story About the Half Cripple). Shanghai: Juvenile Press.

Liu Xinshi. *Hai yan* (Sea Eyes). Shanghai: Juvenile Press.

————. *Meizhou lai de gerunbu* (Columbus from America). Chengdu: Sichuan People's Press.

Qiu Guohua. *Jinse de meng* (A Golden Dream). Fuzhou: Fujian People's Press.

Rao Zhonghua and Lin Yaochen, eds. *Kexue shenghua: 1976–1979 kexue huanxiang zuoping ji* (Science Myths: SF Stories and Abstracts 1976–1979). Beijing: Ocean Press.

Sichuan People's Press, ed. *Shui de jiao ying* (Whose Footprints). Chengdu: Sichuan People's Press.

Tong Enzheng. *Xueshan modi* (The Magic Flute on the Snowy Mountain). Beijing: People's Literature Press.

Wang Chuan. *Moguihu de qiji* (The Miracle of the Demon Lake). Nanjing: Jiangsu People's Press.

Xiao Jianheng. *Meng* (Dream). Nanjing: Jiangsu People's Press.

————. *Milin huzong* (Tiger Traces in the Thick Forest). Shanghai: Juvenile Press.

Xie Shijun. *Han tian buo yu* (Spaceflight Rainmaking). Shenyang: Liaoning People's Press.

Yan Jiaqi. *Kuayue shidai de feixing* (Flight Spanning the Ages). Shanghai: Shanghai People's Press.

Ye Yonglie. *Diule bizi yihou* (After Losing His Nose). Shanghai: Juvenile Press.

————. *Fei xiang Minwangxing de ren* (The Voyager to Pluto). Guangzhou: Guangdong People's Press.

————. *Qiguai de binghao—Ye Yonglie zuoping xuan* (An Odd Patient—Selections of Ye Yonglie's Works). Chengdu: Sichuan People's Press.

————. *Shijie zuigaofeng de qiji* (The Miracle on the World's Highest Mountain). Beijing: People's Literature Press.

————. *Weilai shijie manyou ji* (A Trip to the Futureworld). Shijiazhuang: Hebei People's Press.

You Yi. *Weilai changxiang qu* (Song of the Future). Shanghai: Shanghai People's Press.

Zhang Shilin. *Mima shengming* (A Coded Life). Jinan: Shandong People's Press.

Zhang Xiaotian. *Huilai ba, Luolan* (Come Back, Roland). Shenyang: Chunfeng Literature and Art Press.

Zhang Yiwu and Wei Liao. *Shengming qu* (Song of Life). Guangzhou: Guangdong Science and Technology Press.

Zheng Wenguang. *Fei xiang Renmazuo* (Forward Sagittarius). Beijing: People's Literature Press.

————. *Hai guniang* (The Sea Girl). Beijing: Popular Science Press.

————. *Shayu zhencha bing* (Shark-Spies). Beijing: Chinese Juvenile Press.

## 1980

Bei Xing, et al. *Mohai dieying* (Espionage on the Devil Sea). Harbin: Heilongjiang Science and Technology Press.

Chinese Youth Press, ed. *Kexue huanxiang xiaoshuo xuan* (Selections of Science Fiction). Beijing: Chinese Youth Press.

Dai Shan, et al. *Tianshi yu yeshou* (Angels and Beasts). Shanghai: Shanghai Science and Technology Press.

Dou Xintian. *Sunwukong waizhuan* (Unofficial Biography of Monkey King Sunwukong). Harbin: Heilongjiang People's Press.

Fujian People's Education Press, ed. *Mogui sanjiao qi an* (The Strange Case of the Bermuda Triangle). Fuzhou: Fujian People's Education Press.

Fujian People's Press, ed. *Kongzhong qi an* (A Strange Case in Space). Fuzhou: Fujian People's Press.

Gao Shiqi and Zheng Wenguang, eds. *Kexue wenyi zuoping xuan* (Selections of Scientific Literature and Art, vols. 1 and 2). Beijing: People's Literature Press.

Guo Zhi. *Zhubajie guang xincheng* (Monk Pigsy Strolls around a Star). Beijing: Popular Science Press.

Hubei People's Press, ed. *Sharensan anjian* (The Case of a Lethal Umbrella). Wuhan: Hubei People's Press.

Jiao Qingchang and Shan Quan. *Feidie shang de xianyu* (Dangerous Encounters on a Flying Saucer). Taiyuan: Shanxi People's Press.

Jin Tao, ed. *Bingxia de meng* (Dream Under the Ice). Beijing: Ocean Press.

Lan Fan. *Tiangong youji* (Voyage to the Heavenly Palace). Wuhan: Hubei People's Press.

Liu Xinshi. *Huifei de chengshi* (The Winged City). Chengdu: Sichuan People's Press.

———. *Sicheng de chuangshuo* (Legends About the City of the Dead). Beijing: Chinese Juvenile Press.

Lu Ke. *Ke zi tianwai lai* (Guests from Outer Space). Beijing: Popular Culture Press.

———. *Shui diu le weiba* (Who Has Lost His Tail). Chengdu: Sichuan People's Press.

Miu Shi. *Qiguai de "qianshuiyuan"* (An Odd "Diver"). Nanjing: Jiangsu People's Press.

Qiu Guohua and Chai Haibin. *Xingji qiyu* (Interstellar Adventures). Fuzhou: Fujian People's Press.

Rao Zhonghua, ed. *Kexue shenghua: 1979–1980 kexue huanxiang zuoping ji* (Science Myths: SF Stories and Abstracts 1979–1980). Beijing: Ocean Press.

Ren Daxing. *Dajie shang de long* (The Dinosaur on the Street). Tianjin: New Budding Press.

Shi Hequn and Zhu Yuqi. *Shizong de ren* (The Missing Person). Changsa: Hunan People's Press.

Tan Yingwu. *Xingkong zai zhaohuan* (The Stars Are Calling). Zhengzhou: Henan People's Press.

Wang Xiaoda. *Shenmi de bo* (The Mysterious Wave). Chengdu: Sichuan People's Press.

Wei Yahua, et al. *"Feitan" de fengbo* (A Storm Out of the "Flying Carpet"). Beijing: Workers' Press.

Xinjiang People's Press, ed. *Kexue huanxiang xiaoshuo ji* (An Anthology of Science Fiction). Wulumuqi: Xinjiang People's Press.

Yan Jiaqi. *Manyou lishi he weilai* (Travels Through the History and the Future). Fuzhou: Fujian People's Education Press.

Ye Yonglie. *Bidao dieying* (Espionage on a Blue Island). Changsha: Hunan People's Press.

———. *Qiaozhuang daban* (Disguised). Beijing: Mass Press.

———. *Shengmi yi* (Magic Clothes). Tainjin: New Budding Press.

Ye Yonglie, et al. *Shengsi weibo: kexue huanxiang dianyin jubeng xuan* (Is He Dead or Not: Selections of SF Scenarios). Zhengzhou: Henan People's Press.

You Yi. *Shengmi de xinhao dan* (The Mysterious Signal Flare). Beijing: Chinese Juvenile Press.

## 1981

Chen Jianqiu. *Yaoyuan de daluosi* (The Far-Off Daedalus [a play]). Beijing: *Ocean SF*, no. 2, Ocean Press.

Chi Fang and Wang Wen. *Huo fenghuang* (The Fiery Phoenix). Beijing: Popular Science Press.

Guangdong Popular Science Writing Association, ed. *Youbu xiaoshi de mei* (Everlasting Beauty). Guangzhou: Popular Science Press.

Hu Jingfang. *Huijian yuzhou ren* (Interview with Aliens [a play]). Staged in Shenyang, Liaoning.

Huang Renjun. *Gebi dieying* (The Shadow of a Flying Saucer over the Gobi Desert). Nanjing: Jiangsu People's Press.

Jin Tao. *Taifeng xindong* (Typhoon Operations). Tianjin: Tianjin Science and Technology Press.

———. *Yueguang dao* (The Moonlit Island). Beijing: Geology Press.

Liu Guoliang. *Dayang guaizong* (Strange Traces in the Ocean). Beijing: Chinese Juvenile Press.

Liu Xinshi. *Wei, dahai* (Hello, You Great Ocean). Beijing: Popular Science Press.

Lu Zhonglu. *Fei wang taikong cheng* (Voyage to Space Cities). Film Script.

Meng Weizai. *Fangwen shizong zhe* (Call on the Missing People). Tainjin: *Zhihuishu* (The Tree of Knowledge); New Budding Press.

Miu Shi. *Luse guaike* (Green Aliens). Fuzhou: Fujian People's Press.

Shandong People's Press, ed. *Shuixia moku* (Underwater Den of Devils). Jinan: Shandong People's Press.

Sun Chuansong. *Mo ying* (The Devilish Shadow). Harbin: *Kexue shidai* (Science Era) Supplementary Issue.

———. *Zang zai wuyun li de languang* (The Blue Light Hidden in the Dark Clouds). Harbin: *Kexue shidai* (Science Era) Supplementary Issue.

Sun Huaichuan. *Qitan yuzhou ren* (Look for Aliens). Huhehaote: Inner Mongolia People's Press.

Tie Cui. *Shaonian kantan dui* (A Young Prospecting Team). Fuzhou: Fujian People's Press.

Tong Enzheng. *Zuizong konglong de ren* (Those Who Chased Dinosaurs). Chengdu: Sichuan Juvenile Press.

Wang Guihau. *Wu gen guo* (Rootless Fruit). Beijing: *SF Ocean*, no. 2, Ocean Press.

Wang Jinhai. *Tebie shenxun* (A Special Interrogation). Fuzhou: Fujian People's Press.

Wang Xiaoda. *Shenmi de Bo* (The Mysterious Wave). Chengdu: Sichuan People's Press. [A different book from the same titled one of 1980.]

Wei Yahua. *Guaidao youhun* (The Spectre on a Freak Island). Wuhan: Hubei People's Press.

———. *Qiyi de anjian* (An Unusual Case). Xi an: Shanxi People's Press.

———. *Wo jueding yu jiqi ren qizi lihun* (Conjugal Love in the Arms of Morpheus). Nanjing: Jiangsu Science and Technology Press.

Wu Guoliang and Li Yaping. *Jiulongbei chuanqi* (The Legend of the Nine-Dragon Cup). Hefei: Anhui Science and Technology Press.

Xiao Fan and Zhang Changyu. *Shennu zhimi* (The Mystery of the Goddess). Nanjing: Jiangsu People's Press.

Xin Bao. *Duotou sheyao* (The Multi-Headed Serpent Monster). Fuzhou: Fujian People's Press.

Ye Yonglie. *An dou* (Veiled Strife). Chengdu: Sichuan Juvenile Press.

———. *Guobao qi an* (A Strange Case of Pandas). Shenyang: Liaoning People's Press.

———. *Hei ying* (The Black Shadow). Beijing: Geology Press.

———. *Mimi zhongdui* (The Secret Column). Beijing: Mass Press.

———. *Qiuchang wai de jiandie an* (The Spy Case Outside the Football Field). Hangzhou: Zhejiang Science and Technology Press.

Ye Yanglie, ed. *Zhongguo jingxian kexue huanxiang xiaoshuo xuan* (Selections of Chinese Detective Science Fiction). Nanjing: Jiangsu Science and Technology Press.

Zheng Wenguang. *Dayang shen chu* (Ocean Depths). Beijing: People's Literature Press.

———. *Gumiao qi ren* (An Odd Guy in an Old Temple). Hong Kong: Zhaomin Press.

———. *"Mingyun" yezonghui* ("Destiny" Nightclub). Beijing: *Xiaoshuo jia* (Fiction Circles).

———. *Zheng Wenguang kexue huanxiang xiaoshuo xuan* (SF Book of Zheng Wenguang. Vol. 1. Tianjin: Tianjin Science and Technology Press.

———. *Zheng Wenguang xinzuoxuan* (The Newly-Written Works of Zheng Wenguang). Changsha: Hunan People's Press.

Zhu Yuqi. *Chen chuan jiu bao* (Retrieving the Treasure from a Sunken Ship). Fuzhou: Fujian People's Press.

Zhu Yuqi and Shi Hequn. *Gutu qizong* (Strange Traces of an Ancient Map). Fuzhou: Fujian Education Press.

## 1982

Jin Tao. *Ren yu shou* (Man and Beast). Fuzhou: Fujian Science and Technology Press.

Li Ming. *Zuqiuwang de mimi* (Football King's Secret). Shenyang: Liaoning People's Press.

Song Yichang. *Huoxia dakai zhihou* (After the Pandora Box Is Open). Lanzhou: Gansu People's Press.

Wang Tianyun and Wang Runsheng. *A, Zala de xiaolu* (Ah, the Pathway in Zala). Fuzhou: Fujian People's Press.

Xiao Jianheng. *Jinxing ren zhimi* (The Mystery of the Venusians). Chengdu: Sichuan Juvenile Press.

Yang Beixing and Sun Changsong. *Meinushe qi an* (The Strange Case of the Serpent Beauty). Zhengzhou: Henan People's Press.

Ye Yonglie. *Baobao he Beibei* (Baobao and Beibei). Shenyang: Liaoning Juvenile Press.

———. *Bengbengtiao xiansheng* (Mr. Flea). Chengdu: Sichuan Juvenile Press.

———. *Bu yi er fei* (Disappearing Without a Trace). Beijing: Mass Press.

———. *Leng ru bing shuang* (Frosty in Manners). Fuzhou: Fujian Science and Technology Press.

———. *Weilai de zaochen* (A Morning in the Future). Shenyang: Liaoning People's Press.

———. *Yuan xing bi lu* (Showing His True Colors). Changsha: Hunan Juvenile Press.

Ye Yonglie, ed. *Zhongguo kexue huanxiang xiaoshuo xuan* (Selections of Chinese Science Fiction). Shenyang: Liaoning People's Press.

Zheng Wenguang. *Shen yi* (Wondrous Wings). Changsha: Hunan Juvenile Press.


## 1983

Rao Zhonghua, ed. *Kexue shenghua: 1981–82 kexue huanxiang zuoping ji* (Science Myths: SF Stories and Abstracts, 1981–82). Beijing: Ocean Press.

———. *Zhongguo kehuan xiaoshuo daquan* (Compendium of Chinese Science Fiction). Beijing: Ocean Press.

Ye Yonglie. *Bingdi lian* (Twin Lotus). Shenyang: Lioaning Science and Technology Press.

———. *Jiqi lifadian* (A Machine Barbershop). Nanjing: Jiangsu People's Press.

———. *Ru meng chu xing* (As If Just Awakening from a Dream). Beijing: Mass Press.

Yu Zhaoyan, ed. *Mo mao* (A Magic Cap). Beijing: Chinese Juvenile Press.

Zhang Xiguo (Taiwan). Zhang Xiguo duanpian xiaoshuo xuan (Selections of Zhang Xiguo's Short Stories). Nanchang: Jiangxi People's Press.


## 1984

Liu Xinshi, ed. *Zhongguo SF xuan* (Selections of Chinese SF). Chengdu: Sichuan Juvenile Press.

Zheng Wenguang. *Zhanshen de houyi* (Descendants of the Warrior God). Guangzhou: Flower City Press.


## 1985

Cheng Jiazi. *Guxing tu zhi mi* (The Mystery of an Ancient Star Atlas). Beijing: People's Literature Press.

Tong Enzheng. *Xi you xin ji* (New Journey to the West). Tianjin: New Budding Press.


## 1986

Ye Yonglie. *Xiaolingtong zaiyou weilei* (Little Know-It-All Travels to the Future Again). Shanghai: Juvenile Press.


## 1987

Ye Yonglie. *Ai de xuanze* (Love's Choice). Ningxia: Ningxia People's Press.

**1988**

Liu Xinshi. *Shijia kehuan xiaoshuo xiehui zhongguo huiyuan zuopin ji* (Selected Works of Chinese Members of World SF). Taiyuan: Xiwang Press.

Zhang Zurong. *Dongyou ji* (Journey to the East). Beijing: Chinese Culture and Art Society Press.

# About the Editors
# and Contributors

JIANG YUNSHENG is a faculty member of the Songjiang County Branch of the Shanghai Television University. He has publishd a dozen or so science fiction short stories and short story translations from English into Chinese.

PATRICK D. MURPHY is an assistant professor of English at Indiana University of Pennsylvania. He has published on American and fantastic literature in several journals and coedited *Essentials of the Theory of Fiction* and a *Women's Studies* special issue. He is currently editing *Critical Essays on Gary Snyder,* coediting *Critical Essays on American Modernism,* and writing *The Reader's Guide to Joanna Russ.*

FREDERIK POHL's career in science fiction has spanned more than half a century, as editor, literary agent, critic, fan and, most of all, a writer whom Kingsley Amis called "the best science fiction, in its modern form, has yet produced." Pohl has won all the major awards in the field—the Hugo (six times; he is the only person ever to have won that award both as editor and writer), the Nebula (twice), the international Campbell Award (twice), the American Book Award, and many others. His best-known works are *Gateway* and (with the late C. M. Kornbluth) *The Space Merchants.*

TONG ENZHENG is an archaeologist and professor in the History Department of Sichuan University. He has been writing science fiction since

1960 and his best-known story is "Death Ray on a Coral Island," which was adapted into China's first science fiction film. He is a member of the Chinese Writers' Association and of World SF.

WANG XIAODA is an associate professor of metal materials and metallurgy at Chengdu University. He has published about forty stories, and his "The Tragedy of Dr. Dao and the Electronic Lock" won the first-class Nebula Award in China in 1986. He is a member of the Chinese Writers' Association.

WEI YAHUA is a freelance writer and began publishing stories in 1974. He has published two collections of science fiction stories, and some of his stories have generated great controversy in the field. He often crosses genre lines and ventures into the mainstream. He has sold more than one million words so far and has won several literary awards.

WU DINGBO has taught in the English Department at Shanghai International Studies University since 1964. Areas of interest he has written about are American literature and science fiction. More than forty of his articles and translations in Chinese and English have been published in China and the United States. He is a member of World SF.

YE YONGLIE is a professional writer in Shanghai. He has published over one hundred popular science books and science fiction stories, which makes him seem like the Chinese Isaac Asimov. *Little Know-It-All Travels into the Future* is his most popular juvenile science fiction story. He has also directed more than twenty science films. He is a member of the Chinese Writers' Association and one of the trustees of World SF.

ZHENG WENGUANG is a professor of astronomy. He began writing science fiction in 1954. He has produced dozens of science fiction stories and his best-known book is *Forward Sagittarius*. He is a member of the Chinese Writers' Association and of World SF.

Printed in the USA
CPSIA information can be obtained
at www.ICGtesting.com
LVHW010038031023
759921LV00005B/25